Bob Vila's Guide to Historic Homes of the West

Bob Vila's Guides to Historic Homes of America

Bob Vila's

Guide to Historic Homes of the West

LINTEL PRESS

QUILL
WILLIAM MORROW
New York

ISBN: 0-688-12496-8

Library of Congress Catalog Card Number: 93-086128

Printed in the United States of America

First Quill Edition

1 2 3 4 5 6 7 8 9 10

MANAGING EDITOR — JILL TARDIFF
CONTRIBUTING EDITORS — BARBARA WINARD AND PAUL KOZLOWSKI
LAYOUT AND DESIGN BY EVA JAKUBOWSKI

Acknowledgment

$\mathcal{I}$ would like to acknowledge all of the people who helped make the idea of this book become a reality. To my wife Deborah who shares my enthusiasm for everything about history and whose idea of a vacation is incomplete without visiting every historic house along the way. Her encouragement and determination to see every room in every house gave me the idea for this series of guides.

To Ron Feiner who brought us all together long ago and by doing so enriched us all. To Bob Sann and Hugh Howard whose path findings led us to our publishers, a special thanks for enabling us to be spared the normative agony of attempting to get published. Through Hugh's excellent relationships we hope to benefit all.

To my brother Seth, whose expertise in the publishing business facilitated my limited understanding of the industry.

To Jill A. Tardiff, Barbara Winard, and Paul Kozlowski who worked so tirelessly and professionally to make this a reality. I could not have found more skillful people whose strengths complemented my weaknesses.

To my partner Barry Weiner, whose unfailing support allowed us to open the checkbook when the possibility of returns were vague.

To Eva Jakubowski, who makes books and computers come together. If I ever figured out what you do I'd probably thank you even more.

And finally, to my mother Miriam, who aside from being a librarian demonstrated to me at a very early age that a universe of knowledge could be found between the covers of that most marvelous and wonderful of all things...books.

— *Jonathan Russo*
Lintel Press

Table of Contents

Publisher's Note

We hope that this book will serve as more than a conventional guide to historic homes. For while we set out to create a detailed, informative, and unique guide, devoted exclusively to historic houses, we also had higher goals. For those among you who enjoy, and are devoted to, preservation, architecture, decorative and fine arts, what we have attempted will be self-evident. For those who are first becoming interested in the world of historic Americana, we will try to give you a helping hand. For all those venturing across these historic thresholds, we invite you in, knowing that you will not be disappointed.

The following pages contain a wealth of information on the fascinating people—both the famous and not so famous—who lived in these houses, as well as descriptions of the houses and their remarkable collections. What can also be found within this book, beyond the listings of locations, hours, and tour information, is the most elusive of all things—wonder. For behind each and every house listing lies a world of wonder. Not the manufactured kind, packaged and sold to replace the imagination. Not the superficial kind which manipulates the emotions at the expense of the intellect. But wonder on a higher plane.

The first wonder is that any of these houses still exist and that anyone cares at all. Our society has often achieved its enviable position of affluence by focusing on the new and disposing with the old. The desire for the latest architectural styles, furnishings, and conveniences has often meant a bulldozing of the past, to the point where even the recent past is endangered. Of course, this has always been so; Colonial homes were remodeled into Greek Revivals at the expense of their original architecture. But the changes are far more devastating now, instead of remodeling the houses, we are tearing them down altogether. Time after time, when we went to a historic house in a small city or village, our guide's first statement was that the historic society had been formed to prevent the house from being torn down, often to make room for a parking lot. Historic houses have been made into rooming houses, beauty parlors, or high rises. As we walked through a fifteen room, four-story house built in 1840, complete with irreplaceable architectural details, the enormity of the "let's tear it down" mentality became overwhelming.

Of course the houses themselves possess more wonder than anything else. It is a sorrowfully calloused person who cannot experience the past in a historic house. To tour the prosperous ship captain's house in historic Newport, Rhode Island is to wonder at the riches of furniture, decorations, textiles and food stuffs that ships and winds provided. To tour the 18th-century stone houses of Washington, Pennsylvania with their two-foot thick walls is to wonder at the fortitude of their inhabitants as they struggled against attacks and defended themselves against the cold winters. The very cosmopolitanism of mercantile families in Greenwich Village, New York permeates the air of the historic houses there. One can sense the refinement these people must have felt when they sipped brandy and smoked cigars in their impressive parlors. To be told why people used fireplace screens —so that the wax women used as a cosmetic to fill in their pockmarked faces would not melt—is an explanation of a common object that brings the past alive in a personal and wonderful way. The treasures of art, architectural details, furniture, household implements, and costumes contained in these homes also makes us pause in reflection. Things were viewed very differently when they were made by hand and scarce. There is an education for all of us living in a throw-away culture.

So it is to the individuals, organizations and societies who are saving, preserving and displaying historic America that our sense of wonder and gratitude is directed. Sometimes, we would drive by a mall and see endless cars, stores and shoppers, and know that the energy of the town was now clearly centered at the mall. Then we would arrive at our destination, the local historic house, and find we were the only visitors. Despite this daunting competition from today's faster paced entertainments, our guide was cheerful, patient and full of enthusiasm for the wonder of the house.

We admire the volunteers who fundraise, lobby, catalogue, lecture, and guide their fellow citizens. As visitors, we enrich ourselves because of the efforts of the organizations and individuals who have labored to restore and revitalize these fine houses. We wish to thank the individuals who have given us their time and energy on these tours, and have given us their cooperation in putting this book together. If, in some small way, this guide helps you in your efforts, please consider it a thank you.

— Jonathan Russo
Lintel Press

Editor's Note

*O*ur thanks go to all of the individuals and organizations who have dedicated themselves to preserving America's architectural and historical heritage as exemplified in her residential structures and from whom we received the brochures, photographs, histories, drawings, suggestions, and enthusiastic encouragement without which there would be no book. We only hope that we have been faithful to their stories, their houses, and their mission.

We have tried to make the entries as easy to use as possible, and have included the latest and most accurate information made available to us by the homes themselves. Even so, we highly recommend that you contact a house before planning a visit to verify its hours of operation, scheduled activities, and especially its wheelchair access status—for many older structures, wheelchair access means limited access to the first floor only. Wherever possible we have made mention of other houses located in a given city or town that are worth visiting; these homes appear under the heading "Additional Information."

Though the book is necessarily incomplete—after all, every human habitation is in some sense historical and none are truly permanent—we have tried to include as many of America's most noteworthy homes as possible. If we have omitted any of your favorites, please let us know.

 *Introduction*

All buildings have character, some seem friendly while others have a forbidding feel. Many big buildings demand your attention, while more than a few small ones seem content to let you pass by them unnoticed. Buildings can be eccentric, exotic, familiar, unassuming, warm and welcoming, or cold and sinister; but their individuality is there for all who choose to recognize it.

Since the Bicentennial celebration, millions of Americans have come to appreciate another element of the architectural personality. Like people of a certain age, antique buildings have survived wars and changes and visitors, wanted and unwanted alike. Their very characters are reflections of times past. Some buildings, like some people, have aged gracefully; some have seen happy and sad times, but all of them have something to teach us, about their histories and even ourselves. The truth is that all old houses have something in common with your house and mine.

I fell in love with houses and buildings early in my life—I studied architecture long before *This Old House* and *Bob Vila's Home Again* introduced millions to some intriguing rehabilitation jobs with which I've been involved. My fondness for buildings in general and my experience with old houses in particular only heightens my appreciation of the houses you'll meet in these pages, and the uncompromising approach the many historical societies, community organizations, individuals, and groups have taken to getting the houses restored just right.

These houses represent an immense range of the American experience. Every one has a story to tell, whether it's of the people who built the house or those who lived there; the community that is the context for the place; or even the events that led to its preservation; which so often involve battles with developers or others insensitive to the value and merit in a tumbledown, antique structure.

Each of these houses provides a unique opportunity to step back in time, to learn about how our ancestors lived. Which is another way of saying, these houses offer a glimpse of history, that wonderful state of mind that explains, in part, why and who we are today. I hope in some way we can help inspire you to visit these houses and those other eras that have so much to teach us.

—*Bob Vila*

Alaska

1. Anchorage
Oscar Anderson House

2. Big Delta
Rika's Roadhouse

3. Hatcher Pass
Independence Mine Manager's House

4. Juneau
House of Wickersham

5. Ketchikan
Totem Bight

Oscar Anderson House

420 "M" Street
Anchorage, AK 99501
(907) 274-2336

Contact: Anchorage Historic Properties, Inc.

Open: Mid May–mid Sept., daily
Noon–4 p.m.; first two weekends of
December same hours; year-round by
appointment for school and group tours

Admission: Adults $2.00; seniors and
children (5-12) $1.00; group rates available

Activities: Guided tours, special seasonal
events, third grade educational program,
changing exhibits

Suggested Time to View House: 30 minutes

Facilities on Premises: Picnic area and
playground in park

Description of Grounds: Located in the
north corner of Elderberry Park with a
sweeping vista of Cook Inlet

Best Season to View House: Summer

Number of Yearly Visitors: 4,000+

Year House Built: c.1915

Style of Architecture: National, "Cape Cod"
bungaloid style

Number of Rooms: 8

On-Site Parking: Yes **Wheelchair Access:** Yes

Description of House

Swedish immigrant Oscar Anderson was the eighteenth person to arrive
in the tent city of Anchorage in 1915 and promptly built this wood-frame
house. He lived here for over fifty years, until his death in 1969. Anderson,
a butcher, became a successful supplier of food and fuel to his fellow settlers:
he operated the Ship Creek Meat Corporation until the 1950s and was one
of the principals of the Evan Jones Coal Company. He was also involved in
newspaper publishing and early aviation up north. The house was donated
to the Municipality of Anchorage in 1976 by Anderson's widow, Mrs.
Elizabeth A. Anderson.

This twenty-by-forty-foot, one-and-a-half-story house is one of the first
privately built permanent residences in Anchorage. It faces south to take
maximum advantage of the scant winter light. Upstairs, a single dormer
window faces west; the rest of the windows are set under the moderately
pitched front and side gables. Wood shingles painted green cover the roof
and purlins are used as a decorative touch. The exterior is painted yellow.
Inside, the house features hardwood floors of Douglas fir, wainscotting

downstairs, and the original first flush toilet and bathtub in Anchorage. Over the years the house has survived earthquakes and Alaska's harsh weather; it was completely restored in 1982 to an interpretation of the period 1915 to 1925, when Anchorage was being settled. The Oscar Anderson House is Anchorage's only historic house museum.

The furnishings include a number of original pieces, among them a built-in Victorian-style buffet in the dining room and a Hallett & Davis player piano c.1917.

Notable Collections on Exhibit

On display is a large assortment of household items and artifacts donated by the Anderson family. In addition, one can view a collection of over a hundred antique piano rolls, numerous photographs depicting the early days of Anchorage, a small collection of toys, and several Sydney Laurence prints.

Additional Information

The Oscar Anderson House is listed on the National Register of Historic Places. It is one of the principal sites on a walking tour of Anchorage sponsored by Anchorage Historic Properties, Inc. This tour includes a number of fine buildings, including: the Old City Hall (1936), the Kimball Building (1915), the Wendler Building (1915), the Leopold Davis House, and the Fourth Avenue Theatre (1941).

Rika's Roadhouse

**Milepost 275 Richardson Highway
Big Delta near Fairbanks, AK 99737
(907) 895-4201**

Contact: Alaska Department of Natural Resources, Division of Parks and Outdoor Recreation
Open: Summer, daily 9 a.m.–5 p.m.
Admission: Free
Activities: Guided and self-guided tours
Suggested Time to View House: 1 hour
Facilities on Premises: Museum, gift shop, cafeteria and bakery
Description of Grounds: Restored roadhouse and several log outbuildings located on the banks of the Tanana River
Best Season to View House: Summer
Number of Yearly Visitors: 62,313
Year House Built: 1909
Number of Rooms: 16

Style of Architecture: National, log
On-Site Parking: Yes **Wheelchair Access:** Yes

Description of House

Gold seekers headed from the port at Valdez to Alaska's inland gold fields during the first decades of the 20th century had to travel on the muddy, slow, and frequently dangerous Valdez-to-Fairbanks Trail; they were grateful for any respite from their toilsome journey. An entrepreneur daring enough to cater to these travelers was John Hajdukovich, who built this roadhouse in 1909 to 1910 on the banks of the Tanana River. In 1917, he hired Rika Wallen, recently arrived from Sweden, to run his roadhouse. Six years later he sold it to her and Rika's roadhouse stood for years as a favorite stopping-place for all who took the trail running outside its door. When the Richardson Highway was completed in 1947, it bypassed the roadhouse, business dropped off, and Wallen decided to close down shortly thereafter. She did, however, continue to live here until her death in 1969. It has been completely restored and now forms the centerpiece of Alaska's Big Delta State Historical Park.

The roadhouse is a large, two-story round log structure which features a gabled front; the eave line continues across the gable and gives the three-bay facade a pedimented look. Inside, the house features a kitchen, dining and sitting room, and staff sleeping quarters on the main floor, and the individual bedrooms upstairs. The restored interior is interpreted to the 1920s.

Notable Collections on Exhibit

The old blacksmith shop in the park houses the Delta Historical Society's museum which features a collection of pioneer and native Athabascan artifacts.

Additional Information

Further information can be obtained by writing the Alaska Division of Parks and Outdoor Recreation, Northern Region Office, 3700 Airport Way, Fairbanks, Alaska, 99709.

Independence Mine Manager's House

Independence Mine State Historical Park
Hatcher Pass near Palmer, AK 99645
(907) 745-2827

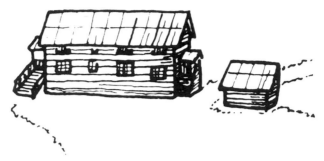

Contact: Alaska Department of Natural Resources, Division of Parks and Outdoor Recreation

Open: Summer hours only

Admission: Free

Activities: Interpretative walk

Suggested Time to View House: 2 hours

Facilities on Premises: Visitor center and museum

Description of Grounds: 271 acre historic mine and mill complex

Best Season to View House: Summer

Number of Yearly Visitors: 112,426

Year House Built: 1939

Style of Architecture: National, frame

Number of Rooms: 8

On-Site Parking: Yes **Wheelchair Access:** Yes

Description of House

In September of 1906, Robert Lee Hatcher discovered gold and staked the first lode claim in the Willow Creek Valley approximately sixty miles north of the landing which would become the city of Anchorage. Lode mining was too expensive for a single operator to engage in because of the capital outlay required to build tunnels and transport heavy equipment to the site. In 1938, two mines in the Willow Creek district near Hatcher's original stake were brought together under one company, the Alaska-Pacific Consolidated Mining Company. In its heyday, the mine employed over two hundred men; many lived here, in the buildings of the Independence Mine State Historical Park, and twenty-two families lived in the nearby community of Boomtown. During World War II, the mine was shut down. It never fully recovered even after the war ended and was closed for good in 1951.

This twenty-by-fifty-foot two-story wood frame house was built to accommodate up to to twelve people—the mine manager, his family, and important visitors. Outside, casement windows are flanked by fixed sash windows; the beveled shiplap siding tightens the house against harsh winters. The interior is dominated by a two-story living room outlined by a balcony and featuring open beam construction. The walls in the living room and stairwell are covered in random-width tongue-and-groove paneling; the rest of the house is covered in celotex painted white. Because the house serves as the park's visitor center it does not contain many furnishings, nor is it made up to look like it did when used as a family residence.

Notable Collections on Exhibit

The Mine Manager's House is only one of the structures in Independence Mine State Historical Site; others include representative bunkhouses, utility shops, a mill, and the assay office which now serves as a museum. The museum houses an extensive collection of implements and artifacts related to gold mining.

Additional Information

The Independence Mine Site is listed on the National Register of Historic Places. For further information write to the Alaska Division of Parks and Outdoor Recreation, South Central Region Office, 3601 C Street, Suite 1080, Anchorage, Alaska, 99503.

House of Wickersham

213 Seventh Street
Juneau, AK 99801
(907) 586-9001

Contact: Alaska Department of Natural Resources, Division of Parks and Outdoor Recreation

Open: May-Sept., Sun.-Fri. Noon–5 p.m.; other times by appointment

Admission: $2.00 per person

Activities: Guided tours

Suggested Time to View House: 45 minutes

Description of Grounds: Sited on grassy yard with many flowers, shrubs and trees. Spectacular view.

Best Season to View House: Early spring-early fall

Number of Yearly Visitors: 1898

Year House Built: 1898

Number of Rooms: 15, first floor rooms open to the public

Style of Architecture: Victorian Queen Anne
On-Site Parking: No **Wheelchair Access:** Yes

Description of House

When Frank Hammond, manager of the Sheep Creek Mining Company, built this large Victorian-style house atop Juneau's "Chicken Ridge" in 1898, the town's housing consisted of log cabins and a few modest frame structures. No wonder townspeople called Hammond's house "the palace." In 1909, Hammond filed for bankruptcy, got out of town, and left the house to his lawyer, J. F. Maloney. After much legal wrangling with a Mr. Albert Gabbs, the house was finally sold to the Alaska Gastineau Mining Company, which used it to house its mangers and directors during the boom years of the late 'teens and early 'twenties. In 1928, it was purchased by James Wickersham, a retired U. S. District Judge and seven-term Congressional delegate. Judge Wickersham and his second wife, Grace Vrooman, remodeled the house and became deeply involved in the life of the community. The Judge's career followed the development of his beloved Alaska—he was the first white man to have climbed Mt. McKinley—as he pushed for home rule, the Alaska Railroad, the University of Alaska, and even the notion of statehood as early as 1917, forty-three years before it would become a reality! The Judge died here in 1939 and his widow lived on in the house until her death in 1963. At that time, one of the Judge's nieces, Ruth Allman, began to give tours of the house which was by then called the House of Wickersham. It was sold to the State of Alaska in 1982.

Although the house is large and well-sited, and features some basic elements of the Victorian Queen Anne style such as a high gabled roof and shiplap siding, it hardly has any of the decorative embellishments which we've come to associate with that style. Among its neighbors on "Chicken Ridge," it appears unfashionably plain; its principal exterior feature is a center dormer gable set back from the first-story roof in a pyramid. Inside, the high ceilings and large rooms create an air of graciousness.

Notable Collections on Exhibit

The house is furnished with items which belonged to the Judge, including his wonderful collection of Alaska artifacts and books. In addition to collecting a library of over 10,000 volumes on Alaska, and publishing a bibliography of Alaska Literature, the Judge himself wrote a memoir of his early years in Alaska entitled *Old Yukon: Tales, Trials, and Trails*.

Additional Information

The House of Wickersham is listed on the National Register of Historic Places. Efforts are being made to have the entire "Chicken Ridge" district, which comprises a number of prestigious homes, listed on the National Register as well.

Totem Bight

North Tongass Highway
Ketchikan, AK 99901
(907) 465-4563

Contact: Alaska Department of Natural Resources, Division of Parks and Outdoor Recreation

Open: Spring -fall, daily 8 a.m.–6 p.m.

Admission: Free

Activities: Self-guided tours, occasional special events

Suggested Time to View House: 1 hour

Facilities on Premises: Picnic grounds

Number of Rooms: 1

Description of Grounds: Interpretative trail through forest and beach areas lined with totem poles

Best Season to View House: Spring-fall

Number of Yearly Visitors: 315,812

Year House Built: Original-precontact, reconstructed 1940

Style of Architecture: Northwest Coast Native Clanhouse, plank

On-Site Parking: Yes **Wheelchair Access:** Yes

Description of House

Totem Bight is the name given to this Civilian Conservation Corps reconstruction of a Native village representative of a type common to the Northwest coast in the early 19th century. Under the supervision of an Alaskan architect, fragments of old totem poles were laid next to freshly-cut cedar logs and copied as closely as possible, using traditional hand-made tools as older skilled carvers who had been hired by the CCC taught their craft to a new generation. Fifteen of these poles, telling myths of both the Tlingit and Haida peoples, line the path to a clanhouse, which itself features large ornamented house posts and a totem pole entry. The painting covering the facade of the clanhouse is a stylized Raven with each of its eyes depicting a face; painted house fronts only appeared on dwellings belonging to wealthy clans. The Raven—a trickster who changed shape at will and often symbolized the Creator—is the hero of many Tlingit and Haida stories.

The clanhouse measures forty feet by forty-four feet and would have housed from thirty to fifty people. The land on which it stands was originally a fish camp. Four interior house posts, independent of the exterior walls, support the principal purlins which in turn support the rafters and cedar plank roof. The exterior walls are constructed of cedar planks set vertically and anchored by four corner posts and two mid-wall posts front and back. The interior of the house is one large room with a central fire-pit and three levels of planked flooring. This clanhouse is one of only two true Northwest coast plank houses presently standing in Alaska.

Additional Information

Totem Bight, as a site, is listed on the National Register of Historic Places. Further information regarding Totem Bight can be obtained by writing to the Alaska Division of Parks and Outdoor Recreation, Southeast Regional Office, 400 Willoughby Avenue, Fourth Floor, Juneau, Alaska, 99801.

Arizona

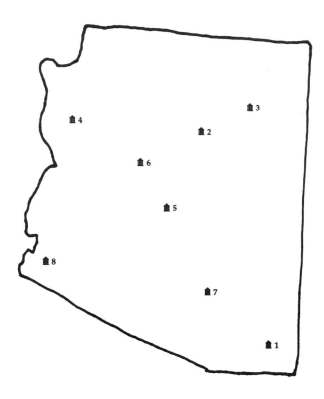

1. **Douglas**
   Slaughter Ranch Museum

2. **Flagstaff**
   Riordan Mansion

3. **Ganado**
   Hubbell Home

4. **Kingman**
   Bonelli House

5. **Phoenix**
   Rosson House

6. **Prescott**
   *Arizona Territorial Governor's
   Mansion*

7. **Tucson**
   Sosa-Carrillo-Frémont House

8. **Yuma**
   *Adobe Annex,
      Captain Jack Mellon House
   Century House Museum and
      Gardens*

Slaughter Ranch Museum

Geronimo Trail
16 miles east of Douglas
Douglas, AZ 85572
(602) 558-2474

Contact: Johnson Historical Museum of the
Southwest

Open: Daily 10 a.m.–4 p.m.

Admission: Adults $4.00; children free

Suggested Time to View House:
2–4 hours

Description of Grounds: Large adjacent
pond and picnic area

Best Season to View House: Spring and fall

Number of Yearly Visitors: 4,000

Year House Built: 1893

Number of Rooms: 9

Style of Architecture: Southwestern Adobe

On-Site Parking: Yes **Wheelchair Access:** Yes

Description of House

The lives of people like John Slaughter have entered into the mythology of the American West; in fact, his life was serialized in a 1958 Walt Disney television production called "Texas John Slaughter." Born in Louisiana in the 1830s and raised in Texas, Slaughter patrolled the range with the infamous Texas Rangers before fighting for the Confederacy during the Civil War. After returning from that conflict, he led the first cattle drive to Arizona along the famous Chisholm Trail. Later, he blazed a new trail to Arizona, subsequently named the Slaughter Trail in his honor. It was in Arizona that Slaughter settled down to become Sheriff of Cochise County, which included the wild town of Tombstone. In 1884, he bought the secluded San Bernardino Ranch, where he lived out his days. During the period Slaughter owned the Ranch, its renown grew when Geronimo surrendered at Skeleton Canyon there in 1896 and Pancho Villa and his army encamped there in 1913 before the battle of Agua Prieta.

The Slaughter Ranch Museum is one of only two remaining 19th-century ranch houses in Arizona, and the only existing cattle ranch from this period. It stands despite the ordinarily limited life of its adobe construction material—it is most likely that only its remote location saved it from the modern "improvements" later pioneers typically wreaked on such structures. The ranch now consists of an ice house, a wash house, a commissary, a cook's house and a granary. Some of the furnishings belonged to the original residents; the remaining artifacts are from the same period.

Additional Information

From Tucson, travel southeast to Tombstone. Continue southeast to Bisbee, then east to Douglas. From Douglas go sixteen miles east on Geronimo Trail to Slaughter.

Riordan Mansion

1300 Riordan Ranch Road
Flagstaff, AZ 86001
(602) 779-4395

Contact: Riordan State Historic Park
Open: May-Sept., daily 8 a.m.–5 p.m.;
Sept.-May, daily 12:30–5 p.m.
Admission: Adults $3.00; youths
(12-17) $2.00; children free
Activities: Guided tours, slide show,
special evening tours for Halloween,
Christmas, Flagstaff Winterfest and
Historic Preservation Week
Description of Grounds: 5 acres consisting
of mansion, lawn, parking lot, visitor
center and paved walkways
Number of Yearly Visitors: 24,331
Suggested Time to View House:
60–90 minutes
Best Season to View House: Year round
Number of Rooms: 40

Style of Architecture: Rustic Craftsman-
American Arts and Crafts Movement
Year House Built: 1904
On-Site Parking: Yes **Wheelchair Access:** Yes

Description of House

When the Riordan Mansion was built in 1904, Flagstaff was no more than a frontier logging town. But the Riordan family had bigger plans for Flagstaff; so they built the largest private residence in town to prove it. Built for two Riordan families, the mansion had forty rooms and over 13,000 square feet of living space. As Flagstaff grew, so did the fortunes of the three Riordan brothers. The relationship between their family and the town of Flagstaff can be characterized as mutually beneficial: Dennis Riordan was instrumental in creating Coconino County in 1891; Michael Riordan served in the Arizona State Legislature; and, Timothy Riordan operated the town's largest industrial company, the Arizona Lumber and Timber Company.

The Riordan home incorporated traditional American architectural styles with the then-most modern advances in technology. The rustic exterior of the mansion features log-slab siding, volcanic stone arches, and hand-split wooden shingles. Inside, however, there are built-in electric light fixtures, central heating, a huge skylight, and indirect lighting. The quality of the interior light was further enhanced by the unique photo-pane window transparencies in the game room and the Tiffany stained glass windows on the first floor.

Notable Collections on Exhibit

The Riordan Mansion is filled with thousands of original pieces—furniture, clothing, rugs, turn-of-the-century books and magazines, photographs and paintings—all belonging to the family. There is an exceptional collection of Craftsman furnishings, including numerous c.1903 pieces constructed by the "Father of the American Craftsman Movement," Gustav Stickley.

Additional Information

The Riordan Mansion is listed on the National Register of Historic Places.

Hubbell Home

Route 264, P.O. Box 150
Ganado, AZ 86505
(602) 755-3475

Contact: Hubbell Trading Post National Historic Site

Open: Winter, daily 8 a.m.–5 p.m.; summer, daily 8 a.m.–6 p.m.

Admission: Free

Activities: Guided tours, slide program, special programs

Suggested Time to View House: 45 minutes

Description of Grounds: Courtyard is presently paved in flagstone, replacing the historic wood paving

Best Season to View House: Fall

Year House Built: Started 1897, final phase completed 1915

Number of Rooms: 12

Number of Yearly Visitors: 200,000

Style of Architecture: Anglo-Territorial with Spanish Colonial influence

On-Site Parking: Yes **Wheelchair Access:** Yes

Description of House

This Spanish Colonial style adobe home exemplifies the tastes and mores common to the Southwest at the turn of the century—the period when Don Lorenzo Hubbell made his living selling general goods to Native Americans at this site.

The home developed from two separate structures. The first phase of construction began in 1897 and continued off and on for some six years. At the end of this period, two buildings had been completed: one housed the Hubbell family—it consisted of a living and dining area, four bedrooms, and a kitchen. The other contained the staff dining room, meat house, south porch, and root cellar. In 1903, and continuing until 1915, the second phase of construction got underway. This phase consisted of adding three contiguous extensions to the original two-part structure: a schoolroom, the present kitchen, and an inner courtyard between the two building halves.

The house has two end porches. The northern one is of frame construction and evolved, first from the original post-and-beam design into a screen porch, then finally into a wainscot and screen-paneled design by the 1920s. The southern porch was always screened. The massive walls—in places they reach a thickness of nearly two feet—are made from local adobe brick. The roof, except for that over the north porch, is framed with peeled log vigas.

For the most part, the living quarters are furnished with pieces originally owned by the Hubbells. The house did, however, undergo some refinements in the twenties and thirties and some of the furnishings date from that period.

Bonelli House

430 East Spring Street
Kingman, AZ 86401
(602) 753-3195

Contact: Mohave Museum of
History and Arts

Open: Thurs.-Mon. 1–4 p.m.;
closed major holidays

Admission: Donation

Activities: Guided tours

Description of Grounds: Large lawn area
with flowers, fruit and shade trees
surrounded by white picket fence

Best Season to View House: Year round

Number of Yearly Visitors: 1,300

Year House Built: 1915

Suggested Time to View House:
30–45 minutes

Number of Rooms: 8

Style of Architecture: Anglo-Territorial with
Victorian-style features

On-Site Parking: Yes **Wheelchair Access:** Yes

Description of House

In January 1915, a frame house belonging to Kingman's Bonelli family caught fire—perhaps due to a malfunction in the electrical system—and burned to the ground. George Bonelli, a prominent local businessman who owned a general store, a jewelry and engraving business, and a meat market in Chloride, immediately hired a contractor named Prendergrast to build another house for his family, this time in the popular Anglo-Territorial style using locally-quarried tufa stone for the walls. Bonelli was descended from a Swiss family, the Bommelis, who became Mormons in Switzerland, changed their name to Bonelli, and emigrated to the United States in the middle part of the century, settling in Nevada on orders from Brigham Young. George was born in Nevada in 1869, moved to Kingman, married Effie Ellen Tarr, and the couple had nine children here. They built their first house—the one that burned—in 1894.

The Bonelli House, in addition to the thick tufa stone walls, which provided excellent insulation against both heat and cold, features a full-width, full-height front porch and balconies to which all rooms have access, and a pyramidal hipped roof. Bonelli had the interior walls plastered with a fire resistant material which made the house virtually fireproof. A cupola, used both as a playroom and lookout, is a later addition. The furnishings are original to the family and date from the turn of the century. The Bonelli House was restored as part of the Bicentennial Project by the City of Kingman and the Daughters of the Mohave Pioneers.

Notable Collections on Exhibit

Among the items on display is a collection of clocks including a large antique wall clock which was, at one time, the only clock in all of Kingman and was loaned to the Santa Fe Railway to be hung in their depot.

Additional Information

The Bonelli House is listed on the National Register of Historic Places.

Rosson House

113 North Sixth Street
Phoenix, AZ 85004
(602) 262-5071

Contact: Heritage Square Foundation, Inc.
Open: Wed.-Sat. 10 a.m.–3:30 p.m., Sun.
Noon–3:30 p.m.; closed month of August
Admission: Adults $3.00; seniors $2.00;
children (6-13) $1.00; special group rates
Activities: Guided tours, exhibits, lecture
series and book signings, craft shows,
annual Victorian Holiday.
Suggested Time to View House: 30 minutes
Facilities on Premises: Foundation and
guild offices, museum, gift and craft shop,
meeting rooms

Description of Grounds: Formal gardens
with various grass, rose, tropical
plantings and shade trees
Best Season to View House: Year round
Number of Yearly Visitors: 20,000
Year House Built: 1895
Style of Architecture: Victorian Queen
Anne-Eastlake
Number of Rooms: 12
On-Site Parking: Yes **Wheelchair Access:** Yes

Description of House

Dr. Roland Lee Rosson built this house in 1895 and he and his family moved in just before he became mayor of Phoenix. Rosson, a native Virginian, had graduated from the University of Virginia Medical School in 1873, served as an assistant surgeon in the U. S. Army in Arizona, and settled in Phoenix upon his discharge in 1879. Here he married Flora B. Murray, the daughter of a prominent Phoenix family, and established a successful practice. His term as mayor was short-lived; he quarreled with the City Council and resigned after only one year in office. Shortly thereafter, he made an unsuccessful run for the office of City Assessor, lost, sold the house, and moved to California. In California, the doctor officially died of gastroenteritis in 1898, but the fact that he had just bought a large life insurance policy caused local officials to look suspiciously upon his wife. The fact that she stayed in Los Angeles and soon built another mansion there only added to these suspicions. From the time that the Rossons sold this house in 1896 to the time that the City of Phoenix bought it in 1975, it went through many owners and tenants, the most prominent of whom were Aaron Goldberg, local merchant and former territorial legislator, and Whitlaw Reid, editor of the *New York Herald Tribune* and Ambassador to Great Britain under President Harrison.

This luxurious four-story house was designed and built by A. P. Petit, a well-known architect who divided his time between California and Arizona; it is constructed of red brick and features a wooden wrap-around porch in the Queen Anne Eastlake style. Other exterior features include a terneplate metal roof, wrought iron cresting, an octagonal turret, lathe-cut ornamentation on the porch, and hooded, paired Italianate-style windows. The interior is a mixture of then modern conveniences, such as hot and cold running water and an early intercom, and fine Victorian Queen Anne detailing: pressed tin ceilings, a golden oak carved staircase, and parquet floors with intricate inlaid oak, walnut, and mahogany. The furnishings are a mix of Victorian and Southwest-style pieces; few of them are original.

Notable Collections on Exhibit

The fully furnished doctor's office has an excellent collection of medical instruments on display.

Additional Information

The Rosson House is one of the major attractions in Heritage Square, a city block of relatively unchanged residences dating from the late 19th century which marks the original townsite for Phoenix. Heritage Square and the Rosson House is listed on the National Register of Historic Places. The Rosson House was featured on a segment of the television program, "This Old House."

Arizona Territorial Governor's Mansion

415 West Gurley Street
Prescott, AZ 86301
(602) 445-3122

Contact: Sharlot Hall Museum and Historical Society

Open: Apr.- Oct., Tues.-Sat. 10 a.m.–5 p.m., Sun. 1–5 p.m.; Nov.-Mar., Tues.-Sat. 10 a.m–4 p.m., Sun. 1–5 p.m.

Admission: Donation

Activities: Group tours, lectures, special events including Folk Arts Fair, Folk Music Festival, and Cowboy Poetry Gathering

Suggested Time to View House: 2 hours

Facilities on Premises: Book and gift shop

Number of Yearly Visitors: 80,000

Description of Grounds: Several exhibit halls

Number of Rooms: 6

Best Season to View House: Spring-fall

Year House Built: 1864

Style of Architecture: National-Folk, hand-hewn log

On-Site Parking: Yes **Wheelchair Access:** Yes

Description of House

The Governor's Mansion, part of the Sharlot Hall Museum complex, was called a "mansion" only in comparison to the tents, wagons, and shacks in which most of Prescott's citizens lived during the 1860s. The mansion was built in 1864 to house officials for the newly created Territory of Arizona. Richard C. McCormick became governor of the territory in 1866, a year after he brought his bride, Margaret, to Prescott. Two years later, twenty-four-year-old Margaret died in childbirth. The French Boursault rose bushes that she planted near the mansion's front door still bloom each year.

The house is made from hand-hewn logs of ponderosa pine cut from a nearby forest. Originally it had six rooms, including a kitchen downstairs and sleeping quarters on the second floor.

Of the rooms currently on exhibit, the most interesting is the West Room, which is dedicated to "Sharlot Hall—A Hobo Soul," in tribute to the fascinating woman who founded the museum in 1928. Sharlot Mabridth Hall, the writer, and chronicler of Prescott's history, made the journey from Kansas to Arizona in 1882 with her family. She was twelve years old. Captivated by the beauty of the land, she dedicated herself to collecting and preserving Arizonan artifacts, encouraging others to follow her example.

Other rooms on display are the dining room, the bachelors' quarters, the Governor's office, the bedroom of Richard and Margaret McCormick, and a sewing room with sewing materials, a quilting block and a piano.

Notable Collections on Exhibit

The West Room contains many items belonging to Sharlot Mabridth Hall including doll's dishes, a piggy bank, and the Blickensderfer typewriter she used. Many of Richard McCormick's furnishings are also on display. The chairs located in the Governor's office are from the first Territorial Legislature.

Sosa-Carrillo-Frémont House

Tucson Convention Center
at 151 South Granada Avenue
Tucson, AZ 85719
(602) 622-0956

Contact: Arizona Historical Society
Open: Wed.-Sat. 10 a.m.–4 p.m.; closed all major holidays
Admission: Free
Activities: Guided tours, walking tours of historic neighborhood, slide programs, holiday exhibit of antique ornaments and dolls
Suggested Time to View House: 30 minutes
Facilities on Premises: Gift shop

Description of Grounds: Large front lawn with trees, benches and Mexican-style fountain. Large landscaped, paved patio and porch in rear with benches.
Best Season to View House: Spring-fall
Number of Yearly Visitors: 10,000
Year House Built: 1880
Style of Architecture: Territorial Adobe with Spanish Colonial and Mexican influences
Number of Rooms: 8
On-Site Parking: Yes **Wheelchair Access:** Yes

Description of House

The site of this house is on property acquired in 1860 by José Maria Sosa, grandson of a soldier stationed at the Presidio of San Augustín del Tucson in 1776. It is not clear whether or not Sosa built a house this plot. In 1878 José Maria's daughter, Manuela Sosa McKenna, sold the property to Jesús Suárez de Carrillo, wife of the civic leader and successful merchant Leopoldo Carrillo. Señora Carrillo built the present adobe house in 1880 and soon rented it to John C. Frémont, the famous Western pathfinder and fifth Territorial Governor of Arizona between 1878 and 1881. It was occupied by Frémont's daughter Elizabeth for five months before she returned to her family back East. After that, and for the next ninety years, the house was home to several generations of the Carrillo family. In 1971, when the house was slated for demolition to make way for the Convention Center, the Tucson Heritage Foundation mounted a successful campaign to save it.

This one-story flat-roofed adobe structure consists of eight rooms, a large back porch, and a spacious rear patio. Characteristic features of the Spanish-Mexican frontier style include the *zaquán* (impressive entry hall), *vigas* (roof beams) covered at right angles by *savinas* (saguaro cactus ribs), and ornamented drain spouts called canales which allowed rainwater to run off. The house has no windows but the front facade has five doors. There are some later details executed in the American Territorial style: the trim around the doors, the lintels fashioned out of mesquite, and the untrimmed pine ceilings. The furnishings are period pieces—among them some superb antiques which belonged to the three families for whom the house is named—mostly dating to the 1880s and made in both the United States and Mexico.

Additional Information

The Sosa-Carrillo-Frémont House is listed on the National Register of Historic Places.

Adobe Annex,
Captain Jack Mellon House

248 Madison Avenue
Yuma, AZ 85364

Contact: Arizona Historical Society
Open: Daily
Admission: Free
Facilities on Premises: Present facility used as offices
Best Season to View House: Spring and winter
Year House Built: 1873, modified 1960s
Style of Architecture: Modified Adobe
Number of Rooms: 3
On-Site Parking: Yes
Wheelchair Access: Yes

Description of House

Captain Jack Mellon was one of the most well-known and skillful steamboat pilots on the Colorado River and his work for the Colorado Steam Navigation Company kept him on his beloved river for more than thirty years. For nine of those years, from 1874 to 1883, he called this one-story adobe building his home.

The house is only twenty feet wide and fifty-five feet deep, with a pair of double doors flanked by a six pane window on each side. Fired brick frames these openings and caps the parapet; the rest of the exterior walls are plastered. A porch extends from the building front to the sidewalk and from the north side of the building to the adjacent Gwynn House. The Captain Jack Mellon House is part of the Brinley Avenue Historic District.

Century House Museum and Gardens

240 Madison Avenue
Yuma, AZ 85364
(602) 782-1841

Contact: Arizona Historical Society

Open: Tues.-Sat. 10 a.m.–4 p.m.;
  closed holidays

Admission: Free

Activities: Guided tours, lectures,
  audiovisual programs, "living history"
  programs, special events

Suggested Time to View House: 1 hour

Facilities on Premises: Library and archives

Description of Grounds: Small yard with
  native grasses and trees

Best Season to View House: Spring and
  winter

Year House Built: c. 1870, modified
  between 1915 and 1925

Number of Yearly Visitors: 15,000

Number of Rooms: 11

Style of Architecture: Adobe, bungaloid style

On-Site Parking: Yes **Wheelchair Access:** Yes

Description of House

Century House, a one-story adobe building, was the home of E.F. Sanguinetti, one of Yuma's most prominent businessmen during the first half of the 20th century. The house was built in 1870 and probably consisted of two adobe rooms; it was remodeled twice, in 1915 and 1925. It now has a shingled roof with hip and gable components and a centrally located shed dormer resting on the front pitch of the roof. The central doorway faces Madison Avenue and is flanked by a tall narrow window. Adobe bricks trim this entry and continue around the main facade, almost like an exterior wainscotting. There is a mixture of late 1800s and early 1900s furnishings in the period rooms. Especially interesting are the pieces of Victorian-style Eastlake and Renaissance Revival furniture.

Notable Collections on Exhibit

A collection of drawings in varied mediums c. 1870s by Fort Yuma soldiers is on exhibit, as well as photographs and artifacts showing life on the Lower Colorado River from 1540 to the present.

California

1. **Benicia**
   Fischer-Hanlon House

2. **Carmel**
   Tor House and Hawk Tower

3. **Chico**
   Bidwell Mansion

4. **City of Industry**
   John Rowland Home
   La Casa Nueva
   Workman House

5. **Clayton**
   Joel Clayton House

6. **Danville**
   Tao House

7. **Death Valley**
   Scotty's Castle-Death Valley Ranch

8. **Escondido**
   Hoffmann House

9. **Fresno**
   Kearney Mansion Museum
   Meux Home Museum

10. **Glen Ellen**
    House of Happy Walls and Wolf House

11. **Goleta**
    Stow House and Sexton Museum

12. **Hayward**
    McConaghy House

13. **Independence**
    Commander's House

14. **Jenner**
    Rotchev House and Kuskov House

15. **Long Beach**
    Rancho Los Alamitos Historical Ranch and Gardens
    Rancho Los Cerritos Historic Site

16. **Los Angeles**
    Avila Adobe
    Frank Lloyd Wright's Hollyhock House
    Sepulveda House

17. **Martinez**
    Muir House

18. **Mendocino**
    Ford House Visitor Center

19. **Monterey**
    Cooper-Molera Adobe
    Larkin House
    Stevenson House

20. **Newhall**
    William S. Hart Museum— La Loma De Los Vientos

21. **Oakland**
    Camron-Stanford House
    Pardee Home Museum

22. **Pasadena**
    Fenyes Mansion
    Gamble House
    Tournament House

23. **Paso Robles**
    Call-Booth House

24. **Redlands**
    Kimberly Crest House and Gardens

25. **Sacramento**
    Governor's Mansion
    Leland Stanford Mansion State Historic Park

Fischer-Hanlon House

135 West G Street, P.O. Box 5
Benicia, CA 94510
(707) 745-3385

Contact: Benicia State Park Interpretive Volunteers

Open: Sat. and Sun. Noon–4 p.m.; group tours with one month notice

Admission: Adults $2.00; seniors and children $1.00

Activities: Guided tours

Suggested Time to View House: 30 minutes

Facilities on Premises: Books available in Benicia capitol building

Description of Grounds: Garden and carriage house

Best Season to View House: Spring

Number of Yearly Visitors: 4,000+

Year House Built: 1848, remodeled 1858, restored 1975

Style of Architecture: Spanish Colonial with Federal-style elements

Number of Rooms: 10

On-Site Parking: No **Wheelchair Access:** No

Description of House

Although the Fischer-Hanlon House had its first incarnation as a former Gold Rush river saloon and rooming house where rooms let for 25 cents a night, Joseph Fischer, a Swiss immigrant, transformed it into a monument honoring the timeless values which first-generation Americans held in pursuing their dreams of the good life.

Joseph Fischer was a local butcher and quarry owner who married Catherine Hall from Ireland; the couple had three children. Fischer bought and remodeled the house in 1858 after transporting it a safe distance from the evils of the waterfront. Although the original design was typical of a Spanish Colonial-style building with its open verandas, he altered it by attaching a front inspired by the Adam style he'd seen and admired on a trip back East. During the next 110 years, successive families—the Fischers, Quinns and Hanlons—occupied the house and, as might be expected, the house itself changed with each change in ownership. Such things as electric lights, new bathrooms and central heating were installed. Most recently, the house has been restored to the 1880 period and many of the original Fischer furnishings have been put on exhibit. There is a typical c.1890 parlor and dining room and three bedrooms interpretative of the 1860 to 1880 period, one of which contains smoky oak furniture purchased in 1902 from a Sears & Company catalog. The 1902 bathroom has been restored and a c.1880 kitchen includes a wood burning stove still used to bake Christmas cookies.

Notable Collections on Exhibit

Also on exhibit are family photographs and memorabilia, and a Square Grand Steinway piano signed and dated 1867. Four family-made quilts are also displayed. Such was the pride of the Fischer family regarding these quilts that each was given a name: the "North Carolina Lily" completed in 1823, the "Pineapple Cover" completed c.1880, the "Crazy Quilt" completed in c.1880 and "Grandmother's Garden" completed c.1890.

Additional Information

The Fischer-Hanlon House is listed on the National Register of Historic Places.

Tor House and Hawk Tower

25304 Ocean View Avenue
P.O. Box 2713
Carmel, CA 93921
(408) 624-1813

Contact: Robinson Jeffers Tor House
Foundation

Open: Fri.-Sat. 10 a.m.–3 p.m.

Admission: Adults $5.00; college students
$3.50; high school students $1.50

Activities: Guided tours, annual Spring
Garden Party and October Festival

Suggested Time to View House: 75 minutes

Facilities on Premises: Book shop

Description of Grounds: Beautiful
"old-world" gardens with stone tower

Best Season to View House: Year round

Number of Yearly Visitors: 4,000

Year House Built: 1918 with subsequent
additions.

Style of Architecture: Eclectic Devon-style
stone farmhouse

Number of Rooms: 5 open to the public

On-Site Parking: Yes **Wheelchair Access:** No

Description of House

"...We must uncenter our minds from ourselves; we must unhumanize our views a little, and become confident as the rock and ocean that we were made from." Robinson Jeffers, the well-known and reclusive American poet, wrote these lines in his poem, "Carmel Point," and they describe what a visitor might feel when coming upon Tor House and Hawk Tower for the first time.

Jeffers was born in Pittsburgh, Pennsylvania, in 1887, far from the wild oceanside beauty of Carmel that became his soul's home. Here, in his California paradise, Jeffers built his forty-foot-high tower over a twenty-four-year span. He built it as a gift to his beloved wife—his partner and a major influence on his poetry—Una Call Kuster. In order to be able to move the massive boulders from the shore below the building's site, Jeffers had to adopt the building methods that the Egyptians used in erecting their pyramids. Besides these stones from the nearby beach, the tower also contains stone fragments from the Great Wall of China and the Pyramid of Cheops in Egypt, lava rock from Vesuvius and Kilawea, and marble from

Ireland and Hadrian's villa. Inside is a carved stone head from the temple at Angkor Wat and a Babylonian tile from the temple at Uruk dated c.2100 B.C.

Tor House was built by M. J. Murphy, a local builder who taught Jeffers "to make stone love stone," from sketches that Jeffers made of a structure that somewhat resembles a Tudor-style barn. The house had neither gas nor electricity until 1949, but Jeffers was comfortable enough to work in the house year round and entertain a series of guests that included Edna St. Vincent Millay, Carl Sandburg, Ansel Adams, Ira and George Gershwin, Vladimir Horowitz, Dylan Thomas, and Judith Anderson, who performed in Jeffers' famous drama, *Medea*, when it opened in New York. After Una's death in 1950, Jeffers' twin sons, Donnan and Garth, stayed at Tor House with their father until he died in his sleep here in 1962.

Notable Collections on Exhibit

Many tokens and mementos given by personal friends of the Jefferses' can be seen in the house and the tower, including a Roman statue of a boy riding a dolphin previously owned by the American artist, John Singer Sargent, an octagonal window from the ship on which Napoleon escaped from Elba (the ship was wrecked off the California coast near Monterey), numerous bits of tile, medieval stone, and lava rock scattered and embedded in various parts of the house and grounds. Visitors can also see the more than 2,000 trees that Robinson Jeffers planted around Tor House and Hawk Tower.

Additional Information

The Tor House and Hawk Tower are listed on the National Register of Historic Places.

Bidwell Mansion

525 Esplanade
Chico, CA 95926
(916) 895-6144

Contact: Bidwell Mansion State Historic Park

Open: Mon.-Fri. Noon –5 p.m., weekends and holidays 10 a.m.–5 p.m.; closed Thanksgiving, Christmas, and New Year's Day

Admission: Adults, $2.00; children (6-12), $1.00; under 6 and public school groups, free

Activities: Guided tours; June-Aug., seasonal "living history" and environmental programs, audio-visual presentations

Suggested Time to View House: 45–60 minutes

Facilities on Premises: Visitor center

Description of Grounds: 8 acres of landscaped grounds includes gazebo, carriage house, and gardens. A self-guided tour of the grounds is available.

Best Season to View House: Spring and summer

Number of Yearly Visitors: 35,000

Year House Built: Started 1865; completed 1868

Style of Architecture: Italianate Villa, towered

Number of Rooms: 26

On-Site Parking: Yes **Wheelchair Access:** Yes

Description of House

John Bidwell (1819-1900) was well-known during his lifetime. An early California pioneer, he made his fortune mining gold on the banks of Feather River, then won his fame, first as a patriot in the struggle for California statehood, then as a Congressman and Civil War Brigadier General. The land he loved was the rich farmland flanking the Chico Creek in the upper Sacramento Valley; he bought 28,000 acres of this land in 1847 with money from his Gold Rush stake. Bidwell became the state's leading agriculturalist, introducing many new crops and successful farming methods to the people of California.

Bidwell started construction on the twenty-six-room mansion in 1865 shortly before his departure to Washington, D.C. In Washington he met and courted Miss Annie Ellicott Kennedy, the daughter of a socially prominent family. Although Miss Kennedy was considerably younger than Bidwell and deeply involved in local Washington social causes, she finally agreed to marry him and travel to the remote California frontier of Chico County. The couple became involved with many social issues including election reform, the education and the employment of the Meedhoopda Indians, the Women's Suffrage Movement and Prohibition. Such was the couple's hospitality that personages as different as the President and Mrs. Rutherford B. Hayes, Susan B. Anthony, John Muir, and General William T. Sherman frequented the home.

Designed by General Henry W. Cleveland—the same architect who designed the original Palace Hotel of San Francisco—the mansion was considered to be very modern for its day; its conveniences included a gas lighting system, indoor plumbing, and bathrooms. The ground floor is composed of an entry hall, a formal parlor, a dining room, a library and the General's office. The second floor contains six bedrooms, two bathrooms, the servants' quarters and a room in which Mrs. Bidwell taught Meedhoopda girls to sew. The third floor contains a ballroom and a private office.

Notable Collections on Exhibit

Chinese artifacts from the Bidwell collection include a dressing screen, several vases and lanterns. The collection also includes many Maidu Indian baskets, and over 1,000 books.

Additional Information

The Bidwell Mansion is listed on the National Register of Historic Places.

John Rowland Home

16021 Gale Avenue
City of Industry, CA 91745
(818) 336-2382

Contact: La Puente Valley Historical Society

Open: House is closed indefinitely due to structural deterioration, but can be viewed from the outside

Activities: Annual La Puente Valley Historical Society Barbeque

Year House Built: 1855, remodeled 1897

Style of Architecture: Modified Italianate with Greek Revival-style influence, brick and adobe

Description of Grounds: Adjacent to the Dibble Museum

On-Site Parking: Yes **Wheelchair Access:** No

Description of House

John Rowland and William Workman arrived in La Puente Valley in 1841 as leaders of the first American wagon train from New Mexico to Southern California. On their journey, they passed Rancho La Puente, one of the largest ranches built by Spanish colonists in California and once owned by the San Gabriel Mission. When they learned that ownership of the ranch had not been allotted, Rowland rode to Monterey with the necessary documents, and $1,000 in gold, to apply for the land grant. The friends and partners became owners of nearly 50,000 acres of rich farm and pasturelands.

John Rowland's first home was made from adobe; it was built directly north of the present site. In 1855, Rowland built a new brick house, the first in the area, with a detached adobe kitchen for his second wife, Charlotte Gray Rowland. Later in 1897, Rowland's daughter, Victoria, and her husband, Josiah Hudson, remodeled the house by changing the slope of the roof, stuccoing the bricks and adding an attached kitchen. A remarkable collection of original family furniture spanning three generations remains in the house.

Notable Collections on Exhibit

The Round House, once the ranch's water tank, is now a children's museum with many local Californian and Native American artifacts, as well as ranch equipment, on display.

Additional Information

The John Rowland House is the oldest standing brick house in the area.

La Casa Nueva

15415 East Don Julian Road
City of Industry, CA 91745
(818) 968-8492

Contact: Workman and Temple
Homestead Museum

Open: Tues.-Fri.1–4 p.m.; Sat. and
Sun.10 a.m.–4 p.m.; closed major
holidays and fourth weekend of
every month

Admission: Free tours

Activities: Guided tours, lectures,
demonstrations, workshops

Suggested Time to View House: 1 hour

Facilities on Premises: Research library
available by appointment

Description of Grounds: Access by
guided tour

Best Season to View House: Spring-fall

Number of Yearly Visitors: 18,000

Year House Built: Started 1919,
completed 1925

Number of Rooms: 24

Style of Architecture: Eclectic Spanish
Colonial Revival

On-Site Parking: Yes **Wheelchair Access:** Yes

Description of House

Walter Temple was the grandson of William Workman who, with John
Rowland, led the first American wagon train full of settlers into the San
Gabriel Valley. Temple assumed ownership of his grandfather's homestead
and built La Casa Nueva in 1917 with profits obtained from the oil acciden-
tally discovered on his farm. La Casa Nueva, which is located just a few
yards from the original Workman home site, is an outstanding example of
the Spanish Colonial Revival style with numerous decorative elements:
stained and painted glass accents, wrought iron rail work, carved wood,
elaborate plaster work and Mexican and American made tiles. La Casa
Nueva featured the then-new conveniences of electric lighting, central air
and solar cooling and heating systems. The tepee-shaped office is a rare
example of pragmatic regional architecture!

Notable Collections on Exhibit

Architectural crafts and early 20th century decorative arts are on display, including many pieces of furniture in the Spanish and American
Colonial, French and Mission styles.

Additional Information

La Casa Nueva is listed on the National Register of Historic Places.

Workman House

15415 East Don Julian Road
City of Industry, CA 91745
(818) 968-8492

Contact: Workman and Temple
Homestead Museum

Open: Tues.-Fri. 1–4 p.m., Sat.and Sun.
10 a.m.–4 p.m.; closed major holidays
and fourth weekend of every month

Admission: Free tours

Activities: Guided tours, lectures,
demonstrations, workshops

Suggested Time to View House: 1 hour

Facilities on Premises: Research library
available by appointment

Description of Grounds: Access by
guided tour

Best Season to View House: Spring-fall

Number of Yearly Visitors: 18,000

Year House Built: 1842,
remodeled 1872

Number of Rooms: 8

Style of Architecture: "Picturesque" Gothic
Revival with elements of the Italianate

On-Site Parking: Yes **Wheelchair Access:** Yes

Description of House

William Workman journeyed far in life, both in geographical and financial terms. He was born in England in 1800 and arrived in the United States at the age of twenty-two. He found work as a fur trapper and trader in the New Mexico territory before he joined John Rowland to guide a group of settlers to the San Gabriel Valley. The two business partners bought Rancho La Puente, a farm extending from the present Whittier Hills north to the present San Bernardino Freeway, and from the City of Walnut west to the San Gabriel River.

The house that Workman built for his family in the 1840s was a three room, one-story Mexican-style adobe; it was remodeled in the 1870s into a picturesque Californian "country" home by Ezra F. Kysor, an architect from Los Angeles. Although the exterior had been restored with particular attention paid to the false brick and stone wall finishes, the interior of the house was not restored. However, many of the interior architectural elements have survived; mainly, the marble fireplaces, the wooden doors, and the decorative wood trim. The exterior has been restored to its 1870 appearance.

Additional Information

The Workman House is listed on the National Register of Historic Places.

Joel Clayton House

6101 Main Street, P.O. Box 94
Clayton, CA 94517
(510) 672-0240

Contact: Clayton Historical Society
Open: Wed.and Sun. 2–4 p.m.; also by
appointment; closed New Year's Day,
Easter and Christmas Day
Admission: Free
Activities: Guided tours, walking tour,
speakers and seasonal events
Suggested Time to View House: 1 hour
Facilities on Premises: Gift shop including
books, small research library
Description of Grounds: Small flower
garden, old local jail and outhouse,
horse-drawn agricultural machinery
Best Season to View House: Spring and
summer
Number of Yearly Visitors: 3,000+
Year House Built: 1860
Number of Rooms: 10

Style of Architecture: Folk Victorian
On-Site Parking: Yes **Wheelchair Access:** No

Description of House

The founder and namesake of the town of Clayton, Joel Clayton was a mining engineer who made his fortune in California. Originally lured to the area by the rumor of coal deposits on Mount Diablo, Clayton stayed on to buy land and settle down. He soon became a successful grape farmer, and a dairy and cattleman.

In 1860, Clayton built a Victorian "cottage" for his wife and ten children. Much of the interior is authentic, including the pine floor boards and the square nails used in the tongue-and-groove construction of the house. Recently, efforts to restore the ground floor and the slanted upstairs ceiling have shown that the house underwent several add-on phases. The present day rooms are furnished with late 19th century pieces donated by Clayton residents; these include a Square Grand rosewood piano c.1870; a pump organ and church pew, both c. 1900; a barber chair and post office furniture c. 1861; and several period wedding gowns and frock coats reminiscent of the early days of Clinton.

Notable Collections on Exhibit

Many Native American artifacts, mainly from the Bay Miwok, are on display.

Tao House

1000 Kuss Road, P.O. Box 280
Danville, CA 94526
(510) 838-0249

Contact: Eugene O'Neill National
Historic Site
Open: Wed.-Sun. guided tours 10 a.m. and
12:30 p.m. reservation required; closed
Christmas, New Year's Day
Admission: Free
Activities: Ranger guided tours
Suggested Time to View House: 2½ hours
Facilities on Premises: Visitor center,
bookstore
Description of Grounds: 13 acre site with
landscaped courtyard and orchards
Best Season to View House: Spring and
summer
Number of Yearly Visitors: 4,000
Number of Rooms: 20

Style of Architecture: Spanish Eclectic and
Monterey
Year House Built: 1937
On-Site Parking: No **Wheelchair Access:** Yes

Description of House

The American Nobel-prize winning playwright Eugene O'Neill (1888-1953) wrote some of his best work here in the Tao House, including *A Long Day's Journey Into Night* and *The Iceman Cometh*. He lived here in the San Ramon Valley—which he pronounced his "final home and harbor"—from 1937 to 1944 with his wife, Carlotta; it is easy to see how the playwright found the serenity he needed to work in this setting and in this house, with its Chinese-inspired interior design echoing his own love of Chinese art and philosophy.

The exterior of the Tao House is in the Monterey variant of the Spanish style, with its walls painted white to resemble adobe but its roof tiles dark and meant to suggest the tiled roofs of the Orient. Not all of the rooms are furnished, but those that are reflect O'Neill's deep interest in Chinese art and artifacts. There are also some wonderful Art Deco-style pieces on display. All of the pieces suggest the years when O'Neill lived here. The ceilings are painted a dark blue which symbolizes the heavens.

Additional Information

The Tao House is listed on the National Register of Historic Places.

Scotty's Castle
Death Valley Ranch

**Death Valley National Monument
on State Highway 72 near Olancha
Death Valley, CA 92328
(619) 786-2392**

Contact: National Park Service

Open: Year-round, daily 7 a.m.–6 p.m.

Admission: Park entrance free, $5.00 per vehicle; castle tour fee, adults $6.00; children (6-11) $3.00; Golden Age Access Card $3.00

Activities: Guided "living history" tour, campfire programs

Suggested Time to View House: 1 hour

Facilities on Premises: Visitor center, gift and book shop, snack bar

Description of Grounds: Death Valley ranch site consisting of the main house, annex and other outbuildings

Number of Yearly Visitors: 100,000

Best Season to View House: Spring, fall and winter

Number of Rooms: 32

Year House Built: Between 1921 and 1931

Style of Architecture: Spanish Eclectic and Craftsman

On-Site Parking: Yes **Wheelchair Access:** Yes

Description of House

Walter Scott, also known as Death Valley Scotty, was the inspiration for this thirty-two room mansion done in a mix of the Spanish Eclectic and Craftsmen styles. When Scott, a cowhand who once performed in Buffalo Bill's Wild West Show, decided to try his hand at gold-mining he caught the attention of Chicago millionaire Albert Mussey Johnson. Johnson and his wife, Bessie, enjoyed the cowboy's tales of the wild West and backed his search for gold. Ultimately, they built a winter retreat in Death Valley and decided to name their house after their entertaining friend.

The Castle is really two separate buildings, the Main House and the Annex, connected by a second-story bridge. The construction is frame and hollow tile, sheathed in mesh and reinforced stucco. Red Mission-style tiles line the gabled roof, and the floors are finished with red quarry tiles. The Johnsons had originally commissioned Frank Lloyd Wright to design their castle, but didn't like his plans and wound up rejecting them. They went through a number of architects before the house was built.

Scotty's Castle employs a number of design elements and materials that were not widely used at the time, including redwood, stucco, decorative ceramic tiles, and hand-forged wrought iron hardware. Inside the castle, it's a wildly eclectic mix of European antiques (mostly 16th and 17th century Spanish and Italian pieces), Native American pieces, and custom-made furnishings modeled after Spanish Colonial or Provincial prototypes. Many of these custom pieces were crafted by regional artisans. Given the Castle's location, perhaps the most important features are the three interior fountains, the covered porches, and the ingenious cooling system.

Hoffmann House

321 North Broadway
Escondido, CA 92025
(619) 743-8207

Contact: Escondido Historical Society
Open: Thur.-Sat. 1–4 p.m.
Admission: Free
Activities: Private tours available, please call in advance
Suggested Time to View House: 20–30 minutes
Facilities on Premises: Gift shop in Santa Fe depot; new Center for the Arts scheduled for completion in 1993
Description of Grounds: Historic Grape Day Park includes the 1888 Santa Fe depot, a railroad car, barn
Best Season to View House: Year round
Number of Yearly Visitors: 15,000
Year House Built: 1890
Style of Architecture: Victorian Queen Anne-Eastlake

Number of Rooms: 8
On-Site Parking: Yes **Wheelchair Access:** Yes

Description of House

Reverend Hoffman was a Lutheran minister in Escondido who lived in this house with his wife and eight children for fifty years; little else is known of the family except that their home reflects the life and activities of an average California family of the late 19th century. The Reverend and Mrs. Hoffman's wedding daguerreotype hangs in the family parlor accompanied by Mrs. Hoffman's wedding dress trimmed in black, in memory of her sweet sister who died suddenly only a few weeks before the Hoffman wedding.

The two-story Victorian house is a rather unique structure with no less than seven gables, beautiful spindlework trim, and the original leaded glass windows. Although more comfortable than many Californian homes of the same period, the Hoffmann House does not contain many significant furnishings or artifacts.

Kearney Mansion Museum

7160 West Kearney Boulevard
Fresno, CA 93706
(209) 441-0862

Contact: Fresno City and County
Historical Society
Open: Fri., Sat.-Sun. 1–4 p.m.;
closed Easter and Christmas
Admission: Adults $3.00; students $2.00;
children $1.00
Activities: Guided tours
Suggested Time to View House: 40 minutes
Style of Architecture: Eclectic Period
Revival, French Renaissance-American
Chateauesque

Facilities on Premises: Museum store
Description of Grounds: 240 acre National
Register Park with many unusual
plantings, including Australian
eucalyptus trees, royal palms,
flowering oleander and pampas
Best Season to View House: Spring-fall
Number of Yearly Visitors: 15,000
Year House Built: 1900
Number of Rooms: 14
On-Site Parking: Yes **Wheelchair Access:** Yes

Description of House

Martin Theodore Kearney (c. 1842-1906) had a dream: to build a French-style chateau and formal gardens in what was essentially a desert. Here, at least in part, his dream was realized. Although Kearney died tragically before his "chateau" was built, the impressive Kearney Mansion—really the caretaker's residence—still stands as a memorial to that dream and to the accomplishments of this great man, known as the "Raisin King of California."

Kearney started his career as a trunk manufacturer in Boston. After he moved West, he became the manager of an enterprise which sought to establish an agricultural colony that would create a system of small farms. Through his promotional efforts, hundreds of farmers were drawn to the Fresno area; soon, the county became known as the richest agricultural region in the nation. Eventually, Kearney had amassed enough capital from his mining and real estate interests to bring his personal dream to fruition.

He began by building the eleven-mile, three-lane, Chateau Fresno Boulevard, designed by Rudolph Ulrich, then planting over 50,000 trees and shrubs. He also laid out the 240-acre Chateau Fresno Park; this beautiful park once boasted of more than five hundred varieties of roses.

The two buildings that Kearney lived to see completed—the Kearney Mansion and a smaller building consisting of servants' quarters and kitchen—are fine examples of French Renaissance-style architecture, executed in adobe brick. The several architects who worked on the elaborate project were thought to be strongly influenced by the Schwab Residence of New York City, itself a copy of the Chateau de Chenonceaux. This influence is evident in the sophisticated high roof lines and dormers, and the ornate pinnacles. The interior wall finishes were designed in accordance with Kearney's suggestions and imported from France; decorative papier mache details accent the ceilings. Many of the furnishings are shown on the original house plan.

Notable Collections on Exhibit

Some of the many early 20th-century pieces of fine and decorative art remain in the Kearney Mansion are an Art Nouveau painted clay bust of a female figure, a large Art Nouveau pottery bowl, a collection of prints and antique frames, and a unique three-light fixture designed in the shape of a "goddess" figure signed "Par Aug. Moreau" and entitled "Fruits d'Automne."

Additional Information

The Kearney Mansion is listed on the National Register of Historic Places.

Meux Home Museum

1007 "R" Street, P.O. Box 70
Fresno, CA 93707
(209) 233-8007

Contact: Meux Home Corporation
Open: Fri.-Sun. Noon–3:30 p.m.;
summer hours include Thurs.
Admission: Adults $3.00; juniors (13-17)
$2.00; children (under 12) $1.00
Activities: Guided tours, school tours,
weddings, receptions, garden parties,
meetings, concerts in yard
Suggested Time to View House: 1 hour
Facilities on Premises: Gift shop
Description of Grounds: Planted with
flowers authentic to the era
Best Season to View House: Spring
Year House Built: Started 1888,
completed 1889
Number of Rooms: 12

Number of Yearly Visitors: 10,000-15,000
Style of Architecture: Eclectic mix of Gothic
Revival and Queen Anne-Eastlake
On-Site Parking: No **Wheelchair Access:** Yes

Description of House

On February 27, 1889, the *Fresno Weekly Exposition* described the nearly completed Meux Home as "probably the most elaborate residence in Fresno..." The reporter noted that the final cost would be approximately $12,000, a true fortune in those days!

The man who built the house was Thomas Richard Meux, born in 1838 and a native of Tennessee. He attended the University of Virginia and the University of Pennsylvania Medical School. During the Civil War, Meux served in the Confederate Army as an assistant surgeon. In 1887, Dr. Meux moved his family from Tennessee to Fresno due to his wife's poor health. Here Dr. Meux practiced medicine well into his seventies.

The Meux Home is a charming architectural example of the Victorian era. To the Victorians, "charm" had to possess an element of surprise and the Meux Home fulfills this intent. The roof lines and chimneys thrust skyward at odd angles and the walls are covered in materials of various textures: horizontal clapboards, fish-scale design shingles, and ornamental floral relief work. The large porch is supported with spindlework decorated with gingerbread detailing and the octagonal master bedroom is topped with a turreted roof. The Meux Home Museum is listed on the National Register of Historic Places.

Notable Collections on Exhibit

Two original stoves are still in the kitchen, along with many of the original kitchen utensils. An extensive costume collection is displayed on a rotating basis; the collection includes the wedding gown of Dr. Meux's daughter, Mary, who was married in the Meux Home in 1907, and other period wedding dresses and christening gowns. A true modern day "surprise" in the costume collection is the presence of a black gown once owned by Lillie Coit of San Francisco! There is also a wonderful collection of bisque and porcelain antique dolls.

House of Happy Walls and Wolf House

2400 London Ranch Road
Glen Ellen, CA 95442
(707) 938-5216

Contact: California Park Service

Open: Daily 10 a.m.–5 p.m.; closed Thanksgiving, Christmas, New Year's Day

Admission: $5.00 per vehicle; seniors $4.00 per vehicle

Activities: Self-guided tours

Suggested Time to View House: 30–60 minutes

Description of Grounds: 40 acre park consisting of the gravesite of American author Jack London, the ruins of Wolf House and Charmian London's House of Happy Walls

Best Season to View House: Spring

Year House Built: Between 1919 and 1922

Number of Rooms: 11

Number of Yearly Visitors: 75,000

Style of Architecture: Spanish Eclectic

On-Site Parking: Yes **Wheelchair Access:** Yes

Description of House

The House of Happy Walls was built by Charmian London, wife of the famous author Jack London (1876-1916) who is perhaps best known for his adventure novels *The Call of the Wild* and *The Sea Wolf*. This Spanish-style house features distinctive roof tiles and walls of volcanic stone. It is filled with London memorabilia and with furniture that had originally been designed for London's own dream house, the Wolf House, the ruins of which can be seen about a mile from the House of Happy Walls.

Wolf House was designed by the San Francisco architect Albert Farr. It was constructed of native materials such as maroon lava, unpeeled redwood logs, dark red Spanish roof tiles, red stone walls, and interior redwood paneling. The Wolf House was planned to be much larger than the House of Happy Walls; the dining room alone was designed to accommodate as many as fifty guests at a sitting. The house was built on a very thick concrete slab, and the walls were made of concrete too. This was probably done to stabilize the house in case of an earthquake. On the eve of its completion, the house was set on fire, probably by arsonists.

After Charmian London's death in 1955, her will directed that the ruins of Wolf House be left as a memorial to her husband, and that the smaller House of Happy Walls be used to house her collection of photographs and papers and other personal items which now comprise the Jack London collection. The Jack London State Historic Park was created in 1959 through a gift from Irving Shepherd, the author's nephew and an heir to his estate. Just a short distance from the Wolf House is Jack London's gravesite; it is a quiet, simple grave, surrounded by more than 800 acres of his beloved land.

Stow House and Sexton Museum

304 North Los Carneros Road
Goleta, CA 93117
(805) 964-4407

Contact: Goleta Valley Historical Society

Open: Sat. and Sun. 2 –4 p.m.;
or by appointment

Admission: Donations $1.00; children
(under 12) free; $2.00 at Christmas,
Fourth of July and Fiddlers' Convention

Activities: Guided tours, special seasonal
events including the October Fiddlers'
Convention of Bluegrass Music, and
Christmas Program

Suggested Time to View House: 30 minutes

Facilities on Premises: Gift shop

Description of Grounds: Large lawn and
trees next to house, benches, short walk
to small reservoir, Lake Los Carneros

Best Season to View House: Spring

Year House Built: 1872

Number of Rooms: 13

Number of Yearly Visitors: 5,500

Style of Architecture: Folk Victorian

On-Site Parking: Yes **Wheelchair Access:** No

Description of House

Sherman P. Stow used the money from stocks left to him by his father to start the first commercial lemon groves in California. After both his father and older brother died, Stow managed the family property and continued extensive research on the lemon root stock and on citrus sprays for fruit diseases. Following family tradition, he also served as State Senator during the 1930s.

The exterior of this white frame, two-story structure features several porches. Inside, on the first floor, there is a formal dining room, a butler's pantry, a living room with fireplace, and a study; upstairs, there are several bedrooms and a sewing room. All of the closets, as well as some of the dressers and cabinets, are built-ins, a rather unique feature for a home of this period. Some of the original furnishings are on display.

Notable Collections on Exhibit

The Sexton Museum features a maritime display, several 18th and 19th century cannons, farm machinery, tack and carriage pieces, and a reconstructed smithy. The Stow House exhibits a collection of wedding gowns dating from 1860.

McConaghy House

Contact: Hayward Area Historical Society
Open: Thurs.-Sun. 1–4 p.m.; closed
month of January
Admission: Adults $2.00; seniors $1.50;
children (6-12) $.50; special Christmas fee
Activities: Guided tours, antique show;
authentic period holiday decorations
Suggested Time to View House: 1 hour

Facilities on Premises: Gift and book shop
Description of Grounds: Carriage house
and tank house
Best Season to View House: Year round
Year House Built: 1886
Style of Architecture: Victorian Queen Anne
Number of Rooms: 12
On-Site Parking: Yes **Wheelchair Access:** No

Description of House

This twelve-room Victorian-style house was built in 1886; it is of a size and style which nicely illuminates the daily life of a local farm family residing here at the turn-of-the-century. The home is well-preserved—in fact, the original wallpapers are still visible—and fully restored. Many home crafts made by the McConaghy family decorate the rooms of the house; in addition, several oil paintings, some examples of perforated paper embroidery and bead work, and a hair picture, are hung as testaments to the family's good taste within the bounds of late Victorian fashion.

Commander's House

Edwards and Main Streets, P.O. Box 206
Independence, CA 93526
(619) 878-2411

Contact: Eastern California Museum
Open: Memorial Day-Labor Day, Sat.-Sun.
Admission: Donations accepted
Suggested Time to View House: 20 minutes
Description of Grounds: Lawn and small garden
Number of Yearly Visitors: 400
Number of Rooms: 9

Activities: Guided tours
Best Season to View House: Year round
Style of Architecture: Folk Victorian-style farmhouse
Year House Built: c.1880
On-Site Parking: Yes **Wheelchair Access:** No

Description of House

At first glance, the Commander's House appears to be a simple, Victorian-style frame farmhouse, not unlike any number of well-built homes of the late 19th century—but looks can be deceiving: this house is special. It is built on the site of the military installation which was established to protect settlers from the native peoples of Owens Valley.

In 1861, the Paiute Indians declared war on the cattlemen and prospectors who arrived in their valley. To protect these settlers, Lt. Colonel George W. Evans established Camp Independence on July 4, 1862. The Camp was located approximately two-and-a-half miles from the present town of Independence. Here the army built adobe structures as troop barracks, but in 1872 an earthquake destroyed many of the buildings. After the disaster, the Federal Government appropriated $30,000 for the construction of a new camp made up of frame structures instead of adobe. Among the first buildings to go up was the Commander's House. The first inhabitants were the Major Harry C. Egbert and his family, followed by Captain Alexander MacGowan—the letter "M" on the dormers above the front porch are thought to represent his name. The Brooks family sold the house to the City of Los Angeles in 1928, but it remained a private residence until 1961, when the Eastern California Museum Association began its restoration of the site.

The house is built in an L-shape with a front gable and wing; the placement of the main entrance is unusual—it sits on an angle between the main section of the house and the ell. The exterior features cross bracing on the front gable, a single-story extended bay, and four porches. The latter were added over the years. The floor plan includes a parlor, dining room, kitchen, foyer, office, and four bedrooms; the original interior walls have been covered in tacked cloth and papered. The furnishings on display date from 1820 to 1910; some of the pieces were made by soldiers stationed at Camp Independence.

Notable Collections on Exhibit

Exhibits relate the natural and cultural heritage of Inyo County; these include a collection of Paiute-Shoshone basketry and a display documenting the Japanese-American internment camp at Manzanar. Little Pine Village, a recreated pioneer settlement, is located behind the museum and is made up of a general store, a blacksmith shop, and other historic buildings of the 1880s.

Rotchev House and Kuskov House

19005 Coast Highway 1
Jenner, CA 95450
(707) 847-3286

Contact: Fort Ross State Historical Park
Open: Daily 10 a.m.–4:30 p.m.; closed Thanksgiving, Christmas, New Year's Day
Admission: $5.00 per car; seniors $4.00 per car
Activities: Guided tours at Noon and 3 p.m.
Suggested Time to View House: 2 hours
Facilities on Premises: Visitor center, gift and book shop

Description of Grounds: Russian settlement outpost located on original bluff site overlooking the Pacific Ocean
Best Season to View House: Year round
Number of Yearly Visitors: 500,000
Year House Built: Rotchev House-c.1812, Kuskov House-1812
Style of Architecture: Folk, Siberian ostrog style hewn-log
Number of Rooms: Rotchev House-7, Kuskov House-6
On-Site Parking: Yes **Wheelchair Access:** Yes

Description of House

In 1812 Ivan Alexandrovich Kuskov arrived on the shores of California with twenty-five fellow Russians and eighty Native Alaskans from Kodiak Island and the Aleutians. Kuskov represented the Russian-American Company, a commercial hunting and trading company chartered by the tsarist government. While most of the company's trade and exploration in North America took place in and around Alaska, the Russians found that the long winters there exhausted their food supply. So they built Fort Ross to open a supply line to their comrades in Alaska. By the 1830s, Fort Ross—from the word "Rossiia," meaning Russia—was foundering; the supply of otter along the coast had been exhausted and efforts to supply food for the Alaskan settlements failed. Fort manager Rotchev tried to sell the fort, first to the Mexicans, then the Hudson's Bay Company. Finally, in 1841, he sold it to John Sutter, founder of Sacramento, for the equivalent of $30,000.

The Rotchev House is the only original Russian structure in the complex still standing. The one-story house, built of hand-hewn logs, features several interconnected interior chambers. On the outside, each window is made up of over twenty small glass panes, a very luxurious detail in an outpost such as Fort Ross. When the family of Alexander Gavrilovich Rotchev—the last manager of the fort—lived here, there was a "choice library, a piano, and a Mozart score." The house now has no furniture at all; placards are set in each room relating the history of the fort and the lives of its inhabitants.

The Kuskov House was the residence of the first commander and it served as the manager's house until the mid-1870s. The downstairs consists of an armory and storeroom and the upstairs is reserved for the living quarters. Inside, furniture of the early 19th century is displayed. Reconstruction of the Kuskov House was completed in 1983.

In addition, historic Fort Ross consists of several reconstructed gate and blockhouses, and a chapel which was the first Russian Orthodox structure built in North America outside of Alaska.

Additional Information

The Fort Ross site was purchased in 1873 by G. W. Call who established here a large ranch operation, and who built a simple frame house located not far from the fort. He and his son Carlos operated this ranch which included herding, farming and lumbering until 1973. The Call Ranch House is temporarily closed to the public, but may be viewed from the outside. The Rotchev House is listed on the National Register of Historic Places.

Rancho Los Alamitos
Historical Ranch and Gardens

6400 Bixby Hill Road
Long Beach, CA 90815
(310) 431-3541

Contact: Rancho Los Alamitos Foundation

Open: Wed.-Sun. 1–5 p.m.; closed major holidays, Mother's Day, last two weeks of December

Admission: Free; nominal fee for special events

Activities: Guided tours, special programs last Sunday of each month

Suggested Time to View House: 45 minutes

Facilities on Premises: Book and gift shop

Best Season to View House: Spring and summer

Description of Grounds: 7½ acre site; 4½ acre historic gardens designed by noted early 20th-century landscape architects including Florence Yoch,William Hertrich, Alan Chickering, Charles Gibbs Adams

Number of Yearly Visitors: 24,000

Year House Built: c. 1800, additions and remodeling to 1931

Style of Architecture: Spanish Colonial Adobe incorporating Craftsman and Monterey-style facades

Number of Rooms: 17

On-Site Parking: Yes **Wheelchair Access:** Yes

Description of House

The story of Rancho Los Alamitos is the stuff of California history, an extended lesson in the development of the Golden State. The seventeen-room house has been occupied almost continuously since it was first built sometime around 1800 and, as might be expected, each succeeding occupant added something of their own to the original building; because of this constant reshaping and renovating, the house has come to be a rather unique agglomeration of architectural styles.

Rancho Los Alamitos was built on a Spanish land grant of 300,000 acres bestowed to Manuel Nieto in 1784 and used to shelter his ranch hands. Perhaps it was Juan José Nieto, the son of the original grantee, who built the original four-room adobe house that still forms the core of the ranch house. Other residents included José Figueroa (1834-1835), the Mexican Governor of California; his close friend, Francisco Figueroa, brother of José and Nicholas Gutierrez (1835-1842) and himself a former Governor of the territory; Abel "Californio" Stearns (1842-1861), the largest landholder in southern California during the Mexican period; John and Susan Bixby (1881-1906), pioneers from Maine who ran a dairy and sheep operation; and finally, Fred and Florence Bixby (1906-1952), very successful cattle ranchers and oil people. Fred Bixby was also president of the California and National Cattleman's Association, and, most notably, a member of the Cowboy Hall of Fame.

During its illustrious history, the house of Rancho Los Alamitos had undergone many alterations but it was Susan Bixby who influenced most of the interior changes after her husband's death in 1887. Presently, the house is a U-shaped structure with a 40-foot-by-60-foot adobe core serving as the anchor of the central east wing. Fred and Florence Bixby added a second story in 1925, incorporating many Craftsman features on the east facade, and changing the west facade to the Monterey style with a balcony. The south wing is covered with stucco. At one time, this south wing housed the children's bedrooms with an addition built in 1910. The north wing contains the kitchen, the ranch hands' dining room, and the original ranch offices built in 1845 and remodeled in 1931. All of the furnishings on display belonged to the later Bixby family, the last official residents of Rancho Los Alamitos; the furnishings are from the 1920 to 1940 period.

Notable Collections on Exhibit

An interesting exhibit of California and southwest Native American objects are on display, as well as an extensive collection of late 19th-century American pressed glass.

Additional Information

The grounds consists of seven outbuildings dating from the 1920s, including several barns, wagons, and displays of common agricultural tools.

Rancho Los Cerritos Historic Site

4600 Virginia Road
Long Beach, CA 90807
(310) 424-9423

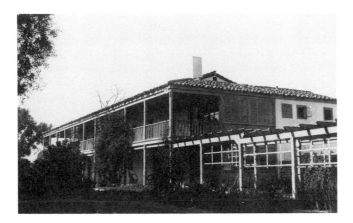

Contact: Rancho Los Cerritos Historic Site
Open: Wed.-Sun. 1–5 p.m.; groups by reservation
Admission: Free
Activities: Guided tours hourly on weekends, special Christmas Candlelight tours
Suggested Time to View House: 1 hour
Facilities on Premises: Reference library

Description of Grounds: Formal garden and picnic areas
Style of Architecture: Spanish Colonial and Spanish Eclectic-Monterey
Best Season to View House: Year round
Number of Yearly Visitors: 15,000
Year House Built: 1844, remodeled 1930
Number of Rooms: 24, 10 open to public
On-Site Parking: Yes **Wheelchair Access:** Yes

Description of House

After months of grueling travel, Manuel Nieto arrived in Alta, California, named by the Spanish in their conquest of the New World, and, in 1784, was awarded a hefty 167,000 acre land grant as reward for his loyal service. Upon Nieto's death in 1804, the grant was divided among his heirs, resulting in the creation of five smaller ranchos. Rancho Los Cerritos was named after the small, rolling hills which distinguished the 27,000 acre parcel of land on which it was situated.

In 1843, Jonathan Temple, a native of Massachusetts and local merchant, purchased Rancho Los Cerritos. With his marriage into a prominent Mexican family, Temple soon became a Mexican citizen and was given responsibility for supervising the Mexican government mint in southern California. Turning his attention to cattle ranching, Jonathan Temple, now calling himself Juan Temple, decided to build a ranch house of adobe brick and redwood. Several years of drought, and then floods, took its toll on his fortunes; he lost most of his cattle herds, resulting in the sale of the ranch in 1866 to Thomas and Benjamin Flint and their cousin, Lewellyn Bixby. The land went cheap at seventy-five cents per acre. Not only were the Flint brothers and their cousin involved in sheep raising and dairy production;

they also managed a land development office and a banking operation. The last resident of Rancho Los Cerritos was Sarah Bixby Smith, the local poet and literary figure who wrote *Adobe Days*, an account of her life on the ranch.

The house features several Monterey style porches and a veranda. While the exterior adobe walls are original, the tile roof and covered walkways were added during the remodeling of the 1930s. The interior staircase is still intact. The parlor, the dining room and the master bedroom are all interpretative of the 1870s. As the Bixby family maintained the longest tenure, most of the furnishings are theirs, with some pieces dating as early as 1866.

Notable Collections on Exhibit

A collection of historical photographs documenting the history of Rancho Los Cerritos from 1872 through the 1930s is on display.

Additional Information

The archives and reference library contains the Sarah Bixby Smith Collection.

Avila Adobe

845 North Alameda Street
Los Angeles, CA 90012
(213) 680-2525

Contact: El Pueblo de Los Angeles
Historic Monument
Open: Tues.-Fri. 10 a.m.–3 p.m.,
Sat.-Sun. 10 a.m.–4:30 p.m.
Admission: Free
Activities: Guided tours, film showing
featuring the early history of Los Angeles
Suggested Time to View House: 15 minutes
Facilities on Premises: Visitor center gift
shop

Description of Grounds: Plaza area was
landscaped and given its circular form in
the 1870s
Best Season to View House: Spring and
summer
Number of Yearly Visitors: 200,000
Year House Built: c. 1818
Style of Architecture: Spanish Colonial
Number of Rooms: 6
On-Site Parking: Yes **Wheelchair Access:** Yes

Description of House

Avila Adobe is the oldest existing house in the Los Angeles area. When it
was built in 1818, the settlement of El Pueblo de la Reina de los Angeles was
already a prosperous colonial capital. Don Francisco Avila, who built the house,
was a native of Sinaloa, Mexico; he came to the small dusty pueblo a decade or
so after the Spanish had founded Los Angeles. First a successful cattle rancher
and owner of Rancho Las Cienegas, he became mayor of Los Angeles in 1810.
Don Francisco Avila married twice: his first wife, Maria del Rosario Verdugo,
died in 1822; his second wife, Maria Encarnacion Sepulveda, died in 1855. She
did, however, outlive her husband, who died in 1832. The Señora and her family
continued to live at the Avila home, leaving it briefly during the Mexican-
American War. In 1847, Commodore Robert F. Stockton, the self-proclaimed
governor of the territory, commandeered the house and the Avila Adobe served
as his residence while peace agreements were negotiated between the California provisional government and the American authorities. Ownership of Avila

Adobe passed through numerous families in the years following, even serving as a boarding house.The property was finally condemned in 1928, but it was rescued from demolition by a local civic leader and, sometime later, fully restored, in part with the support of a direct descendent of the Avila family.

The design of the Avila Adobe—and the materials used in its construction—is a good example of adaptation to conditions in the southern California desert; thick adobe walls offer excellent insulation against the heat, and cross-ventilation is created by exterior doors on either side. The house consists of six rooms and a courtyard: the family room, the office, the kitchen, the master bedroom, the parlor, and the children's room.

Notable Collections on Exhibit

Numerous family pieces are on display. Of particular interest is the beautiful black lacquer table which belonged to Doña Encarnacion; this piece was the work box for her sewing and lace making. In the office, the Avila winery's 1886 account book can be seen.

Additional Information

The famous fur trader, Jedediah Smith, stayed with the Avila family in the year 1826.

Frank Lloyd Wright's Hollyhock House

4800 Hollywood Boulevard
in Barnsdall Art Park
Los Angeles, CA 90027
(213) 662-7272

Contact: City of Los Angeles Cultural Affairs Department

Open: Tues.-Sun. guided tours at Noon, 1 p.m., 2 p.m., 3 p.m.

Admission: Adults $1.50; seniors $1.00; children (under 12) free

Activities: Guided tours

Suggested Time to View House: 1 hour

Facilities on Premises: Bookstore

Description of Grounds: Park setting with Municipal Art Gallery, Junior Arts Center, Gallery Theater, and Barnsdall Arts Center

Best Season to View House: Year round

Number of Yearly Visitors: 15,000

Year House Built: Between 1919 and 1921

Style of Architecture: Eclectic "California Romanza"

Number of Rooms: 13

On-Site Parking: Yes **Wheelchair Access:** Yes

Description of House

Aline Barnsdall, heiress to an oil fortune, met Frank Lloyd Wright in Chicago where she was co-directing an experimental theater company. The architect had just completed Midway Gardens. Barnsdall, a remarkably independent woman, especially for the era during which she lived, and for whom the theater was only one of many enthusiasms—others were travel, socialism, progressive education, and birth control—dreamt of building a community in Los Angeles dedicated to the performing arts and thought she had found in Wright someone who could carry out such a project. Wright, already America's most famous architect, was searching for the ideal expression of his "organic architecture," perhaps looking to build a second Taliesin. On this site, set into a hill in Southern California, with its views of the Los Angeles basin, San Gabriel Mountains, and Pacific Ocean, he built a house in a style he called "California Romanza," employing a musical term to mean "the freedom to make one's own form."

In 1919, work commenced on Olive Hill, the thirty-six-acre site which was planned to include a home for Barnsdall and her daughter, two secondary residences, a theater, a director's house, an actors' dormitory, artists' studios, shops, and a motion picture theater. Unfortunately, these plans were never fully realized; in fact, the only structures to be completed were the Barnsdall residence, called "Hollyhock" after its owner's favorite flower, and the two secondary residences. Failure to complete the rest of the complex was due primarily to the inability of the two principals involved to make decisions, agree on them, and stick by them, even before Barnsdall's financial decline. Their numerous squabbles over design and cost, however, never killed their friendship.

The house was built under the supervision of Wright's son, Lloyd, and his apprentice, Rudolph Schindler, from plans drawn mostly in Japan, where the master was working on the Imperial Hotel. One is immediately struck by its forbidding quality, as though a primitive fortress had been secretly sculpted onto a hillside of delicate beauty. This imposing stucco exterior hides a serene inner courtyard, creating a literal oasis in the middle of a symmetrical floor plan dominated by a dramatic living room which features a fireplace of heroic dimensions. This room, with its pool and skylight, can be said to epitomize Wright's own description of his buildings as "vessels of space." Rooftop terraces celebrate the view in every direction and the eponymous hollyhock can be seen as repeated decorative pattern throughout the house. The house is a masterpiece.

In 1927, the house and eleven acres were given to Los Angeles by Aline Barnsdall. In 1974, it was restored; since then, restoration of some Wright-designed furniture and other related research has taken place at Hollyhock.

Sepulveda House

Main and Olvera Streets
Los Angeles, CA 90012
(213) 680-2525

Contact: El Pueblo de Los Angeles Historic Monument

Open: Mon.-Fri. 10 a.m.–3 p.m., Sat. 10 a.m.–4:30 p.m.

Admission: Free

Activities: Guided tour of historic district, film showing featuring the history of early Los Angeles

Suggested Time to View House: 20–30 minutes

Facilities on Premises: Visitor center gift shop

Description of Grounds: Restored historic city block

Style of Architecture: Spanish Colonial Adobe, renovated Victorian Queen Anne-Eastlake

Best Season to View House: Spring and summer

Number of Yearly Visitors: 200,000

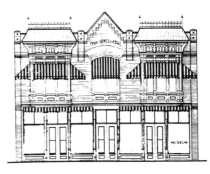

Number of Rooms: 22 private rooms, 2 commercial establishments

Year House Built: 1847, renovated 1887

On-Site Parking: No **Wheelchair Access:** Yes

Description of House

Los Angeles was a boom town in the 1880s; the population exploded from a mere 11,000 to over 50,000 in just ten years. The Sepulveda House was built in response to that rapid growth, and, like the city, the house showed itself a hybrid of Mexican and Anglo traditions. The Sepulveda house was first mentioned in a petition to the Ayuntamiento, or Common Council, by Señora Francisca Gallardo, dated July 24, 1847. She had built a simple adobe on the land granted to her but, by 1870, Señora Gallardo recognized the dramatic changes taking place in Los Angeles and felt the need to match the latest in residential taste, remodeling her traditional one-story, flat-roofed adobe into a two-story structure with a hipped roof.

When the streets of Los Angeles were widened during the 1880s, the Señora's daughter, Eloisa Martinez de Sepulveda, had the original house demolished and a new block-long structure built, with the assistance of architects George F. Costerisan and William O. Merithew. This "house" cost $8,000 and, upon completion, boasted of twenty-two rooms in a unique two-story building combining both businesses and residences, while mixing many Mexican adobe and Victorian-style design elements. It contained two businesses and three private dwelling rooms on the first floor, separated by a courtyard passageway in which part of the old adobe stood. The second floor served as a boarding house with fourteen bedrooms and one bathroom; all of the bedrooms opened into a central hallway lit by two skylights.

The Sepulveda House was inherited by a niece, Eloisa Martinez de Gibbs, in 1901; she and her family lived in the house until 1905.

Muir House

4202 Alhambra Avenue
Martinez, CA 94553
(510) 228-8860

Contact: National Park Service, John Muir
National Historic Site

Open: Wed.–Sun. 10 a.m.–4:30 p.m.;
closed Thanksgiving, Christmas,
New Year's Day

Admission: Adults $1.00; children
(under 17) free

Activities: Guided tours for groups must be
reserved two weeks in advance, film on
the life of John Muir

Suggested Time to View House: 90 minutes

Facilities on Premises: Bookstore

Description of Grounds: 8 acres of
orchards, trees and gardens

Best Season to View House: Spring

Number of Yearly Visitors: 30,000

Year House Built: 1882

Number of Rooms: 17

Style of Architecture: Italianate
On-Site Parking: Yes **Wheelchair Access:** Yes

Description of House

John Muir, a founder of the Sierra Club and patron saint of the American conservation movement, personified the radical shift from that 19th-century pioneer belief which regarded Nature as a storehouse of exploitable commodities to our own age's rather romantic adoration of Nature as a means of spiritual transcendence. Muir's message was clear: "Wilderness is a necessity. Mountain parks and reservations are useful not only as fountains of timber and irrigating rivers, but as fountains of life." He was born in 1838, in Dunbar, Scotland, then immigrated to the Wisconsin frontier with his family at the age of ten. After attending the University of Wisconsin, he turned to the wilds of California for his life course of wilderness study. He literally walked the West, from Canada to the Gulf of Mexico and garnered the nickname, "John of the Mountains." These expeditions provided the inspiration for his numerous writings.

In the 1880s, Muir married Louie Strentzel; the couple had two children, Wanda and Helen. The family settled in this seventeen room house in Martinez but Muir continued to travel and write about the urgent need to save America's vanishing wilderness. Many listened, including President Theodore Roosevelt, who took a personal tour through Yosemite with Muir.

Although the house itself cannot be considered architecturally significant, the 8.8 acre park in Martinez preserves the home and fruit ranch of John Muir as it was when he lived here from 1890 until his death in 1914, and his fame gives it importance. The two-story frame building with redwood siding and a brick foundation was originally painted a light gray with dark green window frames; the porch ceilings were a deep sky blue. After 1890, a three-story addition was built to the south side of the house.

Ford House Visitor Center

735 Main Street, P.O. Box 1387
Mendocino, CA 95460
(707) 937-5397

Contact: Mendocino Area Parks Association
Open: Daily
Admission: Free
Activities: Guided tours, whale watching
Suggested Time to View House: 1 hour
Facilities on Premises: Books and cards for sale
Best Season to View House: Spring-fall

Description of Grounds: A landscaped garden surrounds the house. Large lawn with picnic tables and an ocean view.
Number of Yearly Visitors: 40,000
Year House Built: 1854
Style of Architecture: Victorian
Number of Rooms: 12
On-Site Parking: No **Wheelchair Access:** No

Description of House

A pair of 1891 charcoal portraits hang on the parlor wall of this simple coastal house, the Ford House Visitor Center. These portraits depict Jerome Burley Ford (1821-1890), from Grand Isle, Vermont, and his wife, Margaret Hayes Ford (1831-1890), from Granby, Connecticut, the first occupants of this twelve-room Victorian house. The Ford House, referred to as the "Company House," was one of the first private residences built in Mendocino. The main floor plan consists of a typical Victorian parlor, a bedroom, and an office; the upper floor has three rooms and a bathroom. Interestingly enough, the kitchen and the dining room were originally located in the cellar with only two small half windows on the west side letting in light. Doubtless, this arrangement provided a cool environment for food preparation and storage, and the convenience of having family meals taken so near the kitchen, but it was always dark, and candles and lamps had to be used continuously through day and night—a not inconsiderable expense in those years.

Cooper-Molera Adobe

525 Polk Street
Monterey, CA 93940
(408) 649-7118

Contact: National Trust for Historic
Preservation

Open: Summer, Tues.-Sun. guided tours at
10 a.m., 11 a.m. and Noon; winter,
Tues.-Sun. 10 a.m. and 11 a.m.

Admission: Adults $2.00; children (6-18)
$1.50; special free admission for reserved
school groups through 12th grade

Activities: Guided tours, "living history"
demonstrations, special educational
summer programs, Spring Adobe Tour
and Holiday in Adobes event

Suggested Time to View House: 45 minutes

Facilities on Premises: Visitor center, gift
and book shop

Description of Grounds: 2 acre complex
with several historic outbuildings and
1864 period vegetable and flower garden

Best Season to View House: Year round

Year House Built: 1830

Style of Architecture: Territorial Adobe with
Spanish Colonial-style influence

Number of Rooms: 10, 8 open to the public

On-Site Parking: No **Wheelchair Access:** Yes

Description of House

This three-acre complex of 19th-century colonial farm buildings is perhaps the best interpretation of the merging of Mexican and American
cultures in Monterey. The first inhabitant of this adobe was Manuel Diaz, a
Mexican merchant and politician who lived here in the 1840s. In 1864, the
property was acquired by the sea captain John Rogers Cooper. Cooper, who
originally sailed out of New England, made two trips to China in the 1820s
and a third in 1849, running cargo to Monterey, then California's largest port;
he also sailed from California on a run that took Protestant missionaries to
Hawaii, and returned to those islands several times more before settling on
land. In California, he married Encarnacion Cooper de Vallejo and started
speculating in land. At one time, Cooper owned the land upon which San
Quentin Prison presently sits, the Point Sur Lighthouse, and Rancho El Sur.
It is thought that most of the outbuildings in the complex were built during
Cooper's residency here.

The interior of this house is interpreted to the various periods of occupancy—the downstairs reflects the Diaz and Cooper years, the upstairs appears as it did around the turn of the century and includes the original 1895 electric lights. The wallpaper and carpets are reproductions of the 1850 and 1900 originals. The furnishings which reflect the Diaz years are mainly Empire-style and some Mexican pieces, whereas the Cooper years are reflected in the Victorian-style furnishings with a few odd pieces in the Renaissance, Gothic Revival, and Rococo styles. Virtually all of them were found on the site.

Notable Collections on Exhibit

The Copper-Molera Adobè features an excellent collection of 19th-century California art and the carriage house is home, appropriately enough, to a collection of carriages.

Additional Information

When in Monterey, one should also visit another property which belongs to the National Trust, the Casa Amesti at 516 Polk Street. This walled clay adobe was built in 1834 by the Spanish-born merchant Josè Amesti, one of colonial Monterey's most prominent citizens. The Monterey Art Association conducts weekend tours at Casa Amesti. Call (408) 372-2311.

Larkin House

Calle Principal and Jefferson Street
Monterey, CA 93940
(408) 649-7118

Contact: Monterey State Historic Park
Open: Summer, Fri.-Mon., Wed. guided tours on the hour 2–4 p.m.; winter, Fri.-Mon., Wed. guided tours on the hour 1–3 p.m.; closed Thanksgiving, Christmas, New Year's Day
Admission: Adults $2.00; youths $1.50; children $1.00; two-day ticket available
Activities: Guided walking tours of historic Monterey
Best Season to View House: Year round

Suggested Time to View House: 30–45 minutes
Description of Grounds: ½ acre of English "cottage" gardens with indiguous features
Number of Yearly Visitors: 4,000
Year House Built: Between 1835 and 1839
Style of Architecture: Terrirotial Adobe with Federal-style influence
Number of Rooms: 12
On-Site Parking: No **Wheelchair Access:** No

Description of House

Monterey was the capital of Alta California, a province of Mexico, until July 7, 1846. On that day, Commodore John Drake Sloat came ashore, raised the Stars-and-Stripes, announced the beginning of the Mexican-American War, and proclaimed California a part of the United States. Historic buildings still dot the streets of downtown Monterey, evidence to the fact that the city was once California's capital and main port of entry.

Larkin House is a remnant from those days when California underwent the transformation from Mexican province to American State. Thomas O. Larkin (1802-1858) was an American merchant and the U. S. Consul to Alta California. His home served as the social and political center for Monterey's residents, both Mexican and American; and Larkin kept meticulously detailed records of all that went on. *The Larkin Papers*, published by the University of California Press, is considered one of the most important sources of information on early California history.

The house is a two-story adobe structure with balconies on three sides supported by redwood posts. The house was one of the first in the region to have glass windows. Inside, two of the fireplaces and some of the redwood flooring are original to the 1830s. The Larkin House has been refurbished by Alice Larkin Toulmin, a descendant of Thomas Larkin, with Federal-style pieces that came from Portsmouth, New Hampshire. It is remarkable that these furnishings blend so well with the Spanish Colonial-style architecture.

Notable Collections on Exhibit

On display are fine collections of English prints and engravings, English and American silver pieces, an 1849 portrait of Rachel Larkin, and antique and period decorative art objects.

Additional Information

The many buildings of historic Monterey can best be seen by following the "Path of History," a guided walking tour through the streets of Old Monterey. House tours are offered at the Casa Soberanes, the Stevenson House, the Cooper-Molera complex, and, of course, the Larkin House. The Larkin House is listed on the National Register of Historic Places.

Stevenson House

Contact: Monterey State Historic Park

Open: Summer, Tues.-Sun. guided tours on the hour 2–4 p.m.; winter, Tues.-Sun. guided tours on the hour 1–3 p.m.; closed Thanksgiving, Christmas, New Year's Day

Admission: Adults $2.00; youth $1.50; children $1.00; two-day ticket rate available

Activities: Guided walking tours of historic Monterey

Suggested Time to View House: 30–45 minutes

Facilities on Premises: Visitor center and theater

Description of Grounds: Walled ½ acre of cultivated gardens with large trees, flower beds and many benches

Best Season to View House: Year round

Number of Yearly Visitors: 4,000

Year House Built: 1838

Style of Architecture: Territorial Adobe with Spanish Colonial-style influence

Number of Rooms: 14

On-Site Parking: No **Wheelchair Access:** No

Description of House

Although the famous British author Robert Louis Stevenson only boarded here for a few months in the late summer and fall of 1879, it is now called the Stevenson House. Monterey has claimed Stevenson as its own because this is where he pursued Fanny Osbourne, his future wife. After viewing the house, one might think that Stevenson not only left his heart here, but his furniture as well. In addition, he also left the people of Monterey a memorable portrait of life in their town in his 1879 essay, "The Old Pacific Capital."

Prior to Stevenson's occupancy, the house was owned by Rafael Gonzales, the Mexican Customs Administrator, who lived here from 1840 to 1846. After him, it was owned successively by Walter Colton, Monterey's first American alcade (mayor), then Juan Girardin, a Swiss immigrant who used it as a business and boarding establishment. The house is a typical Spanish Colonial-style two-story adobe structure. Unique features include the original 19th century redwood flooring and the thick angled windows in the exterior walls which create a lovely light effect in the downstairs salon. This salon is done in a 1940s Mexican-style decor, while the rooms upstairs are Victorian.

Notable Collections on Exhibit

Much of the downstairs and all of Stevenson's upstairs room are filled with his furniture, photographs, and personal items, including manuscripts and first editions of his work. There is also a collection of Victorian toys and porcelain dolls.

Additional Information

One block from the Stevenson House is the Cooper Store in the Cooper-Molera complex where an extensive selection of the author's writings can be found. The Stevenson House is listed on the National Register of Historic Places.

William S. Hart Museum— La Loma De Los Vientos

24151 San Fernando Road
Newhall, CA 91321
(805) 254-4584

Contact: Los Angeles County Museum of Natural History

Open: Mid Sept.-mid June, Wed.-Fri. 10 a.m.–1 p.m., Sat. and Sun. 11 a.m.–4 p.m.; mid June-mid Sept., Wed.-Sun. 11 a.m.–4 p.m.; closed Mon., Tues., Thanksgiving, Christmas, New Year's Day

Admission: Free

Activities: Guided tours

Suggested Time to View House: 2 hours

Number of Yearly Visitors: 25,000

Facilities on Premises: Located within a 265 acre park; picnic facilities, hiking and nature trails, 110 acre wilderness area with small herd of bison

Description of Grounds: 265 acre park including outbuildings, picnic facilities, hiking and nature trails, live animals

Best Season to View House: Spring and fall

Year House Built: 1927

Style of Architecture: Eclectic Spanish Colonial Revival

Number of Rooms: 14

On-Site Parking: Yes **Wheelchair Access:** Yes

Description of House

Although born in Newburgh, New York, William Surrey Hart (1872-1946) knew the West intimately. His father, Nicholas Hart, had moved the family from place to place in search of financial security and little Bill lived on what was then the frontier of Wisconsin, Minnesota, Iowa, and Illinois. His childhood companions were often Indian youngsters from whom he learned the rudiments of the Sioux language. This early association also engendered in him a life-long respect for Native Americans and their unique cultures.

When the Hart family settled back in New York, Bill dreamed of becoming an actor. In 1905, he took a role in the "The Squaw Man." It was his first "Cowboy and Indian" movie; this role would ignite his life-long career dedicated to the Western film genre, and which would earn him the nickname, "Two Gun Bill." His great success acting in Westerns led him to the writing, directing and producing of many films. His authentic depiction of the West, based on his memories and devotion to realism, continues to influence the genre to the present day. But, as an actor, he still played "the Frontier Hero," a stereotype more often based on fancy than on fact.

After his retirement from the Silver Screen in 1925, Hart purchased property in Newhall, an area known as a location site, and hired a Los Angeles architect, Arthur Kelly, to design the ranch home which he would name La Loma De Los Vientos or The Hill of the Winds. The two-story split level house was completed in 1927. The exterior details include: wooden balconies with wrought iron railings, a red tile roof, and other features associated with the Spanish Colonial Revival. The interiors, of lath and plaster walls with open beam ceilings, is a showplace for Native American-style art. The house is furnished in its entirety with furniture purchased during Hart's lifetime.

Notable Collections on Exhibit

The home is also filled with pieces reflecting Hart's love of the American West, including Navajo textiles and authentic Native American clothing. Paintings and sculptures from the great names of regional art such as Charles M. Russell, Joe DeYoung, Charles Schreyvogel, Clarence Ellsworth, and Frederic Remington grace the walls. And, of course, Hart's personal possessions and film memorabilia cap the tour.

Camron-Stanford House

1418 Lakeside Drive
Oakland, CA 94612
(510) 836-1976

Contact: Camron-Stanford House Preservation Association

Open: Wed. 11 a.m.–4 p.m., Sun.1–5 p.m.

Admission: Adults $2.00; seniors $1.00; children (under 12) free; first Sunday of every month free

Activities: Guided tours by appointment

Suggested Time to View House: 1 hour

Facilities on Premises: Victorian shop with books and cards

Description of Grounds: Not accessible to the public

Best Season to View House: Year round

Number of Yearly Visitors: 9,500

Year House Built: 1876

Style of Architecture: Italianate

Number of Rooms: 9 open to public

On-Site Parking: Yes **Wheelchair Access:** Yes

Description of House

The residents of the Camron-Stanford House in Oakland form a "Who's Who" of Bay area history. Built by Samuel Merritt in 1876, the house was bought by Alice Marsh Camron and her husband, William Walker Camron. Alice had inherited a fortune from her father, Dr. John Marsh, one of the first doctors in California. William's listing in the Oakland directory simply reads "Capitalist," perhaps referring to his real estate dealings, made possible on the strength of his wife's fortune. After the sudden death of their daughter, Grace, the Camrons left the mansion for a European tour, never to return to their beautiful and gracious home.

In their absence, David Hewes rented the house in 1878. Hewes was known as the man who commissioned the famous gold spike that joined the Central Pacific and Union Pacific Railroads at Promontory, Utah, on May 10, 1869. He and his wife, Matilda French Gray, lived in the house with her daughter, Franklina. They were followed by Horace Seaton, a banker and the deputy treasurer of the Central Pacific Railroad, but his tenure was a brief one. In 1882, the Camrons decided to sell the house to Josiah Stanford, the founder of a chain of stores that supplied gold miners with the basic necessities of life. Stanford also introduced the champagne grape to the region. In 1903, the house was sold again; this time to a retired sea captain and local businessman, John T. Wright. The house was finally purchased by the city of Oakland for use as a museum.

This grand, well appointed Italianate-style two-story mansion was one of many impressive houses built in the Lake Merritt district of Oakland. The partial wrap-around porch was once a welcoming threshold for the rich and the famous of Bay Area society, as well as national celebrities. In late 1880, Matilda French Gray hosted a reception in honor of the President and Mrs. Rutherford B. Hayes here.

Notable Collections on Exhibit

In addition to several family portraits, there are numerous fine examples of American decorative arts; one outstanding item is the silver plate punch bowl and set of six goblets which belonged to Matilda French Gray. This set was brought from the family estate in Warrington, Virginia, and was originally owned by Sarah Scarborough Butler French. The bowl and each goblet are inscribed with her initials.

Additional Information

The kitchen and an adjacent bedroom of the Camron-Stanford Mansion have been restored in the colonial style; these rooms were used as period rooms when the house functioned as a museum. The unusual black mantels were a rather common decorative device of the 1880s. The Camron-Stanford House is listed on the National Register of Historic Places.

Pardee Home Museum

672 Eleventh Street
Oakland, CA 94607
(510) 444-2187

Contact: Pardee Home Foundation
Open: By appointment
Admission: Adults $4.00; seniors $3.00
Activities: Guided tours, archives available
by appointment
Suggested Time to View House:
45–60 minutes
Description of Grounds: Half city block
with original carriage house and tank
house
Best Season to View House: Spring and
summer
Year House Built: 1868, additions 1885
and 1910
Style of Architecture: Italianate Villa,
bracketed
Number of Rooms: 18, 10 open to the
public

On-Site Parking: No **Wheelchair Access:** No

Description of House

Three generations of the Pardee family have occupied this villa for much of the past century. E.H. Pardee, who built the house, was a trained physician who also pursued a very active political career. He served as the mayor of Oakland, a state senator and a local assemblyman. His son, G.C. Pardee, followed, and later surpassed, his father in his accomplishments; first, as a doctor, then as mayor of Oakland, and, ultimately, as Governor of California from 1903 to 1907.

Their two-story home contains the many possessions of the Pardee family. Virtually all the items—the family furniture, housewares, and archives—can be seen just as the family left them, even though a number of high-style decorative elements were added later, as were some of the rooms. The house was entirely redecorated in 1955. The original carriage house and tank house still stand on the half-city-block property.

Notable Collections on Exhibit

Exhibits totaling over 50,000 pieces include an extensive collection of travel mementos from the Pardee family's world-wide excursions, a group of fine paintings, and a exquisite collection of teapots.

Additional Information

The Pardee Home Museum is listed on the National Register of Historic Places.

Fenyes Mansion

470 West Walnut Street
Pasadena, CA 91103
(818) 577-1660

Contact: Pasadena Historical Society

Open: Thurs.-Sun. 1–4 p.m.;
closed major holidays

Admission: Adults $4.00; seniors and
students $3.00; children under 12 free

Activities: Guided tours, exhibits, lectures,
bimonthly luncheons, monthly Sunday tea

Suggested Time to View House:
60–90 minutes

Facilities on Premises: Gift shop, book
store, research library and archives

Description of Grounds: Beautiful
landscaped gardens

Best Season to View House: Year round

Number of Rooms: 18, 10 open
to the public

Year House Built: 1905

Number of Yearly Visitors: 8,000

Style of Architecture: Eclectic Renaissance
Revival, Beaux Arts

On-Site Parking: Yes **Wheelchair Access:** Yes

Description of House

Dr. Adelbert Fenyes and his wife, Eva, commissioned Robert Fargahar to design and build their residence in 1905. The mansion had to be of sufficiently grand proportions to keep company with its luxurious neighbors on Pasadena's "Millionaire's Row." It was; and, since the Fenyes Mansion has not been refurbished or altered in any way, it now stands as a monument to a way of life and a world that no longer exists. The mansion was maintained as a private residence for many years by Eva's widowed daughter, Mrs. Thomas Curtin, and her daughter, Leonora. During the period of Leonora's marriage to George Paloheimo, who had been appointed Finnish Consul to the Southwest, the Fenyes Mansion was used as the Finnish Consulate from 1947 to 1965.

The Fenyes filled their home with many European antiques and art objects dating from the 15th and 16th centuries. In addition, many paintings from well-known American artists—including some 3,000 watercolors painted by Eva Fenyes while on her world travels—line the walls. Since the four generations of the Fenyes family conscientiously maintained their estate, all of the carpets, window coverings, and furnishings are original and in excellent condition.

Notable Collections on Exhibit

The Finnish Folk Art Museum collection is housed in the Fenyes Mansion; it is interpretative of Finnish life in the late 18th century.

Additional Information

The Pasadena History Center is currently under construction; the center will contain a library and archives, lecture hall, and conference rooms. A collection of period costumes will also be stored and exhibited in the new space. The Fenyes Mansion is listed on the National Register of Historic Places.

Gamble House

4 Westmoreland Place
Pasadena, CA 91103
(818) 793-3334

Contact: University of Southern California
Open: Thurs.-Sun. Noon–3 p.m.;
  closed holidays
Admission: Adults $4.00; seniors $3.00;
  students with I.D. $2.00; children
  (under 12) free
Activities: Docent-guided tours
Suggested Time to View House: 1 hour
Facilities on Premises: Bookstore
Description of Grounds: 2 acre property
  with terraces and rose garden
Best Season to View House: Spring and
  summer
Number of Yearly Visitors: 25,000
Year House Built: 1908
Number of Rooms: 12

Style of Architecture: Craftsman Style
On-Site Parking: Yes **Wheelchair Access:** Yes

Description of House

Gamble House was built in 1908 for Mr. and Mrs. David B. Gamble of Procter & Gamble fame. It is widely recognized as a masterpiece of the Arts and Crafts Movement in America and the most complete and best preserved example of the work of architects Charles Sumner Greene and Henry Mather Greene extant.

The Greenes were inspired and guided by Nature rather than by historical styles. In this, they followed the design philosophies of the Swiss and the Japanese, filtered through a thoroughly Southern California sensibility. This easy, graceful amalgam of influences is clearly seen in the Gamble House. Wide terraces, open porches, and cross-ventilation bring the cool scented breezes of a nearby arroyo inside. Wood is used everywhere and the exposed timbers and shingles blend into the landscape—the marvelously varied textures are the result of the wide range of woods employed: teak, maple, Port Orford cedar, redwood, and oak. The iridescent glass in the doors, windows, and light fixtures takes the changing daylight and creates a colored light show throughout the house.

The house was presented to the City of Pasadena in a joint agreement with the University of Southern California by the heirs of Cecil and Louise Gamble in 1966. The Gamble House is listed on the National Register of Historical Places.

Notable Collections on Exhibit

A joint program of the Gamble House, the University of Southern California, and the Huntington Library, an exhibit entitled "Greene and Greene and the American Arts and Crafts Movement" is on permanent display at the Virginia Steele Scott Gallery in the Huntington Library at 1151 Oxford Road in San Marino.

Tournament House

391 South Orange Boulevard
Pasadena, CA 91184
(818) 449-4100

Contact: Pasadena Tournament of Roses

Open: Feb.-Aug., Thurs. 2–4 p.m.

Admission: Free

Activities: Guided tours, audiovisual presentation

Suggested Time to View House: 45 minutes

Description of Grounds: 4½ acre estate consisting of the Tournament House and the Wrigley Gardens which contains hundreds of varieties of roses, camellias, and annuals

Best Season to View House: Year round

Year House Built: Started 1906, completed 1914

Number of Rooms: 22

Style of Architecture: Eclectic Italian Renaissance Revival

On-Site Parking: Yes **Wheelchair Access:** Yes

Description of House

The Tournament House was originally designed for real estate and dry goods tycoon George Stimson; it took over eight years to build this massive 22-room, 18,500-square-foot home. By the time it was completed, most of the Stimson children had grown up and moved away. So, in 1914 Stimson sold his house to William Wrigley, Jr., whose fortune grew out of chewing gum. For Wrigley, the Tournament House was just one of his six residences, and by no means the most grand. But his wife loved this home in Pasadena and spent most of her time here after Mr. Wrigley died in 1932. After her death in 1958, the home and gardens were donated to the City of Pasadena to be used as the permanent headquarters of the Pasadena Tournament of Roses Association.

The Tournament House is constructed of poured concrete and much of the interior woodwork is crafted out of woods that are now extinct. Attention to detail and rich ornamentation is in evidence everywhere. Exterior details include a green tapered Mission tiled roof, a simple hipped roof with a hidden front and center dormer, a wide and open overhang, a balustrade porte cochere, and a balustrade portico which serves as the main entry. The carved Honduras mahogany door is adorned with a lion's head, and the marble stairs in the entry hall have cast bronze railings and a carved mahogany bannister.

Notable Collections on Exhibit

The Rose Bowl Room features a collection of memorabilia related to the most famous games played in that annual collegiate football tournament.

Additional Information

Almost as famous as the Tournament House are the gardens which surround it; the original plantings of specimen trees from around the world were done by an English gardener hired by George Stimson. A storm in the 1930s destroyed many of these magnificent trees, but in recent years the City of Pasadena has restored the gardens for public enjoyment.

Call-Booth House

1315 Vine Street
Paso Robles, CA 93446
(805) 238-5473

Contact: Paso Robles Art Association

Open: Wed.-Sun. 11 a.m.–3 p.m.; closed
month of January

Admission: Donations accepted

Activities: Docent in attendance, exhibits,
artisans demonstrations, special Holiday
Showcase

Suggested Time to View House: 30 minutes

Facilities on Premises: Paintings and crafts
for sale

Description of Grounds: Authentic
Victorian gardens with carriage house

Best Season to View House: Spring-fall

Style of Architecture: Folk Victorian
Queen Anne-style cottage with
Eastlake spindlework

Number of Yearly Visitors: 5,000+

Number of Rooms: 5

Year House Built: c.1893

On-Site Parking: No **Wheelchair Access:** No

Description of House

This cottage was built in 1893 by Dr. Samuel Johnson Call, the Resident Springs Physician at the world-renowned Hotel El Paso de Robles. Many notable personalities of the era—including Teddy Roosevelt and Ignace Paderewski—came to sample the curative effects of the sulphur baths here. In 1904, Dr. Call left California for Hawaii and sold the house to his sister, Susanna Booth. Booth and her husband were cattle ranchers in the Santa Cruz mountains before moving, first to San Luis Obispo, then to this house in Paso Robles. Alfred Booth started the first pharmacy in the town and then became postmaster, a position that his wife would take over when he died in 1906. She died in 1944 at the age of ninety-four and the house became a rental property. It has been restored through the efforts of the couple who purchased it in 1983 and the Booth grandchildren, who provided the documents and photographs detailing the home's appearance at the turn of the century.

This one-story, front-gabled cottage features a full wrap-around porch decorated with Eastlake-style spindlework, gingerbread trim, and a pediment over the front porch entry. The exterior is painted a mustard-yellow highlighted with with dark green trim; inside the wall colors range from beige to burgundy to green. The furnishings are authentic to the late Victorian period and the upholstery matches the interior paints.

Notable Collections on Exhibit

The Call-Booth House is now home to the Paso Robles Art Association; the gallery features pieces done by local contemporary artists.

Kimberly Crest House and Gardens

1325 Prospect Drive
Redlands, CA 92373
(909) 792-2111

Contact: Kimberly-Shirk Association
Open: Thurs.-Sun. 1–4 p.m.; closed
holidays, month of August; other times
by appointment with a 30-day notice
Admission: $3.00 donation for adults
(12 and over)
Activities: Guided tours
Suggested Time to View House: 1 hour
Facilities on Premises: Gift shop
Description of Grounds: 6¼ acres of formal
terraced gardens and orange groves
Best Season to View House: Spring
Year House Built: 1897
Number of Rooms: 20

Number of Yearly Visitors: 6,000-7,000
Style of Architecture: Eclectic Chateauesque
On-Site Parking: Yes **Wheelchair Access:** No

Description of House

This imposing three-story Chateau standing on its hill above Redlands was built in 1897 by a widow from Middletown, New York, Cor-
nelia A. Hill. Mrs. Hill had buried most of her family—they'd died of
tuberculosis—over the preceding ten years, traveled the world, become
a leading member of the Presbyterian Church, and shown a great interest
in the native tribes of California and their artwork. In 1905, her mansion
was purchased by Mr. and Mrs. John Alfred Kimberly and christened
"Kimberly Crest." Alfred Kimberly was one of the four founders of the
Kimberly, Clark & Company. The couple had been wintering in Redlands
since 1899, but by 1905 all their children had married and left home. In
1919, their youngest daughter, Mary Kimberly Shirk, was widowed and
moved back in with her parents. She lived here for the rest of her life.

The Kimberly Crest House was designed by the Los Angeles architectural firm of Dennis and Farwell and it features a stucco and wood trim
exterior over a wood frame with elements common to the Chateauesque
style: a tower, two turrets, cast iron cresting, and decorative wood railing.
On the inside, some of the more notable features are: a French Revival parlor
highlighted with gilt, a glass mosaic tile fireplace, the oval dining room in
the tower, and an oak staircase opening onto a second floor sitting room.
The eclectic mixture of furniture is all original to the Kimberly family. The
Kimberly Crest Gardens are almost more impressive than the house itself;
designed by George Edwin Bergstrom, they have been repeatedly
photographed, painted, and featured in books and magazines.

Notable Collections on Exhibit

Items in the Kimberly Crest Collection include historic costumes c.1915
to 1935, the family archives, paintings by Guy Wiggins, Jessie Arms Botke,
and John E. Bundy, Tiffany lamps, Louis XV and Louis XVI-style furnishings, and American antique furniture c.1858 to 1930.

Governor's Mansion

1526 "H" Street
Sacramento, CA 95814
(916) 445-4209

Contact: Governor's Mansion State
Historic Park

Open: Daily 10 a.m.–5 p.m.; guided tours
on the hour; closed Thanksgiving,
Christmas, New Year's Day

Admission: Adults $2.00; children
(6-12) $1.00

Activities: Daily guided tours, exhibits,
ª living history" programs, special
holiday event

Suggested Time to View House:
45–60 minutes

Facilities on Premises: Carriage house
visitor center

Description of Grounds: Large city block
with Victorian-style plantings

Best Season to View House: Spring

Number of Yearly Visitors: 32,000

Year House Built: 1877, addition 1903

Style of Architecture: High Victorian
Second Empire

Number of Rooms: 30

On-Site Parking: No **Wheelchair Access:** Yes

Description of House

Built in 1877 for Albert Gallatin, a partner in a Sacramento hardware store, this house went on to become California's executive mansion. It was designed by the architect Nathaniel Goodell and built by Uriah Reese. Gallatin sold the house to Joseph Steffens in 1887; Steffens was the father of the famous journalist and author, Lincoln Steffens. The State of California then purchased the house from Steffens in 1903 and Governor George Pardee and his family moved in shortly thereafter. Twelve governors (including Earl Warren, later Chief Justice of the United States Supreme Court) lived here; the last was the future President Ronald Reagan whose occupancy ended in 1975. The interior decor reflects the taste of the three-term governor, Edmund G. "Pat" Brown.

The Governor's Mansion is a three-story, asymmetrical Second Empire-style structure with elements of the Italianate style also in evidence. The exterior features a straight line mansard roof, heavy bracketed cornices with deep overhanging eaves, elaborate dormer and window surrounds, and an entry porch with a curved portico. The mansion has been painted white since the 1940s. Many of the furnishings which once belonged to the various first families who lived here are still in the house, including Governor Pardee's 1902 Steinway piano, hand-tied Persian carpets bought by Mrs. Earl Warren in 1943, marble fireplaces from Italy, gold-framed mirrors from France, and numerous Victorian-style pieces.

Notable Collections on Exhibit

The official state china and silver are on display in the dining room. There is also a fine collection of gowns worn by several of California's First Ladies.

Additional Information

The first governor of California to live here, George Pardee, owned a magnificent Italianate-style villa in the city of Oakland. This house, which was built in 1868, has been fully restored as the Pardee Home Museum which is listed separately in this guide. It is certainly worth a visit.

Leland Stanford Mansion State Historic Park

802 North Street
Sacramento, CA 95814
(916) 324-0575

Contact: California Department of Parks
and Recreation
Open: Limited public tours on Tues.,
Thurs.and Sat.; group reservations
Admission: Free
Activities: Guided tours, holiday program
Suggested Time to View House:
30–45 minutes
Facilities on Premises: Small book and
card concession
Description of Grounds: Not yet restored
Best Season to View House: Year round
Number of Yearly Visitors: 4,000+
Year House Built: 1856,
remodeled 1872
Number of Rooms: 44

Style of Architecture: Eclectic mix of
Italianate and French Second Empire
On-Site Parking: No **Wheelchair Access:** Yes

Description of House

Leland Stanford was a major figure in California's political and academic arenas during much of its early history. He is chiefly remembered as the president of the Central Pacific Railroad Corporation from 1861 to 1890, as the state's eighth governor from 1862 to 1864, and as a United States Senator from 1885 to 1893. Stanford and his wife, Jane, are remembered as the founders of, and major financial contributors to, the university bearing the name of their deceased son, Leland Stanford, Jr.

The Leland Stanford Mansion is currently undergoing major restoration, and will appear much like the rendering of the north elevation upon completion. As one can see, the Leland Stanford Mansion is a beautiful example of the Second Empire style with elaborate embellishments

Notable Collections on Exhibit

On display is a photo exhibit documenting the "before-and-after" process of the current restoration project. This exhibit includes period photographs showing many rooms in the Stanford Mansion as they appeared in 1868 and 1872; it is an added goal of the restoration to bring the interior of the mansion back to its appearance in these photographs.

William Heath Davis House and Park

410 Island Avenue
San Diego, CA 92101
(619) 233-5227

Contact: Gaslamp Quarter Foundation
Open: Tues.-Fri. 12:30–4:30 p.m.,
Sat. 11 a.m.–2 p.m.
Admission: Donations appreciated
Activities: Guided tours, walking tours of the Historic Gaslamp Quarter
Suggested Time to View House: 30–45 minutes

Facilities on Premises: Visitor center, museum
Description of Grounds: Located on city block corner with landscaped grounds
Best Season to View House: Year round
Style of Architecture: Georgian New England "saltbox," prefabricated
Number of Rooms: 4 open to the public
On-Site Parking: No **Wheelchair Access:** Yes

Description of House

William Heath Davis, born in Hawaii into a family of traders, was the visionary who financed the founding of "new town" San Diego, then lost all his money when the wharf there was burnt by soldiers. In his memoir, *Seventy-five Years in California*, he recounts his many adventures; it remains a singular document for those interested in the history of California. Though he never lived in this house which now bears his name, he and his family did live in one identical to it; there were nine such homes shipped from New England on the brig *Cybell* in 1850. They were all cut and framed in Maine, then assembled here. The house was originally purchased by Andrew Gray, a surveyor and close friend to William Heath Davis, lived in for two years by Alonzo Horton, renowned merchant and land speculator, then moved to Eleventh Avenue from its first site at the intersection of State and Market Streets. In 1873, Mrs. Anna Knowles acquired the house and ran a hospital here for indigent patients. The house remained in private hands until 1977; two years later, the Gaslamp Foundation saved it from demolition and reassembled it on its present site.

The William Heath Davis House is the oldest frame house in San Diego—no major structural changes have been made in its history—and the only one of nine New England-built homes which were shipped together on the same mid-century voyage still standing. Each room represents a different chapter in the life of the house; for example, the parlor is interpreted to the Rebirth Period of the Alonzo Horton ownership (1867-1873) and the hallway appears as it did in the 1880s when it was being converted from a hospital. The furnishings reflect the the life led by a modestly well-to-do family in the latter decades of the 19th century.

Notable Collections on Exhibit

Among the many personal items belonging to the various families which inhabited the house, the most notable are the photographs of William Heath Davis, his wife, Maria Estudillo, and Alonzo Horton and his wife.

Additional Information

The William Heath Davis House is now the headquarters of the Gaslamp Quarter Foundation, an organization dedicated to the preservation of San Diego's architectural heritage.

Haas-Lilienthal House

2007 Franklin Street between
Washington and Jackson Streets
San Francisco, CA 94109
(415) 441-3004

Contact: Foundation for San Francisco's Architectural Heritage

Open: Wed. Noon–3:30 p.m., Sun. 11 a.m.–4:30 p.m.

Admission: Adults $4.00; seniors and children $2.00

Suggested Time to View House: 1 hour

Description of Grounds: Located in the Pacific Heights district

Number of Yearly Visitors: 3,000

Style of Architecture: Victorian Queen Anne

Activities: Guided tours, guided walking tours of Pacific Heights District

Facilities on Premises: Bookstore

Best Season to View House: Spring, summer, winter

Year House Built: 1886

Number of Rooms: 18, 10 open to the public

On-Site Parking: No **Wheelchair Access:** No

Description of House

San Francisco has often been called America's most picturesque and romantic city; to view the Haas-Lilienthal House in the city's Pacific Heights district is to confirm that assertion. This house was built in 1886 by William Haas, a Bavarian merchant, and the same family occupied it until 1972. It survived the great earthquake and fire of 1906 and remains a perfectly preserved reminder of life here at the turn of the century. The Haas-Lilienthal House is now owned by the Foundation for San Francisco's Architectural Heritage.

The house is built in the Victorian Queen Anne-Eastlake style and features an extraordinary array of gables and dormers, second-story bays and even a tower. It is shingled throughout and has the typical heavy bracketing under the eaves. Inside, one turns from the rich mahogany and oak woodwork to tiled and carved marble surfaces equally grand. All rooms are fully furnished with Victorian-style pieces.

Additional Information

The Haas-Lilienthal House is listed on the National Register of Historic Places. It is also the starting point for the Foundation's Pacific Heights Architectural Walking Tour.

Octagon House

2645 Gough Street
San Francisco, CA 94123
(415) 441-7512

Contact: National Society of the Colonial Dames of America in California

Open: Every second Sun., every second and fourth Thurs. Noon–3 p.m.; closed all legal holidays, month of January

Admission: Donations accepted; group tour fee $5.00 per person; school groups free

Activities: Group tours

Suggested Time to View House: 45 minutes

Best Season to View House: Year round

Facilities on Premises: Post cards and booklets for sale

Description of Grounds: Situated on city corner, the house is joined by a small award-winning 18th-century-style garden

Number of Yearly Visitors: 2,000

Year House Built: 1861

Style of Architecture: Octagon

Number of Rooms: 4

On-Site Parking: No **Wheelchair Access:** Yes

Description of House

For a brief period in the mid-19th century, houses built after plans published by Orson Fowler in his book *The Octagon House-A House For All* enjoyed a certain vogue in America. Today, fifty-five of these homes are still standing, and two of these are in San Francisco—this one and a private residence.

The Octagon House was built in 1861 by Mr. and Mrs. William C. McElroy; he was a miller and she is thought to have been a housekeeper at the first Hotel St. Francis. The house had a number of owners before it was bought by the Pacific Gas and Electric Company in 1924, who leased it until 1951. In that year, they decided that the property was more valuable than the structure and sold the house to the National Society of the Colonial Dames of America in California. That organization moved the house to its present location across the street from its original site.

The Octagon House is an excellent example of its kind; it features all the main characteristics of the style: the centrally sited stairwell with a skylight and lantern top, the functional arrangement of the rooms, and paired windows. Outside, the Italianate-style window treatments blend well with the Classical Revival-style portico. The use of quoins as a decorative detail is highly unusual. Inside, the present "Maltese Cross" floor plan consists of one large public room downstairs and four private rooms upstairs.

The furnishings have been donated or purchased and all date from 1930 or earlier; they came from New England, New York, and eastern Pennsylvania, in styles that range from William and Mary to Neoclassical.

Notable Collections on Exhibit
Decorative arts of the Colonial and Federal periods are represented here by a large collection of American furniture, portraits, samplers, English and American silver, pewter, imported ceramics, and Oriental rugs and lacquerware. There is also a collection of documents related to Colonial and Early American history.

Additional Information
The Octagon House is listed on the National Register of Historic Places.

Winchester Mystery House

525 South Winchester Boulevard
San Jose, CA 95128
(408) 247-2000

Contact: Winchester Mystery House Gardens and Historical Museum

Open: Mar.-Oct., daily 9 a.m.–5:30 p.m.; Nov.-Feb., daily 9:30 a.m.–4 p.m.; closed Christmas

Admission: Adults $12.50; seniors $9.50; children (6-12) $6.50

Activities: Guided tours, self-guided tours of garden and museums

Suggested Time to View House: 2½ hours

Facilities on Premises: Gift shop, café, two historical museums

Description of Grounds: 4 acres of restored Victorian gardens with many original plantings

Best Season to View House: Year round

Style of Architecture: Eclectic Victorian Queen Anne

Number of Rooms: 160

On-Site Parking: Yes **Wheelchair Access:** No

Description of House

The Winchester Mystery House is indeed a true Victorian-style house. It is also a one-roof amusement park, an exercise in spookiness, a monstrosity, an elicitor of all the superlatives one can think of, and, finally, a reminder that all homes are, to a greater or lesser extent, the embodiment of their owners' characters.

Sarah L. Winchester, daughter of the Pardees of New Haven, Connecticut, married William Wirt Winchester in 1862. William's father made rifles, and, in so doing, made a fortune as well. The couple had one child who died in infancy; and, in 1881, William himself died of tuberculosis. Sarah received an inheritance which made her wealthy beyond her dreams and, in 1884, she moved to San Jose on the advice of a medium that she'd been consulting since her husband's death. The medium also told Sarah that she would be able to ward off the cursed spirits who claimed her husband and child by buying a house and then continually building on it as the spirits directed. She immediately bought an eight-room farmhouse from a Doctor Caldwell and started adding to it. Thus, for the next thirty-eight years, every day for twenty-four hours a day, the Winchester House remained "under construc-tion." On the night that Sarah died, September 5, 1922, construction stopped. She had spent over $16 million—three-quarters of her inheritance—and left behind a 160-room testimonial to her obsessions, and her whims.

There are far too many features—commonplace, bizarre, beautiful, opulent, homely—for even a partial enumeration here; suffice it to say that the visitor will be overwhelmed at every turn. It cannot go unmentioned that at the heart of the design of the house lies the numeral "13." It, or its whole-number multiples, appears everywhere: 13 coat-hooks in each closet, 13 windows in a room, 13 bathrooms in the house, 13 wall or ceiling panels in a room, 13 steps on a staircase, and so on; Sarah even had 13 clauses in her will, which she signed...13 times!

Additional Information
Since early 1973, the Winchester Mystery House and its grounds has been undergoing a thorough restoration. The house is listed on the National Register of Historic Places.

Castro-Breen Adobe

Plaza Hall, P.O. Box 1110
San Juan Bautista, CA 95045
(408) 623-4881

Contact: San Juan Bautista State
Historic Park

Open: Mon-Sun. 10 a.m.–4:30 p.m.; closed
Thanksgiving, Christmas, New Year's Day

Admission: Adults $2.00; children $1.00

Activities: ªLiving history" programs,
audiovisual presentations, special
Father's Day weekend

Suggested Time to View House: 1 hour

Facilities on Premises: Gift shop, bookstore

Description of Grounds: Informal gardens
and orchards

Best Season to View House: Year round

Style of Architecture: Spanish Colonial,
Monterey style with mixed adobe brick
and frame

Number of Yearly Visitors: 350,000

Number of Rooms: 8

Year House Built: c.1838

On-Site Parking: Yes **Wheelchair Access:** Yes

Description of House

The Castro-Breen Adobe looks much the same as it did when General José Maria Castro lived here in the 1830s and 1840s. The General was the interim governor of the Mexican province of Alta California from 1835 to 1836 and interim commandant a decade later.

Although the exterior of this two-story adobe structure is a pure example of the Spanish Colonial style, the interior resonates with the varying styles of those who lived here and witnessed the historic changes that occurred in California during the mid-19th century. The Adobe is furnished to interpret the 1870s, when the Breen family lived here. Patrick and Margaret Breen and their seven children had been part of the ill-fated Donner party, stranded in the Sierra Nevada Mountains for 111 days during the terrible winter of 1846. They arrived in San Juan Bautista penniless and were taken in by the mission. Two years later, their sixteen-year-old son, John, found $10,000 worth of gold dust in the hills of California and presented this find as a gift to his parents. They bought the Castro Adobe and 400 acres of prime land in the San Juan Valley. The Breen family lived in this house until 1933, and then it became part of the San Juan Bautista State Historic Park.

The original adobe structure—and wood frame addition—features a Monterey-style full-width balcony, a red tile roof, and six-over-six fenestration. It has changed little since it was built.

Additional Information

The San Juan Bautista State Park consists of several houses and buildings; the mission church was founded in 1797 by Padre Fermin Francisco de Lasuen and forms the center of the complex. Other buildings include the Plaza Hotel (originally an 1813 barracks), the Plaza Stable, and Plaza Hall.

Alvarado Adobe

1 Alvarado Square
San Pablo, CA 94806
(510) 215-3080

Contact: San Pablo Historical and Museum Society

Open: Year-round, Sun. 1–5 p.m.; other times by appointment; closed major holiday weekends

Admission: Free

Activities: Guided tours, slide program on local history

Suggested Time to View House: 30 minutes

Facilities on Premises: Books on local history and gifts

Best Season to View House: Year round

Description of Grounds: Part of a landscaped civic center complex

Number of Yearly Visitors: 700

Number of Rooms: 4

Style of Architecture: Territorial Adobe with Spanish Colonial and Mexican influences

Year House Built: 1845

On-Site Parking: Yes **Wheelchair Access:** Yes

Description of House

The Castro family was one of the most prominent families in California during the Mexican period of the early 19th century. Francisco Maria Castro was granted the 18,000 acre Rancho San Pablo in 1823, after serving as the mayor of the pueblo of San Jose, and as the foreman of the Mission Dolores. Two of Castro's sons, Victor and Juan José, were granted adjoining land grants including that of the Rancho El Sobrante. Here, the Castro family operated a large ranch and farming enterprise; they raised cattle, sheep, and horses, grew acres of wheat and potatoes, and planted vineyards and pear orchards. The Castro family sold their livestock and produce to the Russians at Fort Ross in northern California and to American companies from New England. The original adobe was built in 1845; it became the home of Martina Castro and her husband, Juan Bautista Alvarado, the Mexican governor of California from 1836 to 1842. It was Alvarado who bravely proclaimed the colony of California a free and sovereign land as a protest against Spanish-Mexican rule.

The exterior of the Alvarado house is a good example of a typical adobe structure, with its characteristic low-pitched, tile-shingled roof and the long and narrow porch. However, the interior is interpretative of a family history which spanned many decades of California's development and many decorative styles. The house features several period rooms; two notable ones are the territorial, Rancho-style bedroom and the Victorian parlor. Fortunately, the house contains some original family furnishings as well as these period collections.

Additional Information

The San Pablo Historical and Museum Society also maintains the Blume House, a restored 1905 farmhouse located at the opposite end of the Alvarado Square complex.

Hearst Castle

**750 Hearst Castle Road
San Simeon, CA 93452
(805) 927-2020**

Contact: California Department of Parks and Recreation, Hearst San Simeon State Historical Monument

Open: Daily 8:20 a.m.–3:20 p.m.; closed Thanksgiving, Christmas, New Year's Day; extended hours in the summer

Admission: Adults $14.00; children (6-12) $8.00

Activities: Guided tours, special evening tours spring and fall featuring a "living history" program

Suggested Time to View House: 75 minutes

Facilities on Premises: Gift shop, snack bar

Description of Grounds: 137 acre compound with terraced gardens, pools and guest houses sited above San Simeon Bay

Best Season to View House: Spring

Number of Yearly Visitors: 1,000,000

Year House Built: Started 1919, "completed" 1947

Style of Architecture: Castle-Eclectic Hispano Moresque, guest cottages-Eclectic Italian Renaissance Revival

Number of Rooms: 165

On-Site Parking: Yes **Wheelchair Access:** Yes

Description of House

Cattle grazing on the slopes of the Santa Lucia mountains do not seem to be bothered by the presence of Hearst Castle, but, for the many visitors to this hilltop retreat, the Castle seems almost like an apparition. Perched 1,600 feet above San Simeon Bay, William Randolph Heart's personal fiefdom houses Greek, Roman and Egyptian sculpture, Medieval and High Renaissance religious art from Italy and Spain, and paintings by the great and not-so-great artists of France, Germany, and Holland. At first glance, the word "excess" springs to mind, but the imaginative mix of several architectural styles, combined with skillful execution and a refined and educated eye for collecting only the best, creates an illusion which rightly justifies the name of the property, La Cuesta Encantada, or the Enchanted Hill.

The Hearst Castle, or La Casa Grande, was designed by architect Julia Morgan. In addition to the main structure, three guest "cottages" add to the fantastical grandeur of the 137 acre estate once called Camp Hill. Other "fantasies" include myriad landscaped gardens with pools shimmering in the California sun, the 345,000 gallon "Neptune" outdoor pool guarded by mythic figures and once frequented by Hollywood screen legends of 1930s and 1940s , and the 205,000 gallon "Roman" indoor pool, decorated with Venetian glass tiles and roof-topped with its own tennis courts. The many architectural stunts are just as fabulous; the visitor looks up to the ceiling and finds that the ornately crafted surfaces are themselves genuine antiques: they have been removed entire from 15th-century European monasteries and castles only to be re-installed in this new American castle. For the most part, the furnishings were collected in France, Italy, and Spain; most date from the 15th through the 18th centuries.

William Randolph Hearst, sole heir to the vast wealth and land holdings which grew from his family's mining ventures, is thought to be the model for the character of Citizen Kane in the Orson Welles' film masterpiece. Though the resemblances are undeniable, Hearst's life was far more fascinating and complex than that of Welles' fictional creation, as a visit to this infamous house will make abundantly clear.

Additional Information

The guest cottages were originally referred to as only "A," "B" and "C," but were later given the names of Casa del Mar, Casa del Monte and Casa del Sol. The Hearst Castle and San Simeon Complex is listed on the National Register of Historic Places.

Casa de la Guerra

11 East de la Guerra
Santa Barbara, CA 93101
(805) 965-0093

Contact: Santa Barbara Trust for Historic
Preservation
Open: Currently undergoing archaeological
investigation and restoration; site open to
the public
Admission: Free
Activities: Visitors are welcome to watch
restoration in progress
Facilities on Premises: Visitor center,
gift shop

Description of Grounds: Large center
courtyard with minimal historic
landscaping
Best Season to View House: Year round
Year House Built: Between 1819 and 1828
Style of Architecture: Spanish Colonial
Adobe
Number of Rooms: 25
On-Site Parking: No **Wheelchair Access:** Yes

Description of House

José de la Guerra y Noriega came to Mexico from Spain as a young man;
in the New World his military career flourished and he became the commandant of the Santa Barbara Presidio as well as an important political leader
in Alta California. His influence lasted from the Spanish Colonial era,
through the years of Mexican provisional rule, up to the period of the
American Territorial government.

He built this house between 1819 and 1828; it is a typical large, one-and-
a-half-story, three-sided adobe structure surrounding a central courtyard.
For the thirty years up to 1858, the Casa de la Guerra was visited by all
high-ranking officials who came to California. It remained in the de la
Guerra family until 1925, when the El Paso shopping complex was constructed around it. It suffered major damage during that year's earthquake
and was subsequently rebuilt in the Spanish Colonial style.

The house and property are currently undergoing archaeological ex-
cavation and restoration, and visitors are welcome at the work site. The
interior will be restored to its appearance in the first half of the 19th century.
Some furniture which originally belonged to de la Guerra has been found
and will be featured in the restored structure.

Additional Information

Casa de la Geurra is listed on the National Register of Historic Places.

Fernald Mansion

414 West Montecito Street
Santa Barbara, CA 93101
(805) 966-1601

Contact: Santa Barbara Historical Museums
Open: Sun. 2–4 p.m.; closed Thanksgiving, Christmas
Admission: Donations welcome
Activities: Guided tours, group tours by reservation
Suggested Time to View House: 30 minutes
Description of Grounds: Beautiful landscaped fenced yard with many rare tree specimens
Best Season to View House: Year round
Number of Yearly Visitors: 4,500
Year House Built: 1862, additions 1880
Style of Architecture: Victorian Queen Anne with Gothic Revival-style characteristics
Number of Rooms: 14

On-Site Parking: Yes **Wheelchair Access:** No

Description of House

Judge Charles Fernald built this house in 1862, the year that he married Hannah Fernald. It was constructed by the master builder Roswell Forbush, who was also made the hand-carved staircase and many other interior decorative elements. When Florence Fernald, the Judge's only surviving child, sold the property, it was with the understanding that the house would be torn down after her death. Instead, money was raised to move the house to its present location and the Santa Barbara Historical Museums Women's Project Committee undertook the restoration and refurbishing of the Mansion, which opened in 1962. The house has recently seen a second restoration of the entry hall and second floor.

The mansion consisted of eight rooms on two floors when it was first built, and it also had a separate lean-to kitchen for safety's sake. Over the years, however, numerous additions were made to the house: in 1880 a dining room, parlor, porch, and upstairs bedrooms were added; and in 1927 a long veranda. The entire roof line was also changed to reflect the more fashionable Queen Anne style. Today the house features fourteen rooms, decorative trusses with carved finials, overhanging eaves, and varied window arrangements with bracketed surrounds. The interior has been interpreted to the turn of the century.

Notable Collections on Exhibit

Of the many original furnishings on display, one piece of note is the bedspread in the former bedroom of Florence Fernald; it is said to have been made by slaves on the plantation of President James K. Polk.

Trussell-Winchester Adobe

414 West Montecito Street
Santa Barbara, CA 93101
(805) 966-1601

Contact: Santa Barbara Historical Museums

Open: Sun. 2–4 p.m.; closed Thanksgiving, Christmas

Admission: Donations welcome

Activities: Guided tours, group tours by reservation

Suggested Time to View House: 30 minutes

Description of Grounds: Beautiful landscaped fenced yard with many rare tree specimens

Best Season to View House: Year round

Number of Yearly Visitors: 4,500

Year House Built: 1854, additions 1882 and 1904

Style of Architecture: Folk "Yankee adobe"

Number of Rooms: 6

On-Site Parking: Yes **Wheelchair Access:** No

Description of House

Captain Horatio Gates Trussell, who was born in Orland, Maine, began his career at sea as a ship's carpenter on the trade between the East Coast of the United States and the Hawaiian Islands with stops at various California ports. Soon he had his own ship and was found calling in at Santa Barbara with some frequency. He had fallen in love with Ramona Ayers-Burke, and they married in 1851—Captain Trussell was forty-two and his bride was only sixteen. Three years later Trussell built this house for his wife and they lived here until 1869, when they had to move to larger quarters to accommodate their growing family; the Trussells had ten children. The Winchester family bought the house in 1882 and their descendants lived here until 1955, when the property was deeded to the Santa Barbara Historical Society.

The single-story adobe features an unusual dual-pitched shingled roof and a porch supported by simple posts. Some of the timbers used in the floor and the roof came from the ill-fated ship, the *Winfield Scott*, which ran aground at Anacapa Island in 1853. The adobe core is joined to an entryway storeroom made entirely of wood. This hybrid, which combines features of both Mexican and American styles of architecture and some have likened to the French Colonial style, is affectionately called "Yankee Adobe."

The furnishings are American period antiques and heirlooms from the Trussell and Winchester families.

Notable Collections on Exhibit

Among the antique pieces is an 1820 Osborne and Stewart piano thought to be one of a kind.

Luther Burbank Home and Gardens

Santa Rosa and Sonoma Avenue
P.O. Box 1678
Santa Rosa, CA 95402
(707) 524-5445

Contact: Luther Burbank Home and
Gardens Board

Open: Apr.-Oct., Wed.-Sun.
10 a.m.–3:30 p.m.; gardens open
daily during daylight hours

Admission: Adults $1.00; children (under 12)
accompanied with an adult free

Activities: Guided tours, exhibits relating to
Burbank's life and work, special Holiday
Open House in December

Suggested Time to View House: 30 minutes

Facilities on Premises: Carriage house
museum and gift shop

Description of Grounds: Approximately
2 acres with carriage house, greenhouse
and gardens

Best Season to View House: Late spring

Style of Architecture: Modified Greek
Revival-style cottage

Number of Yearly Visitors: 15,000

Year House Built: c. 1870

Number of Rooms: 8, 4 open to the public

On-Site Parking: No **Wheelchair Access:** Yes

Description of House

Luther Burbank, the famed horticulturist, lived in Santa Rosa for more than fifty years. When he first arrived here in 1875 as a young man, he said, "I firmly believe, from what I have seen, that this is the chosen spot of all this earth as far as Nature is concerned." And it was on this chosen spot that Luther Burbank decided to build his home.

The Greek Revival style "cottage" was the residence of the Burbank family from 1884 to 1906. At this address, Burbank conducted various experiments in plant breeding; work that would introduce to the world more than eight hundred varieties of plants, including fruits, vegetables, nuts, grains, and flowers—all new. Burbank's self-proclaimed goal was to improve the quality of plant species in order to increase food production and supply.

In addition to the cottage, several outbuildings relating to Burbank's life and work lie on the grounds. These buildings include the carriage house—now the museum—and the greenhouse, designed and built by Burbank himself in 1889. It is in this greenhouse, and in the outdoor laboratory that his gardens provided, that Burbank carried out many of his experiments. The house contains numerous pieces of furniture made from "Paradox" walnut, wood from a tree developed by Burbank.

Notable Collections on Exhibit

Many portraits of Luther Burbank, painted by renowned American artists, hang on the walls of the home.

Additional Information

The Luther Burbank Home and Gardens is listed on the National Register of Historic Places.

Lyford House

376 Greenwood Beach Road
Tiburon, CA 94920
(415) 388-2524

Contact: Richardson Bay Audubon
Center

Open: Nov.-Apr., Sun. 1–4 p.m.

Admission: Donation requested

Activities: Guided tours, special
tours can be arranged, art
exhibits, hiking

Suggested Time to View House:
30 minutes

Facilities on Premises: Small gift and
nature book shop, Audubon Nature
Center with hiking trails

Description of Grounds: 9 acre waterfront
tract on Richardson Bay, an estuary off
San Francisco Bay

Best Season to View House: Spring and
summer

Year House Built: c.1876

Style of Architecture: Victorian
Second Empire, towered

Number of Rooms: 8

On-Site Parking: Yes

Wheelchair Access: No

Description of House

John Thomas Reed, an Irishman who had become a naturalized Mexican citizen, was granted the first land parcel in California's Marin County, the Rancho Corte de Madera del Presidio. This grant encompassed the present towns of Tiburon, Belvedere, Strawberry Point and portions of Mill Valley, Corte Madera and Larkspur. It was on Strawberry Point that his daughter, Hilarita, and her husband, Dr. Benjamin Lyford, built the imposing white Victorian structure which served both as their life-long home and as the center of their experiments in, and proselytizing for, hygienic living. Hilarita Reed had inherited her father's estate; when she married an eminent San Francisco physician famous for his advocacy of "healthful living," he decided to leave his practice and put his theories to the test. On part of the estate he established a scientific dairy farm and on another parcel he founded one of the first housing subdivisions in this country. Based on his principles promoting spiritual and bodily health, this development was named "The Lyford Hygeia." These same principles led him to fight for the installation of a city sewage system. In addition to the doctor's efforts on behalf of salubrious living, it is rumored that he conducted "embalming experiments" and discovered a secret formula for tissue preservation.

Sadly, the Lyfords produced no heirs. Dr. Benjamin died in 1906 and his beloved Hilarita followed two years later, in 1908. The house, which had fallen onto hard times, was saved from demolition in 1957 through the efforts of a local conservation league. They had it moved to its present location—a different part of John Reed's original rancho—by barge.

The Lyford House, like all of the original buildings, was painted white, in accordance with Dr. Benjamin's regimen. The house is a magnificent two-story, centered-towered Victorian. The exterior features a "striped" mansard roof alternating diamond and fishscale-shaped shingles in red and natural colors, elaborate carved finials and trim showing urns, fruit clusters, and floral patterns, and a tower topped by a truncated "witches' hat" roof. Inside, there is an exquisite circular staircase and banister executed entirely in mahogany, and gold leaf trim made in the East; the etched glass closet doors and skylight were lifted from the cabin windows of an old sailing vessel. Unfortunately, the four upstairs bedrooms have not been restored.

The furnishings accurately reflect the state of the house at the end of the nineteenth century but only one piece, a couch, is thought to be original. The rest are donations or loaners. The Lyford House now serves as the headquarters for the Richardson Bay Foundation, the Marin Conservation League, and the Marin Audubon Society. It is well worth a visit.

Held-Poage Memorial Home and Research Library

603 West Perkins Street
Ukiah, CA 95482
(707) 462-6969

Contact: Mendocino County Historical
Society, Inc.

Open: Tues., Thurs. and Sat. 2–4 p.m.;
closed on major holidays, fourth
weekend in June

Admission: Free, donations appreciated

Activities: School and special tours

Suggested Time to View House:
15–60 minutes

Description of Grounds: Older plants and
native trees

Best Season to View House: Year round

Number of Yearly Visitors: 500-650

Year House Built: 1903

Style of Architecture: Late Victorian Queen
Anne

Number of Rooms: 7

On-Site Parking: Yes **Wheelchair Access:** Yes

Description of House

William and Ethel Poage Held moved into this Queen Anne-style Victorian house in the small northern California town of Ukiah shortly after their marriage in 1903. "Billy" Held served in the State Legislature from 1904 to 1912, was elected mayor of Ukiah in 1928, and also served for twelve years as Judge of the Superior Court in Mendocino County.

The house was designed and built by the Mssrs. Orr and Evans for the grand sum of $2,000. It has not been renovated or substantially changed since the Held family lived there. The building now serves as a library containing 4,000 books and over 13,500 historical photographic negatives, maps, scrapbooks, and artifacts documenting the history of the region. An exhibit of watercolor and oil paintings by a local artist are on display.

Additional Information

The Held-Poage Memorial Home is listed on the National Register of Historic Places.

Sun House

431 South Main Street
Ukiah, CA 95482
(707) 462-3370

Contact: Grace Hudson Museum

Open: Wed.- Sat. 10 a.m.–4:30 p.m.,
Sun. Noon–4:30 p.m.; July and Aug.,
Tues. 10 a.m.–4:30 p.m.

Admission: Group rates $1.00 per person; all
others suggested donation of $2.00; family
group $5.00

Activities: Guided tours, 10 minute video

Suggested Time to View House:
25–60 minutes

Description of Grounds: Small park with
picnic tables

Best Season to View House: Spring-fall

Number of Yearly Visitors: 13,000

Year House Built: 1911

Style of Architecture: Craftsman-Bungaloid
style and American Arts and Crafts
Movement

Number of Rooms: 6

On-Site Parking: Yes **Wheelchair Access:** Yes

Description of House

The story of the Sun House is the story of Grace and John Hudson, a couple who found their life's work preserving the native culture of the people and the history of Ukiah. Grace Hudson (1865-1937) was born to a socially prominent pioneer family in Potter Valley; as a child, she showed a true talent for art. Grace attended art school in San Francisco and returned home to begin a long career painting portraits, especially of the local Pomo people. This endeavor earned Grace Hudson a national reputation as an painter known for her sensitive portrayal of Native Americans. John Hudson (1857-1936) was a doctor by profession but his passionate avocation was that of amateur archaeologist. He gave up his medical practice and spent the rest of his life as a collector-scholar and ethnologist, specializing in California Indian basketry. Many of the baskets he collected are now found in the collections of major national museums such as the Smithsonian Institution, the Field Museum of Chicago, and the Brooklyn Museum.

The Sun House, a six-room two-story bungalow, is one of four original Craftsman-style houses found in Ukiah. Built by George Wilcox in 1911, the home is a testament to the genuine artistic life of John and Grace Hudson. Although the house does not contain any original American Arts-and-Crafts style furniture, it does have several antique pieces and personal belongings which the couple collected over the years; these include antique Chinese vases and textiles given to them as presents by their Chinese housekeepers.

Notable Collections on Exhibit

The Sun House collections contain hundreds of art works and artifacts collected by the Hudsons shown in rotating exhibits. Also on exhibit are artifacts from several pioneer settlements of central Mendocino County.

Additional Information

There are only three Craftsman-style houses in the United States open to the general public: the Sun House of Ukiah, California, the Gamble House of Pasadena, California, and the Craftsman Farm in Morris Plains, New Jersey. The Sun House is listed on the National Register of Historic Places.

Rudolph M. Schindler House

835 North Kings Road
West Hollywood, CA 90069
(213) 651-1510

Contact: Friends of the Schindler House
Open: Sat. and Sun. 1–4 p.m.; other times by appointment; closed Thanksgiving, Christmas, New Year's Day
Admission: All $5.00
Activities: Guided tours, occasional architectural exhibits
Suggested Time to View House: 45–60 minutes
Facilities on Premises: Bookstore

Description of Grounds: Gardens are early examples of "indoor-outdoor" lifestyle with several outdoor living rooms
Best Season to View House: Year round
Number of Yearly Visitors: 3,000
Year House Built: Started 1921, completed 1922
Style of Architecture: International "modern radical" style
Number of Rooms: 5
On-Site Parking: No **Wheelchair Access:** Yes

Description of House

Rudolf M. Schindler (1887-1953) was born and raised in fin-de-siècle Vienna; after several years of study at the Imperial Academy of Fine Arts there, he came to the United States, where he apprenticed to the internationally famous architect, Frank Lloyd Wright. While working for Wright, Schindler oversaw the construction of the Hollyhock House, a masterpiece of "organic" architecture which is also listed in this guide.

Though Wright's influence on Schindler was incalculable, the vision that the Austrian had for this, his own home, was distinctly original and considerably ahead of its time. The living arrangement he engineered—his partner Clyde Chace, his partner's wife, Marian, and his own wife, Pauline Gibling Schindler, all living in the house as a kind of intimate commune—was considerably ahead of its time, as well. It may be said that architectural innovation was only one of the gifts that Schindler proffered which California eagerly embraced. Among the more famous commissions that Schindler executed are: the Lovell Beach House (1925-1926), the Wolfe House (1928), the Oliver House (1933), the Laurelwood Apartments (1948), and the Bethlehem Baptist Church (1944). Schindler's own home was a frequent stopping place for artists, their patrons, and the critical avant-garde in the decades from the 1920s through the 1940s.

The house features radical elements which have since become commonplace in Southern California buildings: flat roofs, an open floor plan, and all rooms opening to a central garden through sliding glass doors. Schindler designed this house as a permanent "campsite"—the actual structure is a complex of artists' studios—and the communal living was to be done largely out in the garden; people slept in the open air, ate the fruit growing there, and watched their children run free. Built of unpainted concrete and redwood, the Schindler House is still capable of rousing strong emotions in visitors. It has been restored to appear as it did on the date of its completion, June 6, 1922.

Additional Information

The Rudolph M. Schindler House is listed on the National Register of Historic Places.

General Phineas Banning Residence Museum

**401 East Main Street
Wilmington, CA 90748
(310) 548-7777**

1864

Contact: City of Los Angeles Department of Recreation and Parks, Friends of Banning Park

Open: Tues.-Thurs., Sat.and Sun. 12:30–2:30 p.m.; group tours by appointment

Admission: $2.00 donation

Activities: Guided tours, lectures, school programs, kitchen demonstrations, special seasonal events including the Spring Wisteria Festival

Suggested Time to View House: 90 minutes

Description of Grounds: 20 acre park with coaching barn and one-room schoolhouse; elaborate old plantings include eucalyptus trees, date palms, cedars, giant bamboo, and numerous flower varieties

Best Season to View House: Year round

Number of Yearly Visitors: 17,000

Year House Built: 1864

Style of Architecture: Greek Revival

Number of Rooms: 23

On-Site Parking: Yes **Wheelchair Access:** Yes

Description of House

Phineas Banning had wanderlust right from the start. In 1843, at the age of thirteen, Phineas left his parent's homestead at Oak Hill Farm in Wilmington, Delaware, with only fifty cents in his pocket. After settling for a time in Philadelphia, he heard the call of "Go West" and set off for California in 1851, traveling through the treacherous jungles of Panama on the way. From the Pacific coast of the Panamanian Isthmus, he sailed north 3,000 miles to San Pedro Bay at Sepulveda landing. In 1851, Los Angeles was still a rough-and-tumble town where new settlers and established Mexican families vied to cash in on the booming economy and seemingly endless opportunities. Banning jumped into the thick of it and made a fortune by hauling freight from the port of San Pedro to Los Angeles. Over the next thirty years, he was instrumental in the creation of a transportation network that would make Los Angeles one of the most profitable commercial centers of the West. Banning, a patriotic man, became politically influential, supporting the Union cause during the Civil War, serving in the State legislature, and founding the town of Wilmington, California.

The mansion that Phineas Banning built in 1864 is now recognized as the finest extant 19th-century Greek Revival house in southern California. The beautiful three-story house features full-facade porches graced with squared columns and spindlework railings. Many of the rooms have been restored to the Victorian period post-1870 with costumes, textiles, and decorative art objects on display. Through recent efforts, thirty-two pieces of original Banning furniture have been returned to the site; most of the furnishings are made from walnut and mahogany.

Additional Information

The Phineas Banning House was the center of social and political activity. With patriotic fervor and community spirit, Phineas enjoyed celebrating holidays such as the Fourth of July and George Washington's Birthday, in addition to local Mexican fiestas. At one such celebration, it is rumored that the serving pot for the frijoles was so large the beans had to be stirred with a shovel! The Phineas Banning Residence is listed on the National Register of Historic Places.

Filoli

Contact: National Trust for Historic Preservation and Filoli Center

Open: Mid Feb.-mid Nov., Tues.-Sat.

Admission: $8.00 per person (no children under 12); nature hikes: adults $4.00; children $1.00; student classes (over 12) $4.00 per child

Activities: Guided tours, nature hikes, demonstrations, lectures, musical performances, large-scale benefits

Suggested Time to View House: 2 hours

Facilities on Premises: Garden shop and tea shop

Description of Grounds: 654 acres with 16 acres of formal gardens and nature trails with a carriage house, a gardener's cottage and a tea house

Best Season to View House: Year round

Number of Yearly Visitors: 75,000

Year House Built: Started 1915, completed 1917

Style of Architecture: Eclectic Colonial Revival in the Georgian countryhouse manner

Number of Rooms: 43

On-Site Parking: Yes **Wheelchair Access:** Yes

Description of House

"Fight, Love, Live" was the motto of the man who built Filoli, William Bowers Bourn II (1857-1936). This picturesque and secluded site was chosen by Bourn because it reminded him of the Lakes of Killarney in his native Ireland, and because it was in close proximity to the Spring Valley Water Company, a major supplier of water to the city of San Francisco, and a Bourn-owned business. A prosperous entrepreneur, Bourn owned and operated several other Californian businesses, including the Empire Mine in Grass Valley and the Greystone Winery at St. Helena in the Napa Valley. Bourn also happened to be president of the San Francisco Gas Company.

Filoli was modeled after the elegant country estates of William B. Bourn's native land by architect Willis Polk . The formal gardens, equally beautiful, were designed by Bruce Porter with the aid of Isabella Worn. Bourn and his wife lived at Filoli until their deaths in 1936. The estate was purchased in that same year by Mr. and Mrs. William P. Roth. Mrs. Roth was the daughter of the founder of the Matson Navigation Company; her husband was president and chairman of the board of the same. She was an avid horticulturist and greatly extended the fine tradition of formal garden design established at Filoli by the previous owners. Hundreds of new plantings, of both tree and flower varieties, were added during this period.

The house exhibits an eclectic combination of architectural features characterized by arched windowheads, exterior brick laid in Flemish bond fashion, decorative trim reminiscent of the Stuart period, and a tile roof designed in the Spanish tradition. This unusual mix of styles can also be seen in the interior of the house. Each hand-crafted floor is unique: in the study, for example, the koa wood floor is filled with a burnt chain pattern whereas, in the library, the California black walnut floor is designed in an intricate herringbone pattern. The house boasts of no less than seventeen marble fireplaces with eleven chimneys, and the crystal chandeliers are replicas of those found in the Hall of Mirrors at Versailles.

Notable Collections on Exhibit

Both families collected fine art, decorative artifacts, and rare book editions, and their collections reflect sophisticated tastes. The Filoli collection includes: paintings of the 17th-century European masters, 18th-century French porcelains, Chinese porcelain birds and theatrical figurines of the Ch'ing period, 18th-century Chinese export wallpaper panels, and a complete set of Banks' Florilegium. Five murals painted by Ernest Peixotto in 1925 depict several views of the Lakes of Killarney.

Additional Information

Filoli remained in the possession of Mr. and Mrs. William P. Roth until Mrs. Roth deeded the estate to the National Trust of Historic Preservation in 1975.

Colorado

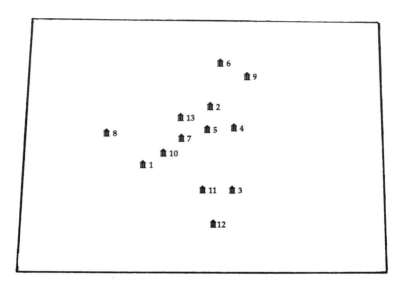

1. Aspen
Wheeler-Stallard House Museum

2. Boulder
Harbeck-Bergheim House

3. Colorado Springs
McAllister House Museum
Orchard House at White House Ranch

4. Denver
Byers-Evans House
Grant-Humphreys Mansion
Molly Brown House Museum

5. Evergreen
Hiwan Homestead Museum

6. Fort Collins
Avery House and Carriage House

7. Frisco
Staley House

8. Glenwood Springs
Edinger-Shumate House

9. Greeley
1870 Meeker Home

10. Leadville
H.A.W. Tabor House Museum

11. Manitou Springs
Miramount Castle Museum

12. Pueblo
Rosemount Victorian House Museum

13. Winter Park
Cozens Ranch House Museum

Wheeler-Stallard House Museum

620 West Bleeker Street
Aspen, CO 81611
(303) 925-6928

Contact: Aspen Historical Society

Open: Mid Dec.-mid Apr., June-Sept.,
Tues.-Sun.

Admission: Adults $3.00; seniors and
children $.50; guided walking tours
$5.00 per person

Activities: Guided tours

Suggested Time to View House: 1 hour

Description of Grounds: Full city block
with indigenous trees

Best Season to View House: Spring

Number of Yearly Visitors: 5,000

Year House Built: 1888,
remodeled c.1950

Style of Architecture: Victorian
Queen Anne

Number of Rooms: 9

On-Site Parking: Yes

Wheelchair Access: No

Description of House

Today, when most people think of the town of Aspen, Colorado, they picture the Rocky Mountain resort of the rich and famous. But in 1888, when Jerome B. Wheeler tried to move his family into their new Aspen home, Mrs. Wheeler blanched...the town was far too uncivilized for her family! Her husband prevailed; he believed in Aspen passionately and banked everything on its future. Unfortunately, he lost it all in the Silver Panic of 1893 and his Victorian home had to be forfeited. It became the property of the Stallard family, then-prominent Aspen citizens.

The house, located in Aspen's West End, was remodeled in the 1950s by Bauhaus architect Herbert Bayer and much of the interior bears his handiwork. The late 19th-century furnishings now on display in the home are those of the Wheeler and Stallard families.

Inside the carriage house black-and-white photographs document Aspen's history, architecture, and culture.

Additional Information

The Aspen Historical Society oversees two ghost towns, Ashcroft and Independence. Both towns are open to the general public year round, but can be reached by car only during the summer and fall. Ashcroft and Independence date from the 1880s. The Wheeler-Stallard House is listed on the National Register of Historic Places.

Harbeck-Bergheim House

1206 Euclid Avenue
Boulder, CO 80302
(303) 449-3464

Contact: Boulder Museum of History

Open: Tues.-Sat. Noon–4 p.m.; other times by appointment; closed New Year's Day, Fourth of July, Thanksgiving, Christmas

Admission: Adults $1.00; children (under 12) free

Activities: Guided tours on request

Suggested Time to View House: 30–45 minutes

Facilities on Premises: Gift shop

Description of Grounds: Located in Beach Park

Best Season to View House: Summer and fall

Style of Architecture: Modified Chateauesque

Number of Yearly Visitors: 2,000

Number of Rooms: 7

Year House Built: 1899

On-Site Parking: Yes **Wheelchair Access:** Yes

Description of House

New Yorker J. H. Harbeck made his fortune in the stock market and as a chain store operator. He and his wife desired a summer home in Colorado for its salutary climate and wonderful scenery. So, in 1899, he commissioned Eastern architects to build a home somewhat in the style of a French Chateau here in Boulder. Harbeck, ever the financier and stock player, also installed a direct phone line to Wall Street in his house. The couple stayed here for two or three months each year until J. H. died in 1910; after that his wife never returned to their summer home. She also wouldn't sell it until twenty years had passed because she didn't want the graves of her beloved pet pug dogs disturbed. When the prescribed period for respecting those gravesites ended in 1939, the house was purchased by Milton Bergheim, the son of the locally renowned pioneer merchant, Jonas Bergheim.

The Harbeck-Bergheim House is built of gray Indiana sandstone and features a huge Dutch-style front door bordered by leaded glass panels. Exterior details include four chimneys, two-story bays, an attic dormer accented with a pair of oval windows, and a portico with balustrade. Inside, one is drawn up the main stairway to a second floor landing dominated by an especially beautiful floral-patterned Tiffany window. Rooms on the second floor include three bedrooms and a large bathroom which features its original tiles and lavatory. Downstairs, there are two fireplaces of Italian marble, a living room ceiling which features decorative plaster moldings, and a built-in buffet in the dining room. The wallpaper presently seen in the house dates to the period 1945 to 1955; samples of the original wallpaper are framed and hung. The house is sparsely furnished in late Victorian pieces.

McAllister House Museum

423 North Cascade Avenue
Colorado Springs, CO 80903
(719) 635-7925

Contact: National Society of Colonial
Dames in the State of Colorado

Open: Sept.-Apr., Thurs.-Sat.
10 a.m.–4 p.m.; May-Aug. Wed.-Sat.
10 a.m.–4 p.m., Sun. Noon–4 p.m.

Admission: Adults $2.00; seniors $1.00;
children (6-16) $.75

Activities: Seasonal guided tours, special
activity program with reservation

Suggested Time to View House:
30–40 minutes

Facilities on Premises: Carriage house
gift shop

Description of Grounds: Large landscaped
yard with rose gardens and picnic tables

Best Season to View House: Summer

Year House Built: 1873

Number of Rooms: 6

Number of Yearly Visitors: 2,100

Style of Architecture: Rural Gothic Revival

On-Site Parking: Yes **Wheelchair Access:** No

Description of House

In 1873 Major Henry McAllister, a Civil War veteran from Pennsylvania, moved his family to Colorado Springs at the behest of General William Jackson Palmer, the town's founder. Here McAllister became the director of the Colorado Springs Company and raised three children. In 1874, the family moved into this brick house, one of the first to be built in the town; the Major lived here until his death in 1921. The house has been restored to its original elegance by the Colonial Dames of America.

This one-and-a-half-story Downing-inspired Gothic cottage is one of the most impressive smaller homes standing in the state of Colorado. The exterior walls are twenty inches thick to provide protection against the extreme Rocky Mountain winters; they're made of brick manufactured in Philadelphia and feature stone quoins. The steeply pitched roof, anchored by iron rods into masonry, has enclosed rafters and purlins and there are two porches, front and rear, trimmed with Gothic Revival-style paired supports. The impression of solidity and permanence is reiterated inside the house, with its unique "doorway" pocket windows, marble fireplaces (also made in Philadelphia), and extremely fine carpentry done by W. S. Stratton, the future mining baron. Most of the structure is unchanged from the days of the McAllister residency; the interior colors reflect the original decor and the furnishings are mostly donated pieces in the various revival styles of the late 19th century: Gothic, Renaissance, and Rococo. A few of the earlier pieces belonged to the McAllister family. The McAllister House Museum is listed on the National Register of Historic Places.

Notable Collections on Exhibit

Items of note are the Major's Civil War memorabilia, an 1870s melodeon, and a small collection of 19th-century "crazy" quilts.

Orchard House at White House Ranch

Garden of the Gods Park
off 30th Street and Gateway Road
Colorado Springs, CO 80905
(719) 578-6777

Contact: Colorado Springs Park and Recreation Department, White House Ranch Historic Site

Open: Early June-Labor Day, Wed.-Sun. 10 a.m.–4 p.m.; Sept.-Dec., Sat. 10 a.m.–4 p.m., Sun. Noon–4 p.m.

Admission: Adults $3.00; seniors $2.00; children (6-12) $1.00

Activities: Guided tours, "living history" farm with demonstrations at 1868 homestead

Suggested Time to View House: 2 hours including house and all outbuildings

Facilities on Premises: Museum shop "general store"

Description of Grounds: Restored homestead with an arboretum featuring native and dry-land plants, nature trails and picnic areas

Best Season to View House: Summer and fall

Number of Yearly Visitors: 63,000

Year House Built: 1907

Style of Architecture: Eclectic Period Revival with Mission and South African Dutch Colonial characteristics

Number of Rooms: 15

On-Site Parking: Yes **Wheelchair Access:** Yes

Description of House

The Gold Rush of 1859 brought thousands of fortune seekers to the territory of Colorado, hell-bent for adventure, dreaming of riches. When the boom went bust, the survivors soon realized that working the rich land itself would produce the wealth which they had vainly sought in gold. The native peoples knew that this ruggedly beautiful "Garden of the Gods" was a precious land, full of game and abundantly watered, but even with these natural gifts, life was extremely hard for the early homesteaders.

In 1867, Walter Galloway moved onto the 160 acre tract which today is known as White House Ranch. For the next seven years, Galloway struggled for survival, battling the elements and the ever-constant threat of raids. It would appear that he tired of the battle; in 1874, Galloway sold his farm to the Chambers family. The new owners named the ranch "Rockledge." With luck on their side, the Chambers turned the ranch into a successful "truck farm," selling fruit and other produce to the Antlers Hotel in Colorado City. At one time, they also let rooms to folks traveling to Colorado in search of cures for their various ailments.

General William Jackson Palmer, founder of Colorado Springs and owner of the Glen Eyrie Estate, purchased the land in 1900. Soon thereafter, he decided to built a house on the property for distant relatives, William and Charlotte Sclater. The unusual design of the three-story stucco structure was in accord with Palmer's wishes; the architect, Thomas MacLaren, took an eclectic, revivalist approach, combining the new Mission style with the more traditional Dutch Colonial style. Orchard House is furnished with items reflecting this eclectic mode; it features furniture and decorative pieces executed in the American Arts & Crafts, Mission, and Colonial Revival styles. The house has been painted its original buff color.

Additional Information

General Palmer's Tudor-style Castle, Glen Eyrie, is now a conference center adjacent to the Garden of the Gods. Depending on the conference schedule, the owners conduct 1¼ hour guided tours of this vastly impressive estate during the summer and on winter Sundays. Rockledge House c.1874 has not been restored and currently serves as a museum shop and general store.

Byers-Evans House

1310 Bannock Street
Denver, CO 80204
(303) 620-4933

Contact: Colorado Historical Society

Open: Tues.-Sun. 11 a.m.–3 p.m.;
  closed holidays

Admission: Adults $2.50; seniors $2.00;
  students $1.00

Activities: Guided tours, introductory video

Suggested Time to View House: 60 minutes

Description of Grounds: Corner lot with
  antique flower gardens and stands
  adjacent to the Denver Art Museum near
  Civic Center Park

Year House Built: 1883 with many
  subsequent additions

Best Season to View House: Summer

Number of Yearly Visitors: 15,000

Number of Rooms: 18

Style of Architecture: Italianate

On-Site Parking: No **Wheelchair Access:** Yes

Description of House

One of Colorado's original 'Fifty-niners, William Newton Byers published Denver's first newspaper, *The Rocky Mountain Times*, just six days after arriving in the fledgling town. He formed a close and lasting friendship with John Evans who, after amassing a fortune in Illinois, came to Colorado where he was installed as the second territorial governor in 1862. The two worked to get Denver a rail line which would connect it to the rest of the country; finally, in 1870, they succeeding in establishing the Denver Pacific Railroad. The two men were also instrumental in the founding of many of Denver's major educational, civic, and religious institutions. By 1883, when Byers built this house on Bannock Street, Denver was a thriving young city, thanks largely in part to the efforts of these two citizens. In 1889, Byers sold the house to his friend's son, William Gray Evans, who would himself become an important Denver business and civic leader. The house remained in the Evans family for ninety-five years; it was donated to the Colorado Historical Society in 1978, but did not come under their stewardship until 1981 when Margaret Evans Davis, the last surviving family member, died.

This well-proportioned two-story Italianate house is built of plum-colored brick and features elaborate wrought iron cresting around the periphery of the flat roof line. There is a front porch with solid brackets, a large second-story bay window, patterned masonry chimneys, and extended rectangular windows with flat lintels. Over the years a number of significant expansions were made, the last in the early 1920s. It is to that period that the house has been restored.

Almost all of the furnishings belonged to the Evans family and include pieces in a variety of styles: William & Mary, Renaissance Revival, and some made by Gustav Stickley. The Byers-Evans House is listed on the National Register of Historic Places.

Grant-Humphreys Mansion

770 Pennsylvania Street
Denver, CO 80203
(303) 894-2506

Contact: Colorado Historical Society
Open: Tues.-Fri. 10 a.m.–2 p.m.; closed holidays
Admission: Adults $2.00; seniors and children $1.00
Activities: Self-guided tours, guided and luncheon tours available
Suggested Time to View House: 45 minutes
Best Season to View House: Summer and fall

Description of Grounds: Located in Humphreys Park with antique flower gardens
Number of Yearly Visitors: 30,000
Year House Built: 1902
Style of Architecture: Eclectic Renaissance Revival, Beaux Arts
Number of Rooms: 30
On-Site Parking: Yes **Wheelchair Access:** Yes

Description of House

This enormous Beaux-Arts mansion was built in 1902 for James B. Grant (1848-1911), the son of an Alabama plantation owner who studied mining in Germany and made his fortune in Leadville, Colorado, as head of the Omaha and Grant Smelting Company. In 1882, the company moved its headquarters to Denver and the following year Grant was elected Colorado's third governor. In 1917, his widow sold the mansion to Albert E. Humphreys, an oil tycoon who had previously made and lost fortunes in logging and mining. Humphreys lived here with his wife, Alice Boyd, and her son, Ira, and his wife. Ira Boyd was the inventor of the Humphreys spiral ore concentrator.

At the turn of the century, James Grant commissioned the architects Theodore Davis Boal and F. L. Harnois to design a home on Denver's "Quality Hill." They built this rather restrained Beaux-Arts masterpiece—it lacks the floral ornamentation common to this style—with a winning combination of elements: an epic front entry featuring a full-height projecting oval supported by six twenty-foot Corinthian columns, exaggerated "tower" chimneys, cornice brackets, a rear entry porte cochere with balustrades, and full-width open porches and balconies on either side cornered with stone pilasters which also serve as quoins. The first floor features floor-to-ceiling windows cased in oval brackets and highlighted with segmented fan lights. The lovely interior woodwork and light fixtures are original; and, in the parlor, one can see the silk damask wallcovering first hung in 1902. In the basement of the mansion is a ballroom and a bowling alley. The house is furnished with a combination of pieces from the Humphreys family and donated items appropriate to the 1920s.

Notable Collections on Exhibit

Portraits of the two famous residents of the mansion, James B. Grant and Albert E. Humphreys, and their wives, are on display.

Additional Information

The Grant-Humphreys Mansion is listed on the National Register of Historic Places.

Molly Brown House Museum

1340 Pennsylvania Street
Denver, CO 80203
(303) 832-4092

Contact: Historic Denver, Inc.

Open: Sept.-May, Tues.-Sat. 10 a.m.–4 p.m., Sun. Noon–4 p.m.; June-Aug., Mon.-Sat. 10 a.m.–4 p.m., Sun. Noon–4 p.m.

Admission: Adults $3.00; seniors $2.00; students (6-18) $1.00; children (under 6) free

Activities: Guided tours, outreach programs, special seasonal events, Victorian dining experiences

Suggested Time to View House: 1 hour

Facilities on Premises: Museum gift shop

Description of Grounds: Small urban lot with an 1889 Victorian home

Best Season to View House: Spring and summer

Number of Yearly Visitors: 40,000+

Year House Built: 1889

Style of Architecture: Victorian Queen Anne

Number of Rooms: 14

On-Site Parking: No   **Wheelchair Access:** No

Description of House

During her lifetime, Margaret Tobin, the woman we know as the "Unsinkable Molly Brown," would travel far from her modest beginnings in Hannibal, Missouri. After moving West to Colorado, Molly fell in love with, and married, the son of Irish immigrants, James Joseph Brown, a successful miner. With money to burn, the couple moved from the small mining town of Leadville to the more civilized state capital, Denver. Here, the Browns fixed themselves at the center of society life, becoming members of the Denver Country Club and traveling frequently to Europe and New York. It was not long, however, before John and Molly separated; when he retreated to his business in Colorado, she embarked on a new round of world travel...beginning with a voyage to Europe on the *Titanic*! It was on this fateful journey that Molly would earn her reputation as a heroine *and* her nickname, "Unsinkable," when she courageously saved and comforted many desperate passengers caught in the life and death struggle aboard that sinking ship and its lifeboats. In 1932, Molly died in New York City while she was staying at the fashionable Barbizon Hotel. After death, she and John were rejoined, having both been buried in the Holy Rood Cemetery, Long Island.

The Molly Brown House was built in 1889, at the time when John and Molly were the toasts of the town. Designed by Denver architect William Lang, this Victorian Queen Anne-style house was rather unusual in its exterior of cut Colorado lavastone with sandstone trim. So different, in fact, that it became a popular place to rent while the Browns were off to Europe. In 1902, the house was rented even by Governor and Mrs. James Bradley Orman and served as the Governor's mansion for two years. Fortunately for future generations, the Browns were intensely proud of their home and photographed the interior with some frequency, thus providing an accurate record of its appearance through the years. The house has been restored with many of the Browns' original possessions and other items appropriate to the period.

Notable Collections on Exhibit

"Fashions from Molly Brown's Trunk" is an informative program featuring vintage clothing from the Historic Denver, Inc. collection.

Additional Information

It is believed that Molly Brown was one of Denver's historic preservationists; in 1930, she purchased the home of poet Eugene Field and donated it to the city as a memorial. The Molly Brown House is listed on the National Register of Historic Places.

Hiwan Homestead Museum

**4208 South Timbervale Drive
Evergreen, CO 80439
(303) 674-6262**

Contact: Jefferson County Open Space
Open: June–Aug., Tues.-Sun.
   11 a.m.–5 p.m.; Sept.-May,
   Tues.-Sun. Noon–5 p.m.
Admission: Free
Activities: Guided tours
Suggested Time to View House: 45 minutes
Description of Grounds: 3 acre grove with
   picnic area
Best Season to View House: Year round
Number of Yearly Visitors: 17,000
Year House Built: c. 1880
Style of Architecture: National, log
Number of Rooms: 17

On-Site Parking: Yes **Wheelchair Access:** Yes

Description of House

Sometime in the 1880s, Mary Neosho Williams, a Civil War widow, traveled to Colorado with her daughter, Josepha, and settled in Evergreen. Here she bought a log building and hired John "Jock" Spence, a Scottish carpenter, to convert it into a summer cottage. Josepha became one of Colorado's first women doctors; she married Canon Charles Winfred Douglas, an Episcopalian curate known for his musical work. Their son, Frederick Huntington, was a collector of Native American artifacts; his collection became the core of the Native American Arts exhibit at the Chappell House, now the Denver Museum. When Josepha died in 1938, the house was sold to Tulsa oilman Darst Buchanan. At that time, the ranch and house were named Hiwan Ranch and Homestead.

The modest log house was originally chinked with mud, sand, and honey; but after Jock Spence finished the remodeling, it stood as a model of elegant workmanship. Some of his improvements included the addition of an octagonal two-story log tower to the master room, the lower level of which served as a sitting room and library, the upper level as a bedroom; and a master staircase made of quarter logs set into a stringer fashioned out of a whole tree. All of the furnishings on display were collected by the Williams and Buchanan families.

Notable Collections on Exhibit

Changing exhibits of artifacts relating to Jefferson County history and a "hands-on" history room for children are some of the highlights of this unique house.

Additional Information

The Hiwan Homestead is listed on the National Register of Historic Places.

Avery House and Carriage House

328 West Mountain Avenue
Fort Collins, CO 80521
(303) 221-0533

Contact: Poudre Landmarks Foundation

Open: Wed. and Sun. 1–3 p.m.; closed New Year's Day, Easter, Christmas

Admission: Free

Activities: Group tours by appointment, exhibits, annual Historic Homes Tour and Christmas Open House

Suggested Time to View House: 45 minutes

Facilities on Premises: Related gift items for sale including the Avery House Cookbook

Best Season to View House: Summer and fall

Description of Grounds: Elaborate gardens with several varieties of antique roses, blue spruce and fruit trees including the largest pear tree in the state. Restored carriage house.

Number of Yearly Visitors: 6,000

Year House Built: 1879, subsequent additions

Style of Architecture: Gothic Revival-style stone cottage

Number of Rooms: 13

On-Site Parking: Yes **Wheelchair Access:** Yes

Description of House

Franklin Avery, like many fellow Easterners, was moved—by the urgings of Horace Greeley and others—to "Go West" and make his fortune. In 1869, he answered an advertisement in the *New York Tribune* seeking settlers to join the Union Colony in Greeley, Colorado. Avery, a skilled surveyor, helped lay out the streets of the colony and soon moved on to Fort Collins where, in time, he became the County Surveyor. He built the Avery Block in downtown Fort Collins and founded one of the town's first banks. In 1876, he married another New Yorker, Sara Edson, and started a family. Three years later, he built this house for $3,000. Descendants of the Avery family lived here until 1962.

This fine example of the Gothic Revival style was originally a two-story structure consisting of a basement, a dining room and entry on the main floor, and two bedrooms upstairs. It was built of colored native Colorado sandstone cut at the Stout Quarry west of Fort Collins: lighter stone for the walls and a darker, reddish stone for the quoins. A number of additions were made over the next twenty-one years, perhaps the most distinctive of which is the Victorian Queen Anne-style tower. The house now features a steep roof line, tall and narrow windows, a center bay extension with a front gable, a small front porch, and dormers with decorative bracketed windows.

The care taken in the interior restoration is clearly evident in the fine reproduced wallpapers copied from samples salvaged when repairs were being made. A detail of note is the curved radiator in the tower. The furnishings comprise an eclectic mix of late Victorian and Eastlake-style pieces in a variety of finishes, as well as an assortment of common household artifacts. One room of the house, appropriately called the Avery Room, contains all its original furnishings and appears exactly as Sara Avery decorated it over one hundred and thirteen years ago.

Notable Collections on Exhibit
The Avery family diary, some of their photographs, and an interesting collection of vintage clothing are on display here.

Additional Information
The Avery House is listed on the National Register of Historic Places.

Staley House

120 Main Street, P.O. Box 820
Frisco, CO 80443
(303) 668-3428

Contact: Frisco Historical Society
Open: Summer, Tues.-Sun. 11 a.m.–4 p.m.;
winter, Tues.-Sat 11 a.m.–4 p.m.
Admission: Free
Activities: Guided tours by reservation,
summer programs
Suggested Time to View House: 1 hour
Facilities on Premises: Museum gift shop
Description of Grounds: Located in the
Frisco Historic Park which contains
several historic buildings including the
Bailey House, and the Log Chapel
Best Season to View House: Summer
Style of Architecture: National-Folk,
pioneer log with clapboard siding
Number of Yearly Visitors: 8,000
Number of Rooms: 6

Year House Built: c. 1890
On-Site Parking: Yes **Wheelchair Access:** No

Description of House

This pioneer-style log home was built in the 1890s. Originally owned by Ben Staley, a miner and long-time resident of Frisco, the house illustrates rather well the not uncommon life that Staley led. He was a working class inhabitant of a typical mining camp town and, as the many basic everyday items once belonging to him and his wife clearly show, his life consisted largely of the struggle to "get by." Peter Prestrud, an entrepreneur of a different class entirely, bought the Staley House about 1910; his local fame rested on two facts: he built the area's first ski jump *and* he was a member of the Colorado Ski Hall of Fame in Vail.

Considered a rather fancy dwelling, the unusual two-story, front-gabled log cabin features a mix of building materials—log and clapboard—and a full-width front porch which differentiates this structure from other mining camp cabins. The Frisco Historical Society has been able to furnish the Staley House with many of the family's original possessions. One such item is a patchwork quilt considered an heirloom, and presented by several local families as a gift to Mrs. Staley in 1900. It can be found displayed in one of the bedrooms.

Edinger-Shumate House

**1001 Colorado Avenue
Glenwood Springs, CO 81601
(303) 945-4448**

Contact: Frontier Historical Society and
Museum

Open: May-Sept., Mon.-Sat. 1–4 p.m.;
Oct.-Apr., Thurs.-Sat. 1–4 p.m.

Admission: Adults $2.00; children
(under 12) free

Activities: Guided tours, audiovisual
presentations, children's specialty
education programs

Suggested Time to View House:
30–60 minutes

Facilities on Premises: Book store,
archives, meeting areas for groups

Description of Grounds: Small yard with
some artifacts displayed

Best Season to View House: Year round

Number of Yearly Visitors: 7,500

Year House Built: 1905

Number of Rooms: 11

Style of Architecture: Folk Victorian

On-Site Parking: No **Wheelchair Access:** No

Description of House

This Folk Victorian-style house was built by Dr. Marshall Dian when he retired from the railroad in 1905. In 1912, a banker and his wife, George and Emma Edinger, bought the house and some years later, they passed it on to their daughter and her husband, Stella and Churchill Shumate. Although this house is a relatively simple and unaffected building, it does have beautiful pocket doors, and all of the downstairs woodwork is in its original state.

Notable Collections on Exhibit

Displays change frequently, highlighting different items from the Frontier Historical Society's collection, mostly household items, vintage clothing, quilts, and period furniture.

1870 Meeker Home

1324 Ninth Avenue
Greeley, CO 80631
(303) 350-9220

Contact: City of Greeley Museums

Open: Mid Apr.-Memorial Day, Labor
Day-mid Oct., Tues.-Sat. 10 a.m.-3 p.m.;
Memorial Day-Labor Day, Tues.-Sat.
10-5 p.m., Sun. 1-5 p.m.

Admission: Adults $1.50; seniors $1.00;
children (6-12) $.50, children (under 6) free

Activities: Guided tours, concerts, lectures,
and special holiday programs

Suggested Time to View House: 45 minutes

Description of Grounds: Public park

Best Season to View House: Spring and
summer

Number of Yearly Visitors: 3,000

Year House Built: 1870.

Style of Architecture: Italianate, adobe

Number of Rooms: 8

On-Site Parking: Yes **Wheelchair Access:** Yes

Description of House

The 1870 Meeker Home was the cornerstone of the Union Colony, an agricultural community founded by Nathan Meeker. An authentic example of frontier pragmatism built out of adobe brick, the design and construction of the house combine elements of romantic architecture with the need to face the realities of living beyond civilization. The peaceful, park-like surroundings in no way indicate the hardships and dangers that the participants of this utopian experiment had to endure. Only the personal belongings of the Meeker family and others hint at the difficulty of their lives; an item of such relevance is the bare thread blanket worn by Meeker's daughter when she was kidnapped by Indians.

Additional Information

The City of Greeley Museums maintains the 1870 Meeker Home, the Centennial Village, and the Municipal Museum. The 1870 Meeker Home is listed on the National Register of Historic Places.

H. A.W. Tabor House Museum

116 East Fifth Street
Leadville, CO 80461
(719) 486-1878

Contact: McVicar Family
Open: May-Sept., daily 9 a.m.–5 p.m.;
Sept.-Apr., Mon.-Thurs. 10 a.m.–5 p.m.,
Fri.-Sun. by appointment
Admission: Adults $2.00; seniors $1.50;
children $1.00
Activities: Self-guided tours
Suggested Time to View House:
20–30 minutes

Facilities on Premises: General Store gift
shop and bookstore
Description of Grounds: Small city lot with
wildflowers
Best Season to View House: Spring-fall
Year House Built: 1877
Style of Architecture: Folk Victorian
Number of Rooms: 6
On-Site Parking: Yes **Wheelchair Access:** Yes

Description of House

Augusta Tabor was a long-suffering woman who shared all sorts of misadventures and deprivations on the difficult, wayward search for mineral wealth with her husband, H. A. W. Tabor—nearly twenty years' work. Her duties included everything from hiding gold dust under her skirt to raising a son under the most unstable conditions as the couple moved from one mining camp to another. And then, when the couple finally struck it rich in silver, she had to put up with Horace's many flagrant infidelities— which didn't keep him from being elected first mayor of Leadville and United States Senator—before finally divorcing him and establishing herself on her own. The affair that led to the divorce involved Horace and a showgirl named Elizabeth Doe who the scandal sheets dubbed "Baby Doe." Augusta, who remained hopeful that Horace would come to his senses and return to his former life, became known as the "First Lady" of Leadville and led a quiet life, entertaining at Unity Church lawn parties and tending to her investments, until her death in 1895 at age sixty-two. When she died she was a millionairess, whereas her ex-husband, the former "Silver King," was bankrupt. As for his young wife Baby Doe—the papers claimed that she froze to death at the Matchless Mine trying to hang on to some vestige of Tabor's once-great fortune.

The H. A. W. Tabor House was built in 1877—the same year that Tabor struck it rich—on a deep narrow lot and consisted of a kitchen, dining room, and parlor on the first floor and two bedrooms and a sewing-sitting room upstairs. There is an adjacent summer kitchen and carriage barn. Two years after being built, the house was moved to its present site on East Fifth Street. The exterior features a small single-story bay extension and is accented with decorative vergeboards. The interior is presently undergoing a restoration of the wallcoverings, window coverings, and painted surfaces. This home was used as the Tabors' second home after the couple bought a house in Denver in 1879.

Notable Collections on Exhibit

The Tabors, who were originally from Northern New England, brought a number of pieces of furniture with them to Colorado; these have been donated by the Tabor family and are on display in the house.

Additional Information

Not far from the H. A. W. Tabor House is the Leadville Historic District which includes the "House with the Eye" built by the French architect Eugene Robitaille in 1879. This house is located at 127 West Fourth Street and the phone number is (719) 486-0860.

Miramount Castle Museum

9 Capitol Hill Avenue
Manitou Springs, CO 80829
(719) 685-1011

Contact: Manitou Springs Historical Society
Open: Summer, daily 10 a.m.–5 p.m.; fall,
11 a.m.–4 p.m.; winter, Noon–3 p.m.;
closed Easter, Thanksgiving, Christmas
Admission: Adults $3.00; seniors $2.50;
children (6-11) $1.00; group rates available
Activities: Guided tours, special seasonal
events including a Victorian Christmas
Suggested Time to View House:
45–60 minutes

Facilities on Premises: Victorian gift shop,
miniature train museum
Description of Grounds: Victorian gardens
Best Season to View House: Spring and
summer
Number of Yearly Visitors: 80,000
Year House Built: 1895
Style of Architecture: Eclectic Period
Revival, predominantely Gothic and Tudor
Number of Rooms: 46, 28 open to the public
On-Site Parking: Yes **Wheelchair Access:** Yes

Description of House

In the early 1890s, Father Jean-Baptiste Francolon, a French-born missionary priest who had retired to Manitou Springs for health reasons, designed this castle-like mansion and commissioned a Scottish contractor, Angus Gillis, to build it. In 1895, the priest and his wealthy widowed mother moved into Miramount and lived here until 1904, when the structure was bought by the Sisters of Mercy and converted into a sanitarium. Forty-two years later, the building was again sold and converted into apartments, which is how it remained until 1976 when the Historical Society acquired it.

This forty-six-room castle is an exuberant amalgam of nine distinct architectural styles built out of locally quarried green stone and yellow pine framing. The styles range from the predominant English Tudor and Domestic Elizabethan to the Venetian Ogee window treatments and the Byzantine arches. Miramount's four floors boast over 14,000 square feet of space but only twenty-eight of its rooms were used by the Francolons. The part of the structure east of the kitchen was completed in 1897. Most of the castle's rooms are oddly-shaped with many more sides than the usual four; typical is the octagonal Chapel, originally the priest's library. The massive and beautiful hallway fireplace weighs 400,000 pounds. The castle was built with indoor plumbing and electricity: in fact, the first electric generator in

El Paso County was built in 1880 by Angus Gillis. Except for a patch in a small closet under the Grand Staircase, the wallpapers in the castle are all documented reproductions. The Manitou Springs Historical Society is doing a representative restoration of Miramount Castle using furnishings and artifacts donated by a number of prominent local families.

Notable Collections on Exhibit

The six-sided conservatory on the third floor now serves as a gallery for the International Museum of Miniatures.

Additional Information

When in Manitou Springs, one should also visit Historic Briarhurst Manor, the former mansion of William Bell, the English doctor who founded the town. The magnificent twenty-three-room English Tudor structure was built in 1876 and now serves as a landmark restaurant on Cripple Creek. Complimentary guided tours are provided to restaurant guests. The Manor is located at 404 Manitou Avenue and the phone number is (719) 685-1864.

Rosemount Victorian House Museum

419 West Fourteenth Street, P.O. Box 5259
Pueblo, CO 81002
(719) 545-5290

Contact: Rosemount Victorian House
Museum, Inc.

Open: June 1-Sept. 1, Tues.-Sat.
10 a.m.–4 p.m., Sun. 2–4 p.m.; Sept.
1-June 1., Tues.-Sat. 1–4 p.m., Sun.
2–4 p.m.; closed January

Admission: Adults $3.00; seniors $2.00;
children (6-16) $1.00, children (under 6) free

Activities: Guided tours, educational and
interpretative programs

Facilities on Premises: Museum shop,
restaurant

Suggested Time to View House: 90 minutes

Description of Grounds: Situated on full
city block, formal grounds not yet restored

Number of Yearly Visitors: 21,000

Number of Rooms: 37

Best Season to View House: Spring-fall

Style of Architecture: Richardsonian
Romanesque

Year House Built: 1893

On-Site Parking: Yes **Wheelchair Access:** Yes

Description of House

At the Rosemount Victorian House, it may be said that East meets West: this massive thirty-seven-room Victorian structure was designed by Henry Hudson Holly and Horatio F. Jellif of New York City and built in rugged Pueblo. Costing $60,750, Rosemount stood in stark contrast to the adobe houses and dirt roads which comprised the town in 1893; it was purely a testament to the enormous financial success of John Tatcher, a local entrepreneur with interests in cattle-raising, mining, and agriculture.

Rosemount shows off the wealth of its owner everywhere. Ten fireplaces accented with silver plate tile, dramatic staircase landings accented with stained and painted glass windows designed by Charles Booth of New York, lighting fixtures crusted with silver and gold plate from the studios of Louis Comfort Tiffany, and intricate woodwork of maple, oak and mahogany done by the Herts Brothers of Philadelphia are but a few of the decorative features found here. The Herts Brothers also designed much of the furniture found at Rosemount. The exterior, fashioned out of locally quarried, pink volcanic stone, is no less dramatic, with its gutters, cornices and flashings of solid copper, main entry delineated by five pink granite columns, and veranda made of basswood with pine carvings. And, as if all this weren't enough...Tatcher had a 2,000-gallon water tank installed in the attic!

Rosemount was so named after the favorite flower of Mrs. Tatcher.

Notable Collections on Exhibit

On his world travels at the turn of the century, businessman and philanthropist Andrew McClelland visited sixty-seven countries and collected numerous treasures. Many of these items—urns, statuary, pottery, other artifacts—are on display, but the one not to be missed is Lady Aset-Beka... an Egyptian mummy!

Cozens Ranch House Museum

77849 U.S. Highway 40
Winter Park, CO 80482
(303) 726-5488

Contact: Grand County Historical
Association

Open: Dec. 15-Apr. 1, Tues.-Sun.
11 a.m.–4:30 p.m.; June 15-Sept. 15,
open daily 11 a.m.–4:30 p.m.; closed
Christmas and New Year's Day

Admission: Adults $2.00; children $1.00;
family $5.00

Activities: Guided tours upon request,
self-guided tours

Suggested Time to View House:
30–60 minutes

Facilities on Premises: Book and gift shop

Style of Architecture: National, homestead
ranch of log and board

Description of Grounds: Ranch work yard

Number of Yearly Visitors: 2500

Number of Rooms: 12

Best Season to View House: Spring-fall

Year House Built: 1874

On-Site Parking: Yes **Wheelchair Access:** Yes

Description of House

The Cozens Ranch Museum provides a unique glimpse of life as it existed in the 19th century West. On display are the frontier diaries of Mary Elizabeth Cozens, the unmarried daughter of William Cozens, rancher and sheriff of Central City. Her diaries record their daily ranch life, and her role as seamstress, laundress, and gardener. These handwritten diaries tell many stories of the weary travelers who stopped and took supper with the Cozenses and their three children. On the parlor walls hang photographs of the family and the Ute Indians who frequented the post office and stage stop.

The two-story ranch house served as both family dwelling and stage stop. The upstairs area had six sleeping rooms; today these same rooms are used for different exhibits illustrating local history. Although the Cozenses' existence was meager by our standards, remnants of such luxury items as a carpet and wallpaper are still in evidence, and the parlor, set with original fabric c. 1875, remains intact. Many of the pieces have been donated by descendants of William Cozens. The walls, floors, and doors are all authentic to the house; so are the kitchen cabinets, storage bins, and the wooden ice chest lined with old newspapers. The Cozens Ranch Museum is listed on the National Register of Historic Places.

Notable Collections on Exhibit

Besides the diaries of Mary Elizabeth, there is a copy of *Caesar's Commentaries*, printed in 1622, on display. This book once belonged to William, Jr., the intellectual of the Cozens family, who disliked ranching and attended St. Louis University.

Hawaii

1. Hilo
Lyman Mission House

2. Honolulu
Chamberlain House
'Iolani Palace
Mission Frame House
Queen Emma Summer Palace

3. Kamuela
Mana and Puuopelu the Main House

4. Lahaina on the island of Maui
Baldwin Home Museum

Lyman Mission House

276 Haili Street
Hilo, HI 96720
(808) 935-5021

Contact: Lyman House Memorial Museum
Open: Mon.-Sat. 9 a.m.–5 p.m.,
Sun. 1–4 p.m.
Admission: Adults $4.50; seniors and
students $2.50
Activities: Interpretative guided tours,
cultural and science exhibits, lecture
series, special Christmas Tradition event
Suggested Time to View House:
60–90 minutes
Facilities on Premises: Gift shop, art gallery
Description of Grounds: Lawn area with
native plants
Best Season to View House: Spring, late
fall and winter
Number of Yearly Visitors: 20,000
Number of Rooms: 10

Style of Architecture: Modified Greek Revival
with Hawaiian Plantation-style influences
Year House Built: 1839
On-Site Parking: Yes **Wheelchair Access:** Yes

Description of House

This house, which stands a few blocks from Hilo Bay on the big island of Hawaii, is the oldest wooden frame building on the island; it was built in 1839 for the missionary couple, the Reverend and Mrs. David Belden Lyman, and their seven children. The Lymans came to Hawaii from New England on one of the later missionary parties and quickly became island notables. Here they entertained Hawaiian royalty and a number of well-known *malihini* (foreigners), including Mark Twain and Robert Louis Stevenson.

The house is patterned after the Greek Revival homes then being built in the Lymans' native New England with the addition of a wide two-story veranda which wraps around three-quarters of the structure. This veranda, its simple post supports, and the home's clean lines, which show very little ornamentation, are closer in spirit to the island's own plantation-style architecture. The first-floor features very large twelve-over-twelve windows which allow for maximum air circulation, and the second-floor veranda is protected from the tropical light by an extended secondary roof-line. The interior has been restored to appear as it did in the late 1860s and contains a number of the Lyman family's own furnishings, including a working melodeon, a set of antique china, and several pieces of handcrafted furniture. The Lyman Mission House is listed on the National Register of Historic Places.

Notable Collections on Exhibit

Next door to the Lyman Mission House is the Lyman Museum which houses a number of fascinating collections which depict the history of Hawaii's native peoples, the era of the missionaries, and the culture of the many immigrant groups who settled on the islands. In addition, there is a first-rate mineral and shell collection, the centerpiece of which is an exhibit of the island's own volcanic formations.

Chamberlain House

553 South King Street
Honolulu, HI 96813
(808) 531-0481

Contact: Mission Houses Museum

Open: Tues.-Sat. 9 a.m.–4 p.m., Sun. Noon–4 p.m.; closed New Year's Day, Easter, Christmas

Admission: $5.00 general fee; state residents, seniors and military personnel $4.00; students $1.00; group rates available

Activities: Guided tours, video orientation program, monthly special events, annual Hawaiian quilt exhibit, spring and fall craft fairs

Facilities on Premises: Visitor center, museum shop, research library, historic cemetery

Description of Grounds: Garden-setting compound of three early-19th-century houses including the Mission Frame House, the Chamberlain House and the 1841 Printing Office located in historic downtown

Suggested Time to View House: 2 hours

Best Season to View House: Year round

Number of Yearly Visitors: 32,000

Year House Built: 1831

Style of Architecture: Modified Greek Revival, brick

Number of Rooms: 11

On-Site Parking: No **Wheelchair Access:** Yes

Description of House

The Chamberlain House is one of three structures which make up the Mission Houses Museum; the other two are the Mission Frame House (which is listed separately in this guide), and the Printing Office. These are the three oldest homes standing in Honolulu and, taken together, provide an excellent introduction to the history of the early-19th-century missionary era in Hawaii. They also provided inspiration for James Michener's epic novel *Hawaii*. These homes were the headquarters of the Sandwich Islands Mission, the first evangelical Christian mission to these islands.

The Chamberlain House was built for the Mission's storekeeper, Levi Chamberlain, and his family. It was also used as a warehouse for the goods he imported from America which were then distributed to the various missionary settlements scattered throughout the islands or traded to the native Hawaiians. The house also served as the island's center of social activity; here Mrs. Chamberlain routinely entertained a parade of guests, foreign visitors, and boarders.

The Chamberlain House was built in 1831 out of coral blocks harvested from the nearby reefs. The three-story structure is built in a vernacular interpretation of the federal style—the typical six-over-six fenestration features green exterior shutters against the white paint on the walls. The house has been fully restored to interpret the period of the 1850s.

Additional Information

Also on the grounds of the Museum is the Mission's Printing Office, built ten years after the Chamberlain House. The work done in this building to preserve the Hawaiian language in written form is one the Mission's great legacies; today one can watch printing and binding demonstrations here. Across the street is the Mission Cemetery, where many of the original community members are buried. The Mission Houses Museum is listed on the National Register of Historic Places.

'Iolani Palace

364 South King Street
Honolulu, HI 96813
(808) 522-0832

Contact: Friends of 'Iolani Palace

Open: Wed.-Sat. 9 a.m.–2:15 p.m.; closed
New Year's Day, Fourth of July,
Thanksgiving, Christmas

Admission: Adults $4.00; children
(5-12) $1.00

Activities: Guided tours

Suggested Time to View House: 45 minutes

Facilities on Premises: Visitor center and
gift shop

Best Season to View House: Year round

Description of Grounds: 11 acres of historic
gardens in the heart of the downtown
area with Indian banyan trees said to
have been planted by Queen Kapi'olani

Number of Yearly Visitors: 65,000

Year House Built: Started 1879, completed
1882

Style of Architecture: High Victorian
Second Empire

Number of Rooms: 104

On-Site Parking: Yes **Wheelchair Access:** Yes

Description of House

The 'Iolani Palace, a Victorian Great House modeled after the great
British houses of the Second Empire and built in last days of the Hawaiian
monarchy, seems somehow to signal the end of that monarchy, with its
borrowed style, heavy ornamentation, and imposing bulk. It is far removed
from the Islanders' native architecture.

The building was begun in 1879 on the site of an earlier palace which
had succumbed to the elements. There Kamehameha III ruled, after moving
the royal court from Lahaina to Honolulu in 1845. The new palace was
completed in 1882 and occupied by the last two Hawaiian monarchs, King
Kalākaua and his sister, Queen Lili'uokalani. The coronation of the King and
his consort, Queen Kapi'olani, was held at the Palace in 1883. Eight years
later, the King died and his sister succeeded him to the throne. However, her
reign lasted only two years; she was deposed in 1893 by foreign-born
residents with United States backing. After the overthrow of the Hawaiian
throne, the Palace was used as the capitol of the Republic, then the Territory,
and finally the State of Hawaii. When a new capitol was built in 1969, the
Palace was vacated and the long process of restoration to its original appearance began.

The royal family worked with three different architects in building their palace; when it was completed, its design was dubbed "American Composite" or "American Florentine." It is an enormous 100-by-140-foot house with a floor plan consisting of public rooms on the main floor, living quarters of the royal family on the second floor, and the utility rooms and servants' quarters in the basement. The interior features a mixture of Victorian opulence, as typified by the "gold" music room, and an interesting use of native materials—the stairway is hand-carved out of local woods. The major rooms have been restored and contain original furnishings. The furniture consists largely of a Gothic Revival-style 225-piece suite made to order for the Palace in 1882 by the A. H. Davenport Company of Boston.

Notable Collections on Exhibit

The Palace boasts a marvelous collection of rare Hawaiian royal family artifacts, such as precious feather cloaks, kâhili, and rare calabashes; this is in addition to the portrait of King Louis Philippe of France given to King Kamehameha III by the French Government in 1848, and the portraits of King Kalâkaua and Queen Lili'uokalani done by the noted American artist William Cogswell.

Additional Information

'Iolani Palace is listed on the National Register of Historic Places.

Mission Frame House

553 South King Street
Honolulu, HI 96813
(808) 531-0481

Contact: Mission Houses Museum

Open: Tues.-Sat. 9 a.m.–4 p.m., Sun. Noon–4 p.m.; closed New Year's Day, Easter, Christmas

Admission: $5.00 general fee; state residents, seniors and military personnel $4.00; students $1.00; group rates available

Activities: Guided tours, video orientation program, monthly special events, annual Hawaiian quilt exhibit, spring and fall craft fairs

Suggested Time to View House: 2 hours

Best Season to View House: Year round

Facilities on Premises: Visitor center, museum shop, research library

Description of Grounds: Compound of three early-19th-century houses including the Mission Frame House, the Chamberlain House and the 1841 Printing Office and museum facilities

Number of Yearly Visitors: 32,000

Year House Built: 1821

Style of Architecture: New England-style frame, prefabricated

Number of Rooms: 7

On-Site Parking: No **Wheelchair Access:** Yes

Description of House

Like the Chamberlain House mentioned above, the Mission Frame House is one the three structures which compose the Mission Houses Museum. This complex portrays the first settlement of Christian missionaries to come to Hawaii and their impact on the life of the native islanders. The Mission Frame House is the oldest of these structures—it was built in 1821—and the most famous; its occupants, the Reverend and Mrs. Hiram Bingham, were used by James Michener as the basis for his fictional characters, the Hales, in his bestselling novel *Hawaii*.

This small wood-frame house was precut in New England and shipped from Boston to Honolulu where it was assembled on this site a half-mile inland from the harbor. The exterior features cross gables and a side porch and balcony; inside the walls are of white-washed plaster and reproduction fabrics and bedclothes are shown in a rotating display. Some of the rooms have been wallpapered and the cellar still features some original adobe. The house has been restored to the period of the 1830s.

Notable Collections on Exhibit

On display at the Mission Frame House are a number of personal items and furnishings which belonged to the Bingham family; among the more notable pieces is a rocking chair fashioned out of koa wood by Bingham and given by him to Queen Ka'ahumanu, an early convert to Christianity.

Additional Information

The Mission Houses Museum is listed on the National Register of Historic Places.

Queen Emma Summer Palace

2913 Pali Highway
Honolulu, HI 96817
(808) 595-3167

Contact: Daughters of Hawai'i

Open: Daily 9 a.m.–4 p.m.; closed major state and national holidays

Admission: Adults $4.00; seniors $3.00; juniors (12-18) $1.00; children $.50

Activities: Docent guided tours, annual fall festival and fund-raiser

Suggested Time to View House: 30 minutes

Facilities on Premises: Gift shop

Description of Grounds: 2½ acre garden with antique plantings and a Victorian cutting garden

Best Season to View House: Year round

Year House Built: 1848

Style of Architecture: Greek Revival, prefabricated

Number of Rooms: 7

On-Site Parking: Yes **Wheelchair Access:** No

Description of House

Queen Emma of Hawaii, the daughter of Fanny Young Naea and High Chief George Naea, was raised by her childless aunt Grace, attended the Chief's Children's School run by Christian missionaries, received tutoring from an English governess, and married King Kamehameha IV in 1856 when she was nineteen. A year later, she inherited this Greek Revival house in the beautiful and historic Nuuanu Valley from her uncle, John Young II, and named it "Hanaiakamalama" (foster child of the god Kalama). In 1858, she gave birth to a son—Prince Edward Kauikeaouli Leiopapa O Kanehameha—who was named Prince Consort to his godmother, Queen Victoria of England. This child was the last heir born to a reigning Hawaiian monarch; sadly, he died of meningitis in his fourth year. Emma herself died in 1885 at the age of forty-nine and her Summer Palace became vacant. It was slated for demolition to make way for a ball park when, in 1919, the Daughters of Hawai'i were granted the home by the Territorial Government with the proviso that it be kept as a museum. A major restoration was undertaken in 1973.

The house that Queen Emma used as a Summer Palace was designed and cut in Boston, then shipped to Hawaii and assembled on its site here in the Nuuanu Valley. The one-story Greek Revival-style structure features a wide front porch ("lanai" in Hawaiian) supported by six Doric columns, a shingled hipped roof, floor-to-ceiling windows with exterior shutters, and a beautiful shuttered front door with an eight-pane, segmented transom light. Inside, the house has seven rooms with high ceilings restored to the mid-19th century; they exhibit a winning combination of Victorian décor and native Hawaiian furnishings. The "Edinburgh Room," a large parlor added in 1869 so the Queen could entertain the Duke of Edinburgh—the party never came off but the room was subsequently used for many lavish socials—is done in a rich wine red color.

Notable Collections on Exhibit

The Summer Palace features many items which belonged to Hawaii's royal family. Some of the more notable are: a large hand-carved koa wood four-poster bed, the Prince's cradle which was made by the craftsman Wilhelm Fischer out of three native woods for the princely sum of $600, a blue agate bracelet containing a lock of Queen Victoria's hair, and a German-made baby grand piano recalling Queen Emma's visit to that county in 1865.

Additional Information

The Daughters of Hawai'i was founded in 1903 by seven daughters of Protestant missionaries to the islands for the purpose of perpetuating "the memory and spirit of old Hawai'i...and to preserve the nomenclature and correct pronunciation of the Hawaiian language." The Queen Emma Summer Palace is listed on the National Register of Historic Places.

Mânâ and Puuopelu the Main House

Puuopelu Road, P.O. Box 458
Kamuela, HI 96743
(808) 885-5433

Contact: Historic Parker Ranch Homes
Open: Daily 10 a.m.–5 p.m.
Admission: Adults $7.50; children (4-11) $3.75; groups rate available
Activities: Guided tours with introductory presentations
Suggested Time to View House: 45 minutes each house
Facilities on Premises: Visitor center/gift shop

Description of Grounds: European-style gardens with tropical flowers
Best Season to View House: Year round
Number of Yearly Visitors: 20,000-30,000
Year House Built: Mânâ-1849, Puuopelu-1862
Style of Architecture: Mana-New England Saltbox, Puuopelu-French Provencial
Number of Rooms: Mânâ-7, Puuopelu-7
On-Site Parking: Yes **Wheelchair Access:** Yes

Description of House

In the Kohala Mountains on the northern side of the big island of Hawaii lies the large cattle ranch established in the 1850s by John Palmer Parker, who arrived in the islands in 1815. Over the next thirty years, Parker assembled his ranch out of two separate land grants (one to him and one to his Hawaiian wife), an outright purchase of 1,000 acres, and the lease of the ahupua'a of Waikoloa. Though Parker adopted many local customs—the first home he and his wife lived in was a traditional Hawaiian ohia and pili grass hut—he also clung to the memories of his early life in New England and his Christian religion. Thus, in 1849, when it came time to build a more permanent house, he built it on the lines of those Georgian saltboxes he remembered from youth. When Parker died in 1861, he left his estate to his two male heirs, son John Palmer Parker II, and grandson, Samuel Parker, with the request that his ranch stay intact. The two heirs, uncle and nephew, were two entirely different characters: John would go on to become one of Hawaii's richest men by building the business side of the ranch whereas Samuel—who came to be called "Colonel"—was the gregarious host who cared little for business. By 1879, they had falling out and gone separate ways; John went to live at Puuopelu in central Waimea and ranch, and the Colonel stayed here at Mânâ and entertained.

Mânâ Hale, John Palmer Parker's small New England saltbox, the house that Samuel Parker loved to open to all visitors, has been reconstructed to reflect the years of its heyday, the 1880s. The replica house features a steep gray slate roof and multi-paned windows, is filled with enough of the contents of the original structure to suggest its authenticity, and sits on a lot adjacent to Puuopelu, the Main House. Puuopelu was built in 1862 by an Englishman and became the home of John Palmer Parker II in 1879, when he left the original ranch to his nephew, Samuel. It is a large home with a yellow "Hawaiian Victorian" exterior masking a voluminous and opulent French Provincial interior. The house has had several major additions and alterations, the most recent in 1969 for its present owner, Richard Smart.

Notable Collections on Exhibit

Puuopela houses a magnificent collection of art objects and paintings ranging from a rich collection of 19th-century French porcelain plates to Ming Dynasty Chinese vases to paintings by noted 20th-century artists like Utrillo and Dufy.

Baldwin Home Museum

695 Front Street, P.O. Box 338
Lahaina on the island
of Maui, HI 96761
(808) 661-3262

Contact: Lahaina Restoration Foundation
Open: Daily 9:30 a.m.–4:30 p.m.; closed
   Christmas, New Year's Day
Admission: Adults $3.00; seniors $2.00;
   families $5.00
Activities: Guided and candlelight tours,
   semi-monthly lei-making demonstrations,
   book signings, art exhibits
Suggested Time to View House: 30 minutes
Facilities on Premises: Gift shop with books
Description of Grounds: Restored c. 1843
   yard and plantings
Best Season to View House: Year round
Number of Yearly Visitors: 40,000-50,000
Year House Built: 1834, additions 1840
   and 1849
Number of Rooms: 7

Style of Architecture: Hawaiian
   plantation-missionary style with veranda
On-Site Parking: Yes Wheelchair Access: Yes

Description of House

In December of 1830, The Reverend Dwight Baldwin, a Connecticut native who had trained at Harvard College in medicine as well as theology, sailed with his bride for Hawaii in the Fourth Company of Missionaries sent by the Sandwich Islands Mission. The Mission had sent its First Company to the islands in 1820, after the death of King Kamehameha I and the subsequent overthrow of the native religion by his son. After serving in Waimea, Baldwin became Pastor of Lahaina's old Wainee Church. He moved into this house in 1838 and lived here until 1871. Baldwin also used his medical training to save scores of people during the smallpox epidemic of 1853.

The Baldwin Home is a simple two-story structure featuring a veranda; it typifies that combination of the New England-based Greek Revival architecture with Hawaiian forms and materials which one sees in many missionary and plantation homes of the period. The construction features thick walls made of coral and stone covered in white stucco over a solid frame of hand-hewn timbers. The home, which stands on the town square facing Lahaina harbor, has been carefully restored to the years of the Rev. Baldwin's residency. The furniture, artifacts, photographs, and other household items present a vivid picture of the Missionary Doctor's busy life.

Additional Information

The Lahaina Restoration Foundation also maintains the Hale Pa'i House, the Wo Hing Museum, which represents the heritage of Hawaii's Chinese immigrants, and the Brig Carthaginian.

Idaho

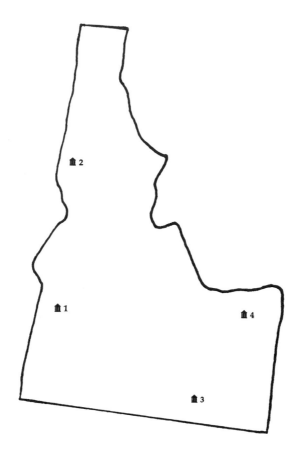

1. Boise
Bishops' House

2. Moscow
McConnell Mansion

3. Pocatello
Standrod House

4. Rexburg
Hess Heritage Home

Bishops' House

2420 Old Penitentiary Road
off Warm Springs Avenue
Boise, ID 83712
(208) 342-3279

Contact: Friends of the Bishops' House, Inc.
Open: Year-round, Mon.-Fri. open by
appointment; closed Easter,
Thanksgiving, Christmas Eve and Day
Admission: Donation
Activities: Guided tours
Suggested Time to View House: 30 minutes
Facilities on Premises: Rental facilities
Description of Grounds: Beautiful
landscaped grounds with period rose
gardens and graceful gazebo
Best Season to View House: Spring-late fall
Number of Yearly Visitors: 9,000
Year House Built: 1889, restyled and
expanded 1899
Number of Rooms: 10

Style of Architecture: Original house-frame,
restyled house-Victorian Queen Anne,
free classic with tower
On-Site Parking: Yes **Wheelchair Access:** No

Description of House

This modest frame house was built in 1889 for the Episcopal Bishop of the Diocese of Idaho and was used as such until the mid 1960s. In 1899, one of its residents, Bishop Funsten, expanded the home for his wife and five daughters. From the time it was given up as a residence until 1970, the structure served as a community center named the Bishop Rhea House after one of its former occupants. In 1974, when the house was threatened with demolition, a citizens' group was organized to save the house; the first thing they did was to move it from its original site at the intersection of Second and Idaho Streets to its present location near the Old Idaho Penitentiary.

The Bishops' House is a two-story Victorian Queen Anne structure with a full basement and attic; it features a cross-gabled roof, overhanging gable extensions with inverted broken pediments, and a tower with a flared, conical-shaped roof topped with a finial showing the Episcopal Church coat-of-arms motif. The windows are mainly simple double-hung sash treatments, but there is a striking Palladian-style window cut into the front gable. There is also a wrap-around porch with grouped classical-style supports, a balustrade and a pedimented entry which nicely counterbalances the prominent gable above. Inside, one finds a typical Victorian floor plan which has the public rooms—including a front parlor, music room, large entry hall, and dining room—downstairs, and the bedrooms up. There are period wallpapers, decorative moldings, paneled doors, and woodwork trim executed in faux Boise oak. The furnishings represent the various periods spanned by the residencies of the Bishops who lived here.

Additional Information

The Bishops' House is listed on the National Register of Historic Places.

McConnell Mansion

110 South Adams Street
Moscow, ID 83843
(208) 882-1004

Contact: Latah County Historical Society
Open: Year-round, Tues.-Sat. 1–4 p.m.; other times by appointment; closed holidays
Admission: Donations requested
Activities: Guided tours, audiovisual presentations, annual Ice Cream Social
Suggested Time to View House: 30 minutes
Facilities on Premises: Museum store
Description of Grounds: Small garden area has a variety of local and period plantings
Best Season to View House: Spring and summer
Number of Yearly Visitors: 3,000
Year House Built: 1886
Style of Architecture: Eclectic mix of late Gothic Revival and Victorian Queen Anne-Eastlake
Number of Rooms: 8
On-Site Parking: Yes
Wheelchair Access: No

Description of House

When William J. McConnell moved to Moscow, Idaho, in 1878, he had modest dreams: he wanted to start a small mercantile store in this up-and-coming town. Perhaps this former miner, vigilante captain, and rancher was too humble in his expectations. By 1886, McConnell was already the area's largest grain dealer and would soon become a state senator, then governor of Idaho. His influence was felt throughout the state when he helped prevent North Idaho from seceding from the Union. As often happens, his good fortune came to an abrupt end during the 1893 depression, resulting in the loss of his business and then his home. Dr. William Adai bought the house in 1901 and rented the rooms to students and faculty from the University of Idaho. In turn, one of his boarders, Dr. Frederic Church, purchased the house in 1941.

McConnell Mansion is an interesting example of late-19th-century transitional architecture with characteristics of both the Gothic Revival and Queen Anne styles: two-story bay windows steeply pitched and ornamented with curved brackets, and elaborately decorated porches and verandas. In fact, the McConnell Mansion is the only example of this particular interpretation in the region. The interior of the house is relatively unchanged: the oak balustrades, red fir shutters, colored glass door panels, and handgrained woodwork are original and fully intact.

Notable Collections on Exhibit

The McConnell Mansion furnishings date from the late Victorian period c. 1880s and include examples of Renaissance and French Rococo Revival styles. Three of the rooms are interpretative of the 1900s and a fourth room is decorated as a university student's bedroom c. 1930. Various exhibits on the second floor illustrate the history of the county.

Additional Information

The McConnell Mansion is listed on the National Register of Historic Places.

Standrod House

648 North Garfield, P.O. Box 4169
Pocatello, ID 83205
(208) 234-6184

Contact: Pocatello Historic Preservation
Commission

Open: Tues.-Fri. 2–5 p.m.

Admission: $1.00 suggested donation

Activities: Self-guided tours

Suggested Time to View House:
30–45 minutes

Description of Grounds: Restored period
gardens

Best Season to View House: Spring-early
fall

Number of Yearly Visitors: 2,000

Year House Built: 1900

Style of Architecture: Late Victorian Queen
Anne, masonry

Number of Rooms: 12

On-Site Parking: Yes **Wheelchair Access:** Yes

Description of House

Drew W. Standrod was an early Pocatello attorney and banker who developed land and helped establish the local utility companies. At the turn of the century he ran for governor of Idaho; though he lost, he remained active in state politics. Standrod and his wife both outlived their children and there were no heirs to their estate.

This fine Victorian Queen Anne-style house was designed by San Francisco architect Marcus Grundfor; it features a round cornered two-story tower which gave the house its nickname, "Standrod Castle," and a smaller tower on the right side of the house with heavy pinnacle ornamentation. The walls are built of light gray and red sandstone. Other exterior details include decorative patterns at the gables and band lines executed in masonry, two partial wrap-around porches—one in front and one in back—showing elaborate spindlework and bracketing, splendid roof cresting, and a center gable keystone with the letter "S" carved into it. The interior, with its golden oak parquet flooring, leaded glass windows, and glazed tiles, also features wash basins and fireplaces made of imported French marble. The center staircase is curvilinear in design. The floor plan consists of a foyer, library, living room, dining room, kitchen, and pantry on the main floor, and five bedrooms, a bath, and the sewing room on the second floor. The donated furnishings are all Victorian in style.

Additional Information

The Standrod House is listed on the National Register of Historic Places.

Hess Heritage Home

275 South Second East
Rexburg near Ashton, ID 83420
(208) 356-5674

Contact: Hess Heritage Museum
Open: Mid Apr.-mid Oct., Mon.,Wed.-Sat. by appointment
Admission: Adults $3.00; children $1.00; group rates available
Activities: Guided tours, audiovisual introduction, special Fourth of July celebration with pioneer craft demonstrations
Suggested Time to View House: 60 minutes
Best Season to View House: Spring-fall

Description of Grounds: Museum complex consists of seven farm buildings with exhibits featuring an outdoor implement park
Number of Yearly Visitors: 8,000
Year House Built: c.1890, additions 1909 to 1919
Style of Architecture: Folk Victorian-style farmhouse
Number of Rooms: 6
On-Site Parking: Yes **Wheelchair Access:** Yes

Description of House

Horace and Mildred Hess were Mormons whose relations had served as missionaries to the Pacific islands; they settled on this homestead in 1909 with their five children and began to add to the modest farmhouse. The farm had been settled earlier in the 19th century and at least two settlers lived here before the Hesses. The home was continuously occupied by the family until 1959, when the "new house" was built next door. The house has been restored by Dan and Mary Hess, direct descendants of the original homesteaders. Mary's grandfather, Thomas Bullock, an immigrant from England and also a Mormon, was one of Brigham Young's followers who settled in Utah's Salt Lake Valley in 1847.

The structure that the Hesses moved into began its existence as a two-room log cabin to which a kitchen lean-to had been added. From the period just prior to their ownership until 1919, rooms were added to the cabin one at time. The original log cabin is now the front parlor of the present house and the kitchen lean-to is a full—though small—attached kitchen. The last additions were: the second bedroom which was named the Liberty Room because its construction was financed by World War I Liberty Bonds, the summer kitchen, and the pump house. Before this pump house was built in 1919, those who lived here had to carry water up from the river in barrels. The house was modernized by adding indoor plumbing and electricity in 1950.

The home is interpreted to the period of 1840 to 1920 and contains many of the original furnishings. Some pieces—the kitchen table and range, the hutch, and the parlor sofa and matching chair—belonged to the Hess family, whereas others were the property of Thomas Bullock's family.

Notable Collections on Exhibit

Among the items belonging to the Bullock family, some of the more noteworthy are: a Victorian bed and desk brought to Utah by Thomas Bullock, who served as personal secretary to both John Smith and Brigham Young, and a Bullock family quilt brought over to America from England. The home also features a collection of Polynesian artifacts collected by various relatives of the Hesses who served as island missionaries for the Mormon Church.

Montana

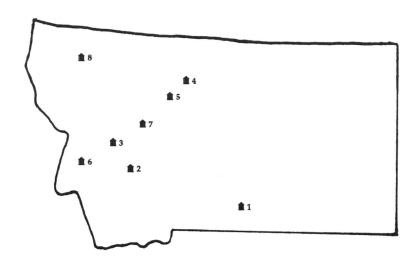

1. Billings
Moss Mansion Museum

2. Butte
William Andrews Clark House

3. Deer Lodge
Grant-Kohrs Ranch House

4. Fort Benton
I. G. Baker House

5. Great Falls
Charles M. Russell Residence

6. Hamilton
Daly Mansion

7. Helena
Original Governor's Mansion

8. Kalispell
Conrad Mansion National Historic Site Museum

Moss Mansion Museum

914 Division Street
Billings, MT 59107
(406) 256-5100

Contact: Billings Preservation Society

Open: Summer, Mon.-Sat., 10 a.m.–5 p.m., Sun. 1–3 p.m.; other times call for seasonal schedules

Admission: Adults $5.00; seniors $4.00; children (under 14) $3.00; group rates available

Activities: Guided tours

Suggested Time to View House: 1 hour

Facilities on Premises: Gift shop

Description of Grounds: 1½ acres of restored landscaped grounds

Best Season to View House: Summer

Number of Yearly Visitors: 10,600

Year House Built: Started 1901, completed 1903

Style of Architecture: Eclectic Renaissance Revival, Beaux Arts with Gothic and Moorish elements

Number of Rooms: 30, 19 open to the public

On-Site Parking: No **Wheelchair Access:** No

Description of House

Upon entering the Moss Mansion, the city of Billings fades into the background and a world full of wealth and grandeur emerges. Preston Boyd Moss created this world. A native of Paris, Missouri, Moss bought into the First National Bank of Billings in 1892; subsequently, he moved his family to the town, founded the newspaper that would become *The Billings Gazette*, and developed the Billings Light and Water Power Company. In addition, he owned and managed 80,000 head of sheep and cattle. His wife, Martha (Mattie) Woodson Moss, was an active community leader and a founder of the local First Church of Christ Scientist. The mansion remained in the Moss family for eighty-one years; during that entire time, it was neither renovated nor redecorated, in fact, it is said that the family never even moved the furniture once!

An impressively massive structure, the Moss Mansion was designed by New York architect Henry Janeway Hardenburgh, one of the only private residences he ever designed; Hardenburgh is best remembered for his New York City buildings, The Plaza Hotel and the Dakota Apartments. The interiors were decorated by the firm of W.P. Nelson Company of Chicago; it took over eleven months to complete the process, with many pieces made especially for the mansion. The results were staggering: a Moorish-style entry hall featuring a Saracenic arch inspired by the Alhambra in Grenada, Spain, and painted burlap walls, main hall walls covered with deep blue velour wallpaper, a ceiling which replicates the interior of an Arabic dome, Louis XVI-style parlors embellished in wall panels of rose-colored damask silk, custom-made Aubusson rugs, Gobelin tapestries, Brussels lace draperies...the seemingly endless list conjures up the image of overwhelming luxury which characterized the world the Mosses called home.

Notable Collections on Exhibit

All of the original leather library and dining room furniture is on display, as well as that in the master bedroom and several other upstairs rooms. A beautiful collection of rugs from every corner of the world is still maintained and Mrs. Moss's personal collection of Salish Indian baskets from Oregon decorates the library.

Additional Information

The Moss Mansion is listed on the National Register of Historic Places.

William Andrews Clark House

219 West Granite Street
Butte, MT 59701
(406) 782-7580

Contact: Copper King Mansion

Open: Daily, 9 a.m.–5 p.m.

Admission: Adults $5.00; seniors and groups $4.50; children $4.00

Activities: Guided tours, bed and breakfast accommodations

Suggested Time to View House: 45 minutes

Facilities on Premises: Gift shop and art gallery

Description of Grounds: Limited access to area

Best Season to View House: Spring and summer

Number of Yearly Visitors: 10,000

Year House Built: Started 1884, completed 1888

Number of Rooms: 34

Style of Architecture: High Victorian Queen Anne, patterned masonry

On-Site Parking: Yes **Wheelchair Access:** No

Description of House

Looking out of the window of the third-floor ballroom of the Copper King Mansion, the visitor can see the copper-rich butte once referred to as "The Richest Hill on Earth." On this site, one of Montana's copper kings, William Andrews Clark, built his palatial residence, a thirty-room mansion complete with billiard room, hand-painted-fresco walls, nine imported French fireplaces, a $30,000 antique pipe organ, and a $100,000 antique crystal collection.

The exterior of this three-story structure features red brick with black pointing; the belting, caps, and trim are white sandstone, and exterior relief panels are terra-cotta. The entrance is a covered portico with hand-carved wood capitals. Inside, the woodwork, walls, and wainscotting are original and fully restored. The newel posts and banisters on the main staircase are hand-carved white oak. The entire house was fitted with both incandescent lighting and gas fixtures; all the glass on the first two floors is beveled French plate. The woodwork was actually removed from a private residence in Chicago belonging to one W. F. Beall.

Anna M. Cote purchased the house in 1951 from the Catholic diocese; for years, it had served as a convent. Anna Cote's daughter maintained the house for thirty years.

Additional Information

The William Andrews Clark House—the Copper Mansion—is listed on the National Register of Historic Places.

Grant-Kohrs Ranch House

North end of Deer Lodge
P.O. Box 790
Deer Lodge, MT 59722
(406) 846-2070

Contact: National Park Service, Grant-Kohrs Ranch National Historic Site

Open: Year-round, daily 10 a.m.–4 p.m.; closed Thanksgiving, Christmas, New Year's Day

Admission: Adults $2.00 or $4.00 per car

Activities: Guided tours, introductory video, summer frontier craft demonstrations

Suggested Time to View House: 60–90 minutes

Facilities on Premises: Visitor center with books and postcards

Description of Grounds: 1,500 acre working ranch with several outbuildings

Best Season to View House: Spring-fall

Year House Built: 1862, addition 1890

Style of Architecture: Modified Greek Revival-style farmhouse with Victorian-style brick rear addition

Number of Rooms: 21

On-Site Parking: Yes **Wheelchair Access:** Yes

Description of House

Johnny Grant, a Canadian trapper and mountain man, came to Montana in the 1850s and began a cattle ranching operation which he moved in 1862 to Deer Lodge. Here he built a two-story log house for his Bannock Indian wife, Quarra, and their large family. Four years later he sold the ranch to the German immigrant Conrad Kohrs for $19,200 and went back to Canada. Kohrs, a butcher by trade, had made his money by supplying local mining camps with beef; in 1868, he went back east to get a wife and found an attractive 19-year-old woman of German extraction named Augusta Kruse. The couple married, then completed the seven-week-long trip back to Montana with Kohrs' half-brother, John Bielenberg.

The two became partners and built a ranching empire founded on principles of scientific range management, selective breeding, and supplemental feeding. They survived the destructive winters of '86 and '88 to become famous cattle breeders with investments in mines, water rights, and land. In 1917, too old to adapt to the closing in of the once-open range, they sold off all but 1,000 acres of their property. Both men died during the following decade but Augusta lived on here until 1945, when she died at the age of ninety-six. By that time, the ranch was being successfully run as a breeding operation by Conrad Kohrs Warren, a grandson of the founder. The ranch was declared a National Historic Site by Congress in 1972 for the purpose of providing "an understanding of the frontier cattle era of the Nation's history."

Johnny Grant's house is built of rough-hewn timber—logs with lime chinking—on a stone foundation, covered in white clapboard siding with green shutters flanking each of its twenty-eight windows. *The Montana Post* of December 16, 1865, called it, "By long odds, the finest house in Montana." The house also features double chimneys on the gabled side walls. The Kohrs addition of 1890 is a two-story brick structure with four bedrooms and a bath upstairs, and a kitchen, dining room, sitting room, and another bedroom and bath downstairs; it turned the house into a T-shaped structure. The house is interpreted to the 1890s.

Notable Collections on Exhibit

The furnishings, ranching equipment, business records, and art objects are original to the house and present a living picture of life on the ranch.

I. G. Baker House

1406 Front Street
Fort Benton, MT 59442
(406) 622-5494

Contact: River and Plains Society
Open: May 15-Sept. 15, daily 10 a.m.–5 p.m.
Admission: Free
Activities: Viewing only
Suggested Time to View House: 15 minutes
Description of Grounds: Located in the Fort Benton Landmark District and a part of the Fort Benton Museum of the Upper Missouri walking tour

Best Season to View House: Summer
Number of Yearly Visitors: 8,000-10,000
Year House Built: 1867
Style of Architecture: National, frontier style with adobe walls
Number of Rooms: 4, 2 open to the public
On-Site Parking: Yes **Wheelchair Access:** Yes

Description of House

By 1867 I. G. Baker, the last agent for the American Fur Company at Fort Benton, had gone into business for himself as a trader, taken a wife, and built this house for her. Their life here was brief; after a only a year his wife returned to St. Louis with their newborn daughter. She was the first white child born outside of the fort. During the steamboat era of the 1890s, Baker became the most successful of Montana's "merchant princes." In the early 1900s, the house was owned by a sheepherder named Conrad. It was given to the city in 1973 by A. E. McLeish.

This simple one-story house is built of adobe; it consists of two original rooms with a double-sided center fireplace to which two more rooms were added in 1869. The whole was remodeled in 1876—the walls and ceilings were plastered and clapboard siding was added to the exterior. At present one of the rooms is interpreted to an 1867 bedroom with exposed adobe walls, an open ceiling, and a fireplace; and a second room is the 1876 parlor with a marble fireplace, a piano, and mannequins in period dress. The Victorian furnishings in the parlor are complemented by the hand-crafted pieces in the bedroom. Some of the pieces came from the Grand Union Hotel.

Charles M. Russell Residence

400 Thirteenth Street North
Great Falls, MT 59401
(406) 727-8787

Contact: C.M. Russell Museum Complex and the Montana Federation of Garden Clubs

Open: Summer, May 1-Sept. 30, Mon.-Sat. 9 a.m.–5 p.m., Sun. 1–5 p.m.; winter, Tues.-Sat. 10 a.m.–5 p.m., Sun., 1–5 p.m.

Admission: $4.00

Activities: Guided tours by appointment

Suggested Time to View House: 30 minutes

Best Season to View House: Summer

Facilities on Premises: Gift shop, bookstore and library facilities

Description of Grounds: Back yard with the log cabin studio

Style of Architecture: National, frame bungalow

Number of Yearly Visitors: 80,000

Year House Built: 1900

Number of Rooms: 10

On-Site Parking: Yes **Wheelchair Access:** Yes

Description of House

Will Rogers once said that Charles Marion Russell could "paint a horse and a cow and a cowboy and an Indian better than any man who ever lived." Russell lived in this house in Great Falls from 1900 until his death in 1926; he painted his version of the American West in the log cabin studio that stands a short distance from the house. Here, he found a sanctuary where he could work, cook cowboy stew, and entertain the many friends he'd made during his early days as a wrangler. The studio, constructed from telephone poles, now contains Russell's sketches, paintings, materials, and personal art collection.

The house itself looks a good deal more respectable than a "Wild West" cabin; it reflects his wife's tastes more than his own. Nancy married Charles when she was eighteen years old and he was thirty-two. It was she who convinced him to leave the trail behind and concentrate on his art. She used monies inherited from her mother's estate to buy land and she supervised the construction of this simple ten room bungalow. After Russell died, the house fell into great disrepair and became a potential fire hazard; it would have been demolished if it hadn't been for the efforts of the citizens of Great Falls.

A compact, two-story structure, the Charles M. Russell Residence has front and side gables with a partial wrap-around porch. Inside, on the first floor, there is a foyer, living room, dining room, bathroom, kitchen and pantry; upstairs, there is a water closet, two full bedrooms, a child's bedroom, and another small bedroom. Although the furnishings are appropriate to the period in which Charles M. Russell lived here, only a lone sewing machine belonging to Nancy Russell remains in the house.

Notable Collections on Exhibit

A number of Charles Russell's works are on display.

Additional Information

Charles M. Russell and his wife built a home in Pasadena, California, named "Trail's End," where they spent their winters. After Russell's death, Nancy and her son, Jack, made this house their permanent residence. The Charles M. Russell Residence is listed on the National Register of Historic Places.

Daly Mansion

45 miles south of Missoula, P.O. Box 223
Hamilton, MT 59840
(406) 363-6004

Contact: Daly Mansion Preservation Trust

Open: May 1-Sept. 30, daily

Admission: Adults $5.00; seniors $4.00; children (5-12) $2.00; groups 20 or more $4.00 each

Activities: Guided tours, "Adopt A Tree" and "Porch Spindle" programs

Suggested Time to View House: 75 minutes

Facilities on Premises: Gift shop

Best Season to View House: Summer

Description of Grounds: 50 acre park with over 500 mature deciduous trees

Number of Yearly Visitors: 8,000-9,000

Year House Built: 1886, remodeled 1889, 1897, and 1910

Style of Architecture: Eclectic Colonial Revival, Georgian style with Neoclassical features

Number of Rooms: 42

On-Site Parking: Yes **Wheelchair Access:** Yes

Description of House

Marcus Daly lived the kind of success story that filled the imaginations of thousands of immigrants who poured into the United States from Europe during the 19th century looking to make their dreams come true. Daly was born in rural County Cavan, Ireland, and came to this country at age fifteen. By the time he was thirty, Marcus had become a foreman at a mine in Utah; soon after, he was hired by the Walker Brothers of Salt Lake City, who sent him to Montana to find a suitable mining operation to invest in. He purchased the Alice Mine in Butte, keeping an interest for himself. By 1890, the mines of Butte were producing over $17 million worth of copper a year and Marcus Daly had joined the ranks of the "Copper Kings."

The Daly Mansion—merely his summer residence—has forty-two rooms and sits on over fifty acres of what was once a 22,000-acre stock farm; it is the largest private residence in Montana. The dimensions are truly impressive: 24,000 square feet of living space on three floors, 24 bedrooms, 15 bathrooms, and 7 fireplaces faced in Italian marble. Designed by A. J. Gibson, with interiors by the Baltimore firm of Hurlbert & Hurlbert, the house was decidedly Victorian, with its gable detailing and wrought-iron roof cresting, but subsequent 19th-century remodelings made it even more so, adding side bay windows, towers, and screened porches. The 1910 remodeling, however, effectively obliterated the Victorian elements and refashioned the exterior in the Neoclassical style.

After Mrs. Daly died in 1941, the house remained unoccupied until it was opened for public viewing in 1987. It had been purchased from the estate of Countess Margaret Sigray Bessenyey, granddaughter of Marcus Daly. The trophies and ribbons on display in the house are those won by the Countess Bessenyey's Hungarian horses. The property includes a carriage house (not open to the public), laundry building, children's playhouse, greenhouse, icehouse, boathouse, and two pools.

Additional Information

The mansion, now owned by the state of Montana, has been designated as a National Historical Site, and listed on the National Register of Historic Places.

Original Governor's Mansion

Sixth Avenue and Ewing Street
Helena, MT 59620
(406) 444-4710

Contact: Montana Historical Society

Open: Apr., May, Sept.-Dec., Tues.-Sat.
Noon–5 p.m.; Memorial Day-Labor Day,
Tues.-Sun. Noon–5 p.m.

Admission: Free

Activities: Guided tours, annual Christmas
Home Tour

Suggested Time to View House: 45 minutes

Description of Grounds: Mature
landscaping and the property contains a
carriage house

Best Season to View House: Early
spring-fall

Number of Yearly Visitors: 9,000

Year House Built: 1888

Number of Rooms: 17

Style of Architecture: Victorian Queen Anne
On-Site Parking: Yes **Wheelchair Access:** No

Description of House

Governor Sam Stewart and his family came from Virginia City, Montana, to reside in this house in 1913. Over the years, Governor Stewart's two daughters provided oral histories, artifacts, and photographs documenting the period of their family's occupation of the house. Between the years 1913 and 1961, nine of Montana's governors and their families lived in the mansion.

The Original Governor's Mansion is a three-story brick building located near downtown Helena. It has a masonry foundation, a pillared porch, and decorative detailing above the windows. Inside, the space has been remodeled several times throughout the years, usually to satisfy the aesthetic considerations of its various inhabitants. Though some of the furnishings are original, many of them are period pieces purchased for the mansion by the state of Montana.

Notable Collections on Exhibit

The dining room set, purchased from the Tobey Furniture Company of Chicago, is original to the house, as is the desk in the den with its carved lion heads and an Atlas motif. A mahogany sleigh bed, chest, and dressing table from the Widdicomb Company of Grand Rapids, Michigan, that was used by the governors is also on display.

Additional Information

When in Helena, look for the Kluge House at 540 West Main Street, one of the last and finest examples of that Prussian log and half-timber construction called "Fachwerk" to be found in this country. Built in the 1880s by a German immigrant, the fully restored house currently serves as a dressmaking and alteration shop; though it displays no furnishings, the architecture is well worth viewing; in fact, it is included on Helena's historic tour train route.The Original Governor's Mansion is listed on the National Register of Historic Places.

Conrad Mansion National Historic Site Museum

Woodland Avenue between
Third and Fourth Streets East
P.O. Box 1041
Kalispell, MT 59903
(406) 755-2166

Contact: Conrad Mansion National Historic Site Museum

Open: May 15-June 14, 10 a.m.–5:30 p.m.; June 15-Sept. 15, 9 a.m.–8 p.m.; Sept. 16 and Oct. 15, 10 a.m.–5:30 p.m.

Admission: Adults $4.00; children $1.00; groups 20 or more $3.20

Activities: Guided tours, special seasonal events including the Pie and Ice Cream Lawn Social, and Christmas bazaar in October, carriage rides

Suggested Time to View House: 1 hour

Facilities on Premises: House shop

Description of Grounds: 3 acres of landscaped gardens surrounded by rock wall with gazebo and concrete walkways

Best Season to View House: Summer

Number of Yearly Visitors: 20,000

Year House Built: 1895

Style of Architecture: Victorian Shingle Style

Number of Rooms: 23

On-Site Parking: Yes **Wheelchair Access:** No

Description of House

Charles Conrad, founder of the city of Kalispell and a true western pioneer, came to the Montana Territory after the Conrad family's Virginia plantation was destroyed during the Civil War. In 1868, he started trading and hauling freight on the Missouri River, eventually building a thriving business supplying goods to other settlers. His wife, Alicia Stanford Conrad, came to the Montana Territory in 1879 from Nova Scotia; they had three children, the youngest of whom donated the house to Kalispell in 1974.

Most homes belonging to Montana's wealthy pioneers have been remodeled over the years, but the Conrad Mansion is a notable exception: though both the exterior and interior have been restored, they have not undergone any architectural changes. Thus, the mansion is thought to be the most authentic example of late 19th-century architecture extant in the Northwest.

Designed by Kirkland Cutter, this three-story Norman-style structure with 14,000 square feet of living space has nine bedrooms, three bathrooms, eight sandstone fireplaces, and a hand pulley elevator. It features woodwork of natural golden oak, windows of leaded diamond-pane Tiffany stained glass, and French wrought iron light fixtures with pineapple globes of Waterford crystal. About ninety percent of the contents of the home are on display, of which less than half are on loan. They are all authentic to the period.

Notable Collections on Exhibit

The furnishings and artifacts on display reflect the lives of a wealthy Western family during the Victorian era. On their world travels, Mr. and Mrs. Conrad collected many unusual and beautiful objects, a number which are on display, as is an extensive collection of the family's original clothing from the 1900s to the 1920s, and a doll and toy collection from the same period.

Additional Information

The Conrad Mansion is listed on the National Register of Historic Places.

Nevada

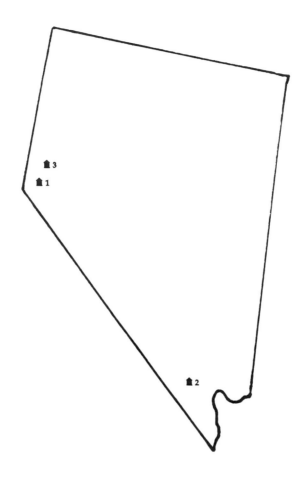

1. Carson City
Historic Bowers Mansion

2. Henderson
Babcock-Wilcox House
Beckley House
Giles-Barcus House
Heritage House
Townsite House

3. Virginia City
"House of the Silver Door Knobs"
MacKay Mansion

Historic Bowers Mansion

4005 Old Highway 395 North
Carson City, NV 89704
(702) 849-0201

Contact: Washoe County Parks and
Recreation Department, Bowers Mansion
Regional Park
Open: Memorial Day-Labor Day, daily
11 a.m.–4 p.m.; spring and fall, guided
tours available by appointment; closed
winter months
Admission: Adults $3.00; seniors and
children $2.00
Activities: Guided tours
Suggested Time to View House: 30 minutes
Facilities on Premises: Visitor center,
gift shop
Description of Grounds: Expansive lawn
area in 46 acre park with picnic area
shelters at base of ridge
Best Season to View House: Spring-fall
Number of Yearly Visitors: 15,000

Year House Built: 1864
Number of Rooms: 16
On-Site Parking: Yes **Wheelchair Access:** Yes

Description of House

The Scottish-born Eilley Orram and her future husband, Lemuel
"Sandy" Bowers, met in Gold Hill, Nevada, married in 1859, became the first
millionaires of the Comstock Lode, built this house in 1864, and lived well
for three more years. In 1867, the world as they knew it came to an end with
disarming swiftness: the mine played out and Sandy died. He was thirty-
five. The following year, Eilley was forced to add a third floor to their house
and open it to the public as a hotel. Even so, within seven years, she had to
sell it at auction to pay off her debts. Sadly, during these years Eilley had to
resort to fortune-telling to try to make ends meet—her crystal ball now sits
on one of the tables in the formal parlor. The "Washoe Seeress" died in 1903.

This two-story granite structure is largely representative of the Italianate
style, featuring a full-width wrap-around porch, a balcony with balustrades, a
hexagonal-shaped cupola, and stone tap quoins. The large windows—eight-
over-eight upstairs and nine-over-nine down—are Georgian-style, and the
double doors at the entry and capped with a glazed transom. Inside, the house
features expansive hallways and wide archways between rooms. The furnishings are mainly in the Victorian Eastlake, Renaissance Revival, and Empire
styles; a few pieces belonged to the Bowerses', but most are donated—by over
five hundred Nevada families. The Historic Bowers Mansion is listed on the
National Register of Historic Places.

Notable Collections on Exhibit

Among the notable items on display are: an 1850 Grovestein piano, an
1876 Brunswick billiards table, several Ansonia clocks, a drawing room harp
c.1900, and a number of Currier & Ives prints.

Babcock-Wilcox House

1830 South Boulder Highway
Henderson, NV 89015
(702) 455-7955

Contact: Clark County Southern Nevada Museum

Open: Daily 9:00 a.m.–4:30 p.m.; closed Christmas and New Year's Day

Admission: Adults $1.00; seniors and children $.50

Activities: Self-guided tours, "hands-on" exhibits

Suggested Time to View House: 1-3 hours

Facilities on Premises: Gift shop with books

Description of Grounds: Museum park complex with five resettled historic houses located on "Heritage Street"

Best Season to View House: Fall-early spring

Number of Yearly Visitors: 45,000

Year House Built: 1933

Style of Architecture: National, frame

Number of Rooms: 3

On-Site Parking: Yes **Wheelchair Access:** Yes

Description of House

The Hoover Dam, considered one of the wonders of the modern world since its completion in 1935, was built with the blood, toil, and sweat of over four thousand workers. During the first year of the massive project, these people were housed in rudimentary tents and suffered cruelly from the heat and lack of sanitary facilities. The outcry was such that the United States Government decided to build a city for the purpose of providing adequate housing for its workers; thus, in 1933, it allocated two million dollars to create a 600-building development called Boulder City. It was under the tight control of the U. S. Marshall and the laws banning liquor, narcotics, and gambling were strictly enforced.

The city was built on 300 acres of land and the overall plan was designed by S. R. DeBoer. The Babcock and Wheeler House was originally built at 441 Hotel Plaza; for years it was owned by the City of Los Angeles Department of Water and Power. In 1943, when it still stood on its original site, the house was listed on the National Register of Historic Places, along with eleven other houses built for Babcock and Wilcox Company employees. These simple one-story frame structures were designed by the architect E. D. Wagner of Akron, Ohio, and built by the contractor Paul S. Webb. In 1987, these houses were auctioned off and demolished to make room for a new post office; fortunately, this one was moved and reassembled in Henderson as part of the Clark County Southern Nevada Museum.

Beckley House

1830 South Boulder Highway
Henderson, NV 89015
(702) 455-7955

Contact: Clark County Southern Nevada
Museum and the Junior League
of Las Vegas

Open: Daily 9:00 a.m.–4:40 p.m.; closed
Christmas and New Year's Day

Admission: Adults $1.00; seniors
and children $.50

Activities: Self-guided tours, "hands-on"
exhibits

Suggested Time to View House: 1–3 hours

Facilities on Premises: Gift shop with books

Description of Grounds: Museum park
complex with five resettled historic
houses located on "Heritage Street"

Best Season to View House: Fall–early
spring

Number of Yearly Visitors: 45,000

Year House Built: 1912, additions 1923
and 1925

Number of Rooms: 4

Style of Architecture: Craftsman, bungaloid
style

On-Site Parking: Yes **Wheelchair Access:** Yes

Description of House

The year was 1908 and Will Beckley arrived in a desert village beside a
railroad track—Watering Stop #19—in southern Nevada and built himself
a tent house with a wooden door, canvas walls, and a roof. Four years later,
Beckley was a successful haberdasher in the new town of Las Vegas, with a
shop in the old Nevada Hotel, later called the Golden Gate Casino. He had
also taken a wife, a mail-order bride from Illinois named Leva Grimes, and
dedicated himself to the social and cultural development of Las Vegas, the
flower of the desert.

The Beckley House was designed in the California Bungalow style, a good
example of the typical house being built in the desert during the early part of
the century. In 1912, the house boasted of four rooms and a front porch. Thirteen
years later, a brick fireplace and chimney, as well as a dining room and
connected kitchen, were added to the house. For years, this relatively modest
structure was the center of social activity in Las Vegas. After the Beckleys died,
there was pressure to develop this land; after all, Las Vegas was a burgeoning
town that needed more housing. So, in 1979, the house was moved here, to the
Clark County Southern Nevada Museum group.

Giles-Barcus House

1830 South Boulder Highway
Henderson, NV 89015
(702) 455-7955

Contact: Clark County Southern Nevada
Museum

Open: Daily 9:00 a.m.–4:30 p.m.; closed
Christmas and New Year's Day

Admission: Adults $1.00; seniors and
children $.50

Activities: Self-guided tours, "hands-on"
exhibits

Suggested Time to View House: 1–3 hours

Facilities on Premises: Gift shop with books

Description of Grounds: Museum park
complex with five resettled historic
houses located on "Heritage Street"

Best Season to View House: Fall-early
spring

Number of Yearly Visitors: 45,000

Year House Built: c. 1905

Number of Rooms: 4

Style of Architecture: National, frame

On-Site Parking: Yes **Wheelchair Access:** Yes

Description of House

The town of Goldfield appeared soon after gold was discovered here in the Columbia Mountains by Billy Marsh and Harry Stimler in 1902. Within six years, Goldfield was home to some 20,000 residents, two stock exchanges, five banks, two daily and three weekly newspapers, three railroads, and four schools. The town peaked—in every way—in 1910; after that, a series of calamities befell the community which effectively ended its prosperity and hope for renewal. These included a disastrous labor dispute, the drying up of the gold veins, a brutal flood in 1913, and, finally, a fire that destroyed fifty-three square blocks in 1923.

The Giles-Barcus House was built in Goldfield during the town's heyday—around 1905—by Edwin Giles, a local surveyor. In 1952, his daughter Edith Giles Barcus moved the house to Las Vegas. It was located at the corner of Hacienda and Giles Streets, where it was home to the Odd Shop Antique Shop. The simple frame structure has since been relocated to the Clark County Southern Nevada Museum.

Heritage House

1830 South Boulder Highway
Henderson, NV 89015
(702) 455-7955

Contact: Clark County Southern Nevada Museum

Open: Daily 9:00 a.m.–4:30 p.m.; closed Christmas and New Year's Day

Admission: Adults $1.00; seniors and children $.50

Activities: Self-guided tours, "hands-on" exhibits

Suggested Time to View House: 1–3 hours

Facilities on Premises: Gift shop with books

Description of Grounds: Museum park complex with five resettled historic houses located on "Heritage Street"

Best Season to View House: Fall-early spring

Style of Architecture: Eclectic Period Revival, Swiss Chalet

Number of Yearly Visitors: 45,000

Year House Built: 1931

Number of Rooms: 7

On-Site Parking: Yes **Wheelchair Access:** Yes

Description of House

By the 1930s, the gold boom in Las Vegas had gone bust and folks were looking to the tourist trade to bring in needed cash. "Glitter Gulch," the downtown casino zone, was beginning to thrive as gamblers abandoned Los Angeles. In addition to the legalization of gambling, Las Vegas also reduced the residency requirements for divorce from three months to six weeks. Both of these policies, and the desert climate, had the desired effect of attracting people, businesses, and development. And the Federal Government's New Deal programs provided the funds for streets, sewer systems, parks, schools, and other public buildings. One of the more elegant homes built in Las Vegas during the decade of the 1930s is the Heritage House. It was designed by the architectural firm of Warner and Nordstrom and built by Jack Hagenson, an employee of the Boulder Club. The house is constructed in the style of a Swiss Chalet, and features a gable roof, jigsaw-work balustrades, and elaborate ornamentation. Pros J. Goumond purchased the house in 1935; he was part-owner of the Boulder Club as well as the owner and operator of a successful dude ranch.

Heritage House was moved to its present location on the South Boulder Highway in 1984 and is currently undergoing restoration to the style of the 1950s.

Townsite House

**1830 South Boulder Highway
Henderson, NV 89015
(702) 455-7955**

Contact: Clark County Southern Nevada
Museum

Open: Daily 9:00 a.m.–4:30 p.m.; closed
Christmas and New Year's Day

Admission: Adults $1.00; seniors and
children $.50

Activities: Self-guided tours, "hands-on"
exhibits

Suggested Time to View House: 1–3 hours

Facilities on Premises: Gift shop with books

Description of Grounds: Museum park
complex with five resettled historic
houses located on "Heritage Street"

Best Season to View House: Fall–early
spring

Number of Yearly Visitors: 45,000

Year House Built: 1942

Number of Rooms: 5

Style of Architecture: National, frame

On-Site Parking: Yes **Wheelchair Access:** Yes

Description of House

Unlike most Nevada towns, Henderson did not come into being as a result of a gold rush, or a change in the divorce laws, or a gambling boom; it was created by bombs. Here the United States Government built a processing plant for magnesium, the principal ingredient in the incendiary bombs used in World War II. In order to house the workers in the $63 million plant, one thousand frame houses were built, along with stores, schools, churches, a hospital, and a bowling alley.

On January 1, 1944, the townsite officially became Henderson, named in honor of Charles B. Henderson, a United States Senator and grandson of Louis Rice Bradley, a Governor of Nevada in the 1870s. Eleven months later, due to a surplus of magnesium, the processing plant shut down operations and the town emptied. Amazingly, Henderson did not become a ghost town; slowly new industries moved in and today it is a thriving suburb of Las Vegas.

The Townsite House was supposed to be temporary, as were all of the houses built in Henderson. The interior walls are made of 1/4 inch plywood with no insulation, and they are covered on the outside with redwood siding. There was no air-conditioning in the house, but the windows were situated to maximize cross-ventilation. This "temporary" house has weathered the years exceedingly well and can now be seen in the complex called the Clark County Southern Nevada Museum.

"House of the Silver Door Knobs"

70 South "B" Street
Virginia City, NV 89440
(702) 847-0275

Contact: The Castle

Open: Memorial Day-Labor Day, daily
10 a.m.–5 p.m.; Labor Day-Oct., daily
11 a.m.–5 p.m.

Admission: Adults $3.00; children
(6-12) $.25

Activities: Guided tours

Suggested Time to View House: 30 minutes

Description of Grounds: Terraced yard
with flowers

Best Season to View House: Spring and
early summer

Year House Built: 1868

Style of Architecture: Modified Second
Empire style modeled after a castle in
Normandy

Number of Rooms: 16

On-Site Parking: No **Wheelchair Access:** No

Description of House

Virginia City in the 1860s was a town awash in silver and gold and the wealth that those precious metals created; some of this money was spent in building magnificent homes, only a few of which survived the engulfing fire of 1875. Perhaps none were as elaborate as this house—certainly none were as determinedly ostentatious after the European fashion—which has come to be called the "House of Silver Door Knobs."

Designed to resemble a Norman castle, the mansion was built in 1868 by Robert N. Graves, the superintendent of the Empire Mine. After Graves moved away in 1872, H. Blauvett, a local banker, bought the house and lived here until his death in 1916. At that time, the McQuirk family acquired it and continue to own it up to the present.

It is hard to believe the lengths to which the builders of the "House of the Silver Door Knobs" went to insure its Continental authenticity: all the furnishings and decorative pieces were purchased in Europe, shipped around the Horn to San Francisco, then carted by mule and ox over the Sierras to Virginia City. In addition, dozens of old world craftsmen and artisans were "imported" to work on the house. Their work was quite beautiful.

The exterior of the house features many elements of the Second Empire style: an asymmetrical plan with a tower, heavily bracketed windows, a front gable with a one-story bay, an entry porch, wood-trimmed quoins, and a roof line which cleverly mixes both the hipped and mansard styles. The interior decor features a profusion of imported materials and European designs—even the silver is imported! The furnishings are all original, as is the carpeting, and even a bit of the white wall paint in some of the rooms.

MacKay Mansion

129 South "D" Street, P.O. Box 971
Virginia City, NV 89440
(702) 847-0173

Contact: MacKay Mansion
Open: Mar.-Oct., daily 10 a.m.–6 p.m.;
Dec.-February, daily Noon–5 p.m.
Admission: Adults $3.00; children (under 12) free, special group rates available
Activities: Guided tours
Suggested Time to View House: 60 minutes
Facilities on Premises: Souvenirs for sale
Description of Grounds: Restored acre with lawn, pond and rock gardens
Best Season to View House: Spring and early summer
Number of Yearly Visitors: 25,000
Year House Built: 1860
Number of Rooms: 15

Style of Architecture: Modified Italianate
On-Site Parking: Yes **Wheelchair Access:** No

Description of House

The MacKay Mansion was built for the Gould and Curry Mining Company in 1860, one year after the discovery of Virginia City's Comstock Lode, that rich vein of gold and silver which made fortunes overnight. Its first occupant was George Hearst, mine superintendent and father of William Randolph Hearst, the newspaper publisher whose California house, "San Simeon," is also featured in this guide. In 1870, John W. MacKay moved in. MacKay, the richest man on the Comstock Lode with holdings reputed to be in the $100 million range, was alternately called the "Bonanza King" and "Boss of the Comstock." He also founded the Postal Telegraph Company.

This three-story Italianate structure is unique for the area: it survived the great fire of 1875 which leveled much of Virginia City and, as such, has escaped any structural alterations. It features a full wrap-around porch and columned veranda, double-hung sash windows with four-by-four panes, and a pyramid-shaped roof with a centered ridge line chimney. Inside, one sees a number of original details: the wallpaper c.1870–c.1900, carpets from the 1880s, wood floors in the kitchen and office, and some of the gold leaf moldings. The house has six fireplaces, its original plumbing—which included running water inside—and electrical wiring. The beautiful window in the transom over the front door is made by Tiffany.

The furnishings reflect a uniquely American taste and sensibility; most pieces, even the Renaissance Revival and Victorian-style parlor and bedroom sets, were manufactured in this country, many of them locally. The chandelier in the dining room is solid Comstock silver.

Notable Collections on Exhibit

The MacKay Mansion includes the original mine office and vault; displayed here are samples of ore from the Comstock vein as well as mine records and other memorabilia.

New Mexico

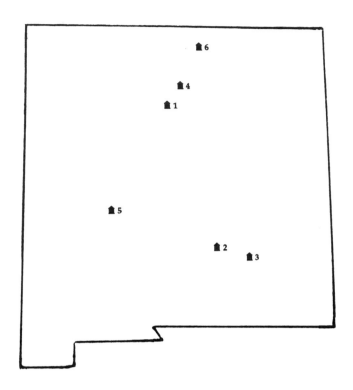

1. La Cienega
Las Golondrinas Placita House

2. Lincoln
Dr. Woods' House

3. Roswell
J.P. White House

4. Santa Fe
El Zaguan

5. Socorro
Historic Socorro Village

6. Taos
Ernest L. Blumenschein Home
Governor Bent House
Kit Carson Home
La Hacienda de Don Antonio Severino Martinez

Las Golondrinas Placita House

15 miles south of Santa Fe
La Cienega, NM 87505
(505) 983-2994

Contact: El Rancho de las Golondrinas

Open: Apr. and Oct. by appointment;
June-Sept., Wed.-Sun. 10 a.m.–4 p.m.

Admission: Adults $3.00; seniors $2.00;
children $1.00

Activities: Guided tours by appointment,
self-guided tours, seasonal festivals and
demonstrations

Description of Grounds: "Living history"
museum complex with several historic
buildings from the early 1700s to 1880

Suggested Time to View House: 1–2½ hours

Facilities on Premises: Museum store,
weekend food service

Number of Yearly Visitors: 40,000

Number of Rooms: 12

Style of Architecture: Spanish Colonial
Adobe, pueblo style

Year House Built: Early 1700s

On-Site Parking: Yes **Wheelchair Access:** Yes

Description of House

El Rancho de Las Golondrinas—The Ranch of the Swallows—owes its existence today as a living history museum to the vision of the Curtin-Paloheimo family who acquired the property in 1932. It is comprised of fully restored historic buildings, the most important of which is the 18th-century placita (courtyard) house, as well as some reconstructed outbuildings and even a few that have been moved here from other sites. The whole presents a detailed portrait of life on a self-sufficient settlement in the Spanish Colony of New Mexico; in addition to the house, it includes another, later house, a molasses mill, several water mills, a blacksmith shop, a wheelwright's shop, and a winery and its vineyards. The land upon which the ranch sits is part of a 1710 royal purchase made by the Spaniard Miguel Vega y Coca; his family later joined the Baca family in marriage and the property passed to their descendants. Located on El Camino Real (the Royal Road which ran between Mexico City and Santa Fe), the ranch was famous as the last stopping place—paraje—on that trail before reaching Santa Fe. In 1778, Juan Bautista de Anza, Governor of New Mexico, spent a night here with his expedition of 150 men as they searched for a direct route to Arizpe, Sonora.

The pueblo-style structure features an original section of three rooms built of stone to which adobe rooms have been added. Virtually all of the elements which make up the Spanish Colonial style are in evidence here: the covered entry, the placita with a well and outdoor ovens, the living room and chapel, *la cocina con fogón de pastor* (kitchen with shepherd's bed and fireplace), the watchtower, weaving workrooms, bedrooms for the residents and guests, and the slaves' quarters (*cuarto de los cautivos*—captives' room). Two of the original stone rooms have later wood plank floors and a tin roof; the other rooms have the older mud floors and flat roofs with vigas. All of the furnishings in these rooms are either collected pieces or reproductions in the Spanish Colonial style.

Dr. Woods' House

Main Street, P.O. Box 98
Lincoln, NM 88338
(505) 653-4025

Contact: Lincoln County Historical Society
and Lincoln County Heritage Trust

Open: May–Sept., daily 9 a.m.–Noon,
1–6 p.m.

Admission: $4.50 fee includes admission to
all town museums

Activities: Guided tours

Suggested Time to View House: 20 minutes

Description of Grounds: Garden with
vegetables

Best Season to View House: Spring–early
fall

Style of Architecture: National,
Lincoln-style Territorial Adobe

Number of Yearly Visitors: 15,000

Number of Rooms: 5

Year House Built: c. 1882

On-Site Parking: No **Wheelchair Access:** No

Description of House

Dr. Earl L. Woods began his medical career at Bellevue Hospital in New York City, moved to Kansas, then Colorado, and finally settled in Lincoln, New Mexico, where he purchased this house in 1925. Here he practiced medicine, ran a drug-store, started a winery during Prohibition, raised chickens, and made his own brand of deodorant soap—"Dr. Woods' Noscents to dissipate all body odors." In his later years, he tried his hand at running an ice cream business and a filling station. Of the numerous tenants and owners through the years, none were as dedicated as Mattie Wright, the woman who bought the house from Dr. Woods in 1940 and nursed him until his death in 1942. She saved his books, medical instruments, and furnishings—even his medical bag.

Records show that Dr. Woods charged $2.50 for a house call, plus $1.00 per mile. Apparently, these rates were more than sufficient remuneration, for the doctor's house was considered quite elegant at the time. Originally built in the early 1880s by George Pieppin, a former sheriff and master mason, the house is an artful mix of traditional southwest adobe construction and "back-east" design. Each room has a door which leads to the outside in the Spanish Colonial style and the second floor has an exterior stairway. Both structures—the house and an annex in which the doctor worked—have walls of adobe built within an existing wooden frame.

In 1976, the Lincoln County Heritage Trust bought the house from Mrs. Wright and furnished it with period pieces, including an 1866 Steinway grand piano bought in St. Louis. The house, and its contents, have been preserved so well that one can easily imagine the doctor still making his rounds at a dollar a mile.

J.P. White House

200 North Lea Avenue
Roswell, NM 88201
(505) 622-8333

Contact: Historical Center for Southeast
New Mexico

Open: Fri., Sat., and Sun. 1–4 p.m.; special
tours by appointment

Admission: Adults $2.00; group rate
available

Activities: Special guided tours upon
request, monthly program meetings,
exhibits

Suggested Time to View House: 60 minutes

Facilities on Premises: Archives

Description of Grounds: Yard with native
shrubs and trees

Best Season to View House: Spring-early fall

Year House Built: 1910

Number of Rooms: 13

Number of Yearly Visitors: 5,000

Style of Architecture: Prairie Style

On-Site Parking: No **Wheelchair Access:** Yes

Description of House

Built in 1910, the home of James Phelps White is a reminder of what life was like for a well-to-do family at the turn of the century in New Mexico. White was born in Gonzales, Texas, in 1856 and came to Roswell in 1881, where he earned his money in cattle ranching and farming. His wife, Lou Tomlinson White, also moved to Roswell from Texas. Together, the couple contributed greatly to the religious, cultural, and civic well-being of their community. Mrs. White lived in this house until her death in 1972 at the age of 92.

This yellow brick house is built in the Prairie Style which had been developed by American architect Frank Lloyd Wright. Exterior features include large wrap-around porches and a hipped roof covered in terra-cotta clay tiles. Inside, beamed ceilings and stained-glass windows decorate the dining room. The original kitchen has been fully restored and now contains hundreds of utensils and a well-stocked pantry. Perhaps the finest interior detail is the hand-carved newel post on the main staircase capped with a splendid Art Nouveau light fixture.

Chaves County residents have contributed antiques and artifacts of the period, including an Edison Amberola phonograph and a buggy footwarmer.

Notable Collections on Exhibit

The upstairs bedrooms are used as exhibit spaces showing fashions of the late 19th and early 20th centuries, as well as a collection of little "adult" toys. The Historical Society's archives are kept on the third floor.

El Zaguan

545 Canyon Road
Santa Fe, NM 87801
(505) 983-2567

Contact: Historic Santa Fe Foundation
Open: May-Sept., daily
Admission: Free, donations welcome
Activities: Docent guided tours available
Suggested Time to View House: 60 minutes
Facilities on Premises: Foundation office and archives, publications for sale
Description of Grounds: Victorian style flower garden

Best Season to View House: Spring and summer
Year House Built: pre-1850
Style of Architecture: Spanish Colonial Adobe, pueblo style
Number of Rooms: 24, including private residences not open to the public
On-Site Parking: No **Wheelchair Access:** No

Description of House

The name El Zaguan comes from an Arabic word meaning "the arches" which describes the large gateway through which horses and wagons entered the house's plaza. Over the years, the words may have also come to refer to the long corridor here which runs between the Bandelier garden and an open patio.

True to its name, El Zaguan's style is Spanish Pueblo, and the hacienda and its gardens are early-19th-century treasures. James L. Johnson, a trader and merchant who came to Santa Fe from Maryland on the famous Santa Fe trail, bought the house in 1849. At the time, it probably consisted of two or three rooms behind four-foot-thick adobe walls. The house and garden grew and changed as the years went by; at one point it boasted of twenty-four rooms and the servants' quarters were sited across Canyon Road. These changes are clearly visible in the varying wall thicknesses, ceiling heights, and different door and wall treatments seen throughout the house. Additional rooms included a "chocolate room," wherein chocolate was freshly ground and served each afternoon, and a library then considered to be the largest in the territory. Johnson's grandson, Colonel James Baca, owned the property until 1927; it was then purchased by Margaretta Dietrich and remodeled and furnished under the direction of Kate Chapman, a local restoration advisor. The hacienda and gardens have served many functions over the years—as a home for a New York theater group, a hotel, a girls' school, and as rental apartments.

The Bandelier Garden was laid out by Adolph Bandelier, the famous Swiss archaeologist. He lived at El Zaguan during the years 1891 to 1892. The garden is a fantastical amalgam of the historical and the exotic; two giant horse chestnut trees brought by James Johnson from Ohio stand beside peonies that were imported from China via Mexico.

Historic Socorro Village

Town Plaza, P.O. Box 923
Socorro, NM 87801
(505) 835-5242

Contact: Socorro County Historical Society, Inc.

Open: Daily

Admission: Donation requested $10.00 includes tour of all historic areas of Socorro village

Activities: Guided tours by reservation

Suggested Time to View House: 1 hour

Facilities on Premises: Historic Socorro includes the plaza area with the Juan Nepomocento Garcia House, the Juan José Baca House, and Fischer House

Year House Built: Nine historic houses dating from 1816-1913

Description of Grounds: Street with the Jesús Maria Torres House, the French Quarter with the Antonio Abeytia House and the Eaton House as well as religious and civic buildings, the San Miguel Mission, the Val Verde Hotel and the Hammel Brewery and Museum

Best Season to View House: Spring

Style of Architecture: Eclectic mix of Spanish Colonial and late nineteenth-century bungaloid styles

Number of Rooms: Not all houses are open to the public

On-Site Parking: Yes **Wheelchair Access:** No

Description of House

Socorro means "help" or "aid" in Spanish, and it is an apt name for this historic village; in 1598 the Pueblo dwellers here gave explorers from the Juan de Onate expedition food and shelter as they made their way north to establish a Spanish colony near modern Santa Fe. The modern history of Socorro begins in 1815, when the governor of New Mexico ordered that the site be resettled; by the 1850s the town had a population of 600. It reached its heyday in the late 19th century, when the Santa Fe railroad was built. The railroad brought boom times and a significant mining industry started up, along with many successful farms and ranches. Once mining declined, Socorro reverted to an agriculturally-based community and the population stabilized at around 9,000.

The self-guided tour of Sorocco includes approximately twenty-six different buildings; among these historic structures are some fine homes. The Juan Nepomocento Garcia House, built in 1916 in the Spanish Colonial style, features adobe construction, a flat roof, and a center courtyard; the Juan José Baca House was built just prior to the advent of the railroad in a similar style, but the original flat roof was later changed to a pitched metal roof; the Jesús Maria Torres House c.1913 is a good example of the Bungaloid style executed in adobe with wood trim, its windows and doors bought via mail-order from the Crab Tree Lumber Co.; the Antonio Abeytia House of La Casa de la Flecha (House of the Arrow) was built around 1890 and is one of only a pair of two-story houses in town—it reflects the boom years of the '90s in its opulence; and the Eaton House, originally built in 1820 in the Spanish Colonial style but radically altered after the 1906 earthquake here. All of these homes, and the other historic buildings which comprise this fascinating restored village, are well worth visiting.

Ernest L. Blumenschein Home

13 Ledoux Street
Taos, NM 87571
(505) 758-0505

Contact: Kit Carson Historic Museums
Open: Summer, daily 8 a.m.–6 p.m.; winter, daily 9 a.m.–5 p.m.
Admission: Adults $3.00; special group rates and senior citizen discounts available
Activities: Self-guided tours
Suggested Time to View House: 1 hour
Facilities on Premises: Gift shop and books
Description of Grounds: Located two blocks west of the Taos Plaza
Best Season to View House: Fall
Number of Yearly Visitors: 100,000
Year House Built: 1797
Style of Architecture: Spanish Colonial Adobe
Number of Rooms: 10

On-Site Parking: No **Wheelchair Access:** No

Description of House

The Ernest L. Blumenschein Home built in 1797 is one of three historic houses that comprise the Kit Carson Historic Museums. All of these homes reflect the personalities of those hardy pioneers who made Taos their home. Ernest L. Blumenschein was the co-founder of the Taos Society of Artists and a leading figure in the movement to establish Taos as a haven for international artists and writers. His paintings, as well as those of his wife, Mary Greene Blumenschein, and their daughter, Helen, are exhibited here among the work of numerous other Taos artists.

This beautifully restored adobe, originally constructed during Spanish rule, is decorated with traditional southwestern-style furniture and European antiques. In addition, there are decorative art objects from around the world in every room.

Additional Information

The Ernest L. Blumenschein Home is listed on the National Register of Historic Places.

Governor Bent House

117 Bent Street, P.O. Box 153
Taos, NM 87571
(505) 758-2376

Contact: Governor Bent Museum
Open: Daily, 10 a.m.–5 p.m.; closed
Thanksgiving, Christmas,
New Year's Day
Admission: Adults $1.00; children (8-15)
$.50; children (under 8) free
Activities: Self-guided tours
Suggested Time to View House:
30–45 minutes

Description of Grounds: Patio area
Best Season to View House: Summer and
fall
Year House Built: 1832
Style of Architecture: Mexican-Territorial
Adobe
Number of Rooms: 5
On-Site Parking: No **Wheelchair Access:** Yes

Description of House

The Governor Bent House was the home of Charles Bent, an admired
and respected figure in early territorial history. Bent—a trader, trapper, and
former mountain man—was known for his generous dealings with the early
settlers of Taos Pueblo. He owned and operated several trading posts in
Santa Fe and Taos and traded supplies for furs and buffalo hides with the
local inhabitants. With assistance from his brother, William, and a close
personal friend, Ceran St. Vrain, he built the fort in Colorado which won
fame as a trading center for many Native American tribes and adventurers,
and came to be called Bent's Fort.

Bent was appointed Governor of the Territory of New Mexico in 1846,
but this new role would soon prove fatal. In January of 1847, an angry mob
protesting American rule attacked the Bent home. While some members of
the Bent family escaped their dwelling by digging a hole through a rear wall,
Bent himself was captured and killed. Virtually all of the family possessions
were destroyed during this hostile raid.

Notable Collections on Exhibit

The Governor Bent House collection exhibits the few remaining
souvenirs left behind by the Bent family including some odds-and-ends,
chairs, trunks, and native artifacts. Perhaps the most fascinating pieces in
this collection are the actual kitchen utensils used during the family's futile
escape, and the original written testimony to the murder of Governor Bent
by his young daughter, Teresina Bent Scheurich.

Additional Information

The Governor Bent House is listed on the National Register of Historic
Houses.

Kit Carson Home

Kit Carson Road, Route 64
Taos, NM 87571
(505) 758-0505

Contact: Kit Carson Historic Museums

Open: Summer, daily 8 a.m.–6 p.m.; winter, daily 9 a.m.–5 p.m.

Admission: Adults $3.00; special group rates and senior citizen discounts available

Activities: Special cultural exhibits

Suggested Time to View House: 1 hour

Facilities on Premises: Gift shop and books

Description of Grounds: Located just a half a block east from the Taos Plaza

Best Season to View House: Fall

Number of Yearly Visitors: 100,000

Year House Built: 1825

Style of Architecture: Territorial Adobe with Spanish Colonial influences

Number of Rooms: 12

On-Site Parking: No **Wheelchair Access:** No

Description of House

The Kit Carson Home is the focal point of the historic museum complex in Taos which bears his name and includes the Martinez Hacienda built c.1804, the Ernest L. Blumenschein Home built in 1797, and the Kit Carson Home built in 1825. All three houses illustrate different facets of the colorful history of Taos.

The person of Kit Carson is familiar to devotees of Old West folklore. Christopher "Kit" Carson was born in Kentucky. As a young man, he became a knowledgeable trapper on the Missouri frontier. Reputed to be skillful in the ways and languages of local native tribes, Carson was chosen by John Charles Frémont to be his principal scout and agent. Carson finally settled in the Taos area when he married his third wife, Josefa Jaramillo, in 1843. Carson purchased this twelve-room adobe home as a wedding gift for his bride. It was here that the Carson family, which included the couple's own eight children as well as several Native American orphans they raised, would remain for the next twenty-five years.

While many of the rooms serve as exhibit space featuring Native American and Spanish history and artifacts, there are three rooms—a parlor, bedroom, and kitchen—dedicated to the Carson period. These rooms are furnished in much the same way as when Kit Carson and his family lived here.

Additional Information

The Kit Carson Home is listed on the National Register of Historic Places.

La Hacienda de Don Antonio Severino Martinez

Ranchitos Road and Route 240
two miles west of Taos
Taos, NM 87571
(505) 758-0505

Contact: Kit Carson Historic Museums
Open: Summer, daily 8 a.m.–5 p.m.; winter, daily 9 a.m.–5 p.m.
Admission: Adults $3.00; special group rates and senior citizen discounts available
Activities: Special cultural exhibits and demonstrations
Suggested Time to View House: 1 hour
Facilities on Premises: Gift shop and books

Description of Grounds: 1 acre along the banks of the Rio Pueblo River
Best Season to View House: Fall
Number of Yearly Visitors: 100,000
Year House Built: c.1804
Style of Architecture: Spanish Colonial Adobe
Number of Rooms: 21
On-Site Parking: No **Wheelchair Access:** No

Description of House

The Martinez Hacienda is one of three historic homes which comprise the Kit Carson Historic Museums in Taos (the other two—the Ernest Blumenschein Home and the Kit Carson Home—have separate listings in this guide). The Hacienda is the oldest of the three and may be the oldest restored hacienda in New Mexico.

Don Antonio Severino Martin—he later changed his last name to Martinez—worked hard all his life transporting goods between Mexico and the territories by mule train and developing his property on the banks of the Rio Pueblo in Taos. The work was rewarded with financial success and the respect of his community; he held the office of "Alcalde" for a number of years. He had two sons: one of them took over his transport business and the other, Antonio José, became a priest who later gained wide recognition as a major religious and social leader in the Northern Rio Grande area. Both brothers served in the New Mexico legislature.

The Martinez Hacienda is located about two miles west of Taos Plaza on land that Don Antonio purchased in 1804. It was originally built to withstand attacks from the Comanches and Apaches, which occurred with some regularity during the early years of the 19th century. The massive walls did their job well: even Don Antonio's livestock survived by being driven through the heavy gates into the inner plaza where they remained until the raids ended. It was difficult to furnish the hacienda because the supplies had to be brought from Mexico on ox-cart by way of the Chihuahua Trail—the trail known as the "Journey of Death." Even so, by the time Don Antonio died in 1827, the hacienda had grown to twenty-one rooms, and all were fully furnished in the Colonial style. The living area surrounds the larger placita, while the servants' quarters and utility rooms faced the smaller placita at the rear of the house.

Notable Collections on Exhibit

Exhibits show the trade routes to the hacienda on the Chihuahua Trail from Mexico in the 1800s. Also on display are exhibits relating the traditions of northern New Mexico and the influence of Spanish culture.

Additional Information

La Hacienda de Don Antonio Severino Martinez is listed on the National Register of Historic Places.

Oregon

1. Astoria
Captain George Flavel House Museum

2. Brownsville
Moyer House

3. Canby
Historic Barlow House

4. Cascade Locks
Original Lock Tender's Residence

5. Lakeview
Schminck Memorial Museum

6. Monmouth
Brunk House

7. Newberg
Hoover-Minthorn House

8. Newport
Burrows House Museum

9. Oregon City
McLoughlin House National Historic Site
Stevens-Crawford Museum
William L. Holmes House

10. Portland
Pittock Mansion

11. Salem
Historic Bush House
Jason Lee House and John D. Boon House at Mission Mill Village

12. Sixes
Historic Hughes House

Captain George Flavel House Museum

**441 Eighth Street
Astoria, OR 97103
(503) 325-2203**

Contact: Clatsop County Historical Society

Open: May-Oct., daily 10 a.m.–5 p.m.;
Oct.-Apr., daily 11 a.m.–4 p.m.

Admission: Adults $4.00; children (6-12)
$2.00; group discount rates available

Activities: Self-guided tours with docent
assistance, special programs

Suggested Time to View House:
45–60 minutes

Facilities on Premises: Gift shop and
summer tea room

Description of Grounds: One full city
block with a eclectic display of century
old trees and carriage house

Best Season to View House: Summer

Number of Yearly Visitors: 26,000

Year House Built: Started 1884,
completed 1885

Style of Architecture: Victorian
Queen Anne, towered with
Italianate features

Number of Rooms: 15

On-Site Parking: No

Wheelchair Access: No

Description of House

Captain George Flavel was born in 1823 in Armagh County in Ireland; at the age of twenty-six, he commanded the brig *John Petty* out of Norfolk carrying goods to San Francisco; unfortunately, when he reached that city, he found that they had no need of his cargo. So he just continued up the Pacific coast and landed at Portland. Here there was a ready market for Eastern manufactured goods and here's where he got the notion that the West coast would be a good place for him to operate. For the next few years he transported miners on the Sacramento River during the gold rush of '49; ran cargo between Mexico, California, and Oregon; got the first branch license issued to a bar pilot; met and married Mary Christina Boelling; and finally settled down to become harbor master of the Port of Astoria. In Astoria, he also formed a partnership with Asa Meade Simpson, the boat builder and founder of the Simpson Lumber Company, and then got involved in local politics, serving as both city councilman and county treasurer. The house stayed in the family after Captain George's death ion 1893 and was donated to the Clastrop County Historical Society in 1936 by his great granddaughter, Patricia Flavel.

Because it has not been subject to any major alterations, the Captain George Flavel House is one of the finest surviving examples of the Queen

Anne-style architecture in the Pacific Northwest. It was designed by the German-born architect Carl W. Leick who had been hired out of San Francisco by Flavel. The exterior features a typical hipped roof with wrought iron cresting, a three-story octagonal tower, variegated red shingles, and is painted in its original colors: antique gold with olive green and chocolate brown trim. The Eastlake-style interior is breathtaking; one can see everything from the sliding doors to six different fireplaces each featuring a distinct tile surround and elaborate hand-carved mantel. The original stained glass transom window over the main entrance, designed as a sailing ship, was done by Cleveland Rockwell, whose work appears throughout the house.

Notable Collections on Exhibit

Most of the period Eastlake-style furnishings are not original to the house; they have been collected by the historical society to reflect the grand appearance of the house at the turn-of-the-century. In addition to these wonderful pieces, one can also view the paintings of John H. Trullinger, an Astoria native who studied in Paris and whose father built the first electric power generating plant in the area.

Additional Information

The Captain George Flavel House Museum is listed on the National Register of Historic Places.

Moyer House

204 North Main Street, P.O. Box 607
Brownsville, OR 97327
(503) 466-3390

Contact: Linn County Historical Museum
Open: Mon.-Sat. 11 a.m.–4 p.m., Sun.
1–5 p.m.; closed New Year's Day, Easter,
Thanksgiving, Christmas
Admission: Donations $1.00
Activities: Audiovisual programs, special
events including the annual "Carriage
Me Back" drama, Tea for the Grand
Marshall Pioneer Picnic Parade, and
Victorian Christmas
Suggested Time to View House: 45 minutes
Facilities on Premises: Gift shop, book store
Description of Grounds: Restored grounds
surrounded with decorative spindle fence
Best Season to View House: Spring
Year House Built: 1881
Number of Rooms: 8

Number of Yearly Visitors: 13,000
Style of Architecture: Italianate Villa, towered
On-Site Parking: Yes **Wheelchair Access:** Yes

Description of House

John M. Moyer arrived in Oregon in 1852, in the little growing community then called Kirk's Ferry or Callapooya. It lay nestled in the fertile Calapoola Valley, yet near to the Cascade Range with its rich timber resource—a perfect place for a carpenter like Moyer to make a living. Here he met and married Elizabeth Brown, daughter of Hugh Brown, when Brown hired him to build a house. Kirk's Ferry would be renamed Brownsville in honor of this native Tennessean who arrived here in 1846.

Shortly after their wedding in 1857, Elizabeth and John built a small box house on 160 acres near town and started farming. Moyer was devoting more time and attention to his construction business, however, and then organized the Linn Woolen Mills, later called the Eagle Woolen Mills. As the mills prospered, the time came for the Moyers to build a grander house. Thus, in 1881, they completed this very fine Italianate villa.

The two-story, asymmetrical frame structure exhibits a meticulousness in its detail which attests to Moyer's skill at carpentry. There are jigsaw-cut corner boards, frieze boards, and eaves brackets—most of the millwork is thought to have been done at Moyer's mill—a cupola which was used as an observatory, and wood siding which has been smoothed and matched to look like stone. Inside, one sees walls covered in hand-painted landscapes, floral designs, and stenciling, light fixtures hung from plaster medallions, and some exceptional examples of fine woodworking, especially on the diagonal wainscotting, the curved walnut banister, and on the newel posts.

After the Moyers died, the house changed hands several times and much of the original detailing was either covered up or destroyed. The Linn County Historical Society has taken on the responsibility for restoring the lost work. The Moyer House is listed on the National Register of Historic Places.

Historic Barlow House

**24670 South Highway 99 East
Canby, OR 97013
(503) 266-4375**

Contact: Barlow House
Open: By appointment
Admission: Adults $2.00; 12 and
under $1.00
Activities: Guided tours
Suggested Time to View House:
60–90 minutes
Facilities on Premises: Gift shop
Description of Grounds: 1½ acres of lawn
trees and shrubs
Best Season to View House:
Spring-summer
Year House Built: c. 1884
Style of Architecture: Italianate, bracketed
Number of Rooms: 12

On-Site Parking: Yes **Wheelchair Access:** No

Description of House

In 1846 Samuel Kinsbrough Barlow built a road on the last one hundred and twenty miles of the Oregon Trail but it was his son, William, who reaped the benefits of such pioneering. William Barlow became one of Oregon's most successful early entrepreneurs and a major landowner in the state. He and his wife Martha Ann built this lovely house in 1884 and their family lived here for the next twenty years. Sam Berg bought it in 1905 and the Berg family lived here for two generations, at which time Mr. and Mrs. Page took ownership and stayed twenty-one years. Finally, in 1972, Virginia Miller bought the house, and began the job of restoring it to its original glory.

This two-and-a-half story jewel of a house features a wide, shallow front section with a central hallway and open stairway and a two-story kitchen wing with a basement. The small front porch entrance is flanked by two almost square bays. The house has six original coal fireplaces, including two made of marble and one of slate, and arched second-story windows built almost entirely of cedar. Some of the furniture is original; there are several pieces in the Renaissance Revival style, including two bedroom sets, a desk with glass doors, and an organ.

Additional Information

The Historic Barlow House is listed on the National Register of Historic Places.

Original Lock Tender's Residence

1 Portage Road, P.O. Box 321
Cascade Locks, OR 97014
(503) 374-8691

Contact: Cascade Locks Historical Museum
Open: June–Sept., daily Noon–5 p.m.; open all year for school children by appointment
Admission: Free
Activities: Early transportation exhibits including photographs and artifacts, home of the "Oregon Pony" locomotive display

Suggested Time to View House: 1 hour
Facilities on Premises: Museum
Description of Grounds: Park setting
Best Season to View House: Summer
Number of Yearly Visitors: 20,000
Year House Built: 1905
Style of Architecture: National, frame
Number of Rooms: 8
On-Site Parking: Yes **Wheelchair Access:** No

Description of House

Those pioneers in the mid-19th century who traveled west on the Oregon Trail and survived the grueling overland trek faced a final and seemingly insurmountable obstacle: the wild Columbia River. Settlers demanded that the Federal Government do something, and, in 1878, monies were appropriated to begin construction on a canal which would allow for easier water passage in the Columbia River Valley. Construction wasn't completed until 1896 because of the harsh winters and difficulty in transporting supplies over the mountains.

As the canal locks were built, a town came into being, first called Whiskey Flat, then Cascade Locks. By 1893, it had grown into a booming "Wild West" town of 1,000 inhabitants. In 1937, when the Bonneville Dam was built just three miles away, Cascade Locks began to fall into decline as a transportation center.

The Cascade Lock Tender's Residence is one of three homes—all are still standing in excellent condition—built in 1905 for the men who operated the navigation locks beside the canal and their families. It is now one of Oregon's finest small museums, partially furnished to interpret the pioneer era of those who built and operated the canal.

Notable Collections on Exhibit

The museum has an antique photo collection depicting steamboats, railroads, highways, portage roads, and numerous articles related to Oregon's early settlers. There is also a large collection of Native American artifacts. Out in front of the museum is *The Oregon Pony*, the first locomotive built on the Pacific coast and the first to pull a train west of the Missouri River.

Schminck Memorial Museum

128 South "E" Street
Lakeview, OR 97630
(503) 947-3134

Contact: Oregon State Society of Daughters of the American Revolution

Open: Feb.-Nov., Tues.-Sat. 1–5 p.m.; closed holidays

Admission: Adults $1.00; young adults $.50; children (6-12) $.25; children (under 6) free; educational groups with teacher free

Activities: Guided tours

Suggested Time to View House: 20–60 minutes

Description of Grounds: Small front and back yards

Best Season to View House: Summer and fall

Number of Yearly Visitors: 1,000

Year House Built: 1922

Number of Rooms: 8

Style of Architecture: Frame bungalow

On-Site Parking: Yes **Wheelchair Access:** No

Description of House

Perhaps Lula and Dalpheus Schminck knew that even the most ordinary items from the early 1900s would be of interest to succeeding generations. They preserved what they loved and used, items ranging from American pressed glass goblets to shaving mugs and quilts, and now visitors to the Schminck Memorial Museum can view their vast and unique collection. Over the years, as others heard about the Schminck collection, they too began to donate items of all sorts to add to it. Now the collection comprises more than five thousand objects and artifacts which encompass all aspects of the lives of early 20th century Oregonians.

Dalpheus Carl Schminck was born in 1876 in California and died in 1960 in Klamath Falls, Oregon. His mother was an early pioneer and his father was a German immigrant. His wife, Artie Lula Foster, was born in Oregon in 1878 and died eighty-four years later here in Lakeview. Her parents were pioneers who came to Oregon on two famous railroad runs of the mid-19th century: her mother on the Applegate Train in 1846 and her father on the "Blue Bucket" Train in 1845. They married in 1901 and remained here for the rest of their lives.

The house that the couple built and lived in for forty years is a modest frame bungalow typical for its era. An extended room forms the front porch, which features square supporting pillars. The stucco on the exterior had deteriorated rather badly and is now covered with aluminum siding.

Notable Collections on Exhibit

The collection of implements, utensils, decorative objects, household items of all sorts, clothing, furnishings, toys, and just about anything else one can think of, is really the reason for stopping by the Schminck Museum. Not to be missed are the 160 pressed glass goblets on display.

Brunk House

5705 Salem-Dallas Highway
Monmouth, OR 97361
(503) 371-8586

Contact: Polk County Historical Society

Open: June 1-Aug. 30, Mon. Wed.-Sun.
Noon–4 p.m., Tues. 9 a.m.–1 p.m.;
guided tours by appointment at any time

Admission: Tours $1.00 per person;
otherwise donation requested

Activities: Guided tours, special events
including annual Quilt Show and
Christmas Open House

Suggested Time to View House: 1 hour

Facilities on Premises: Gift and history
book store

Description of Grounds: Period rose
garden, herb garden, grape arbor and
dahlia beds enhance a farm machinery
shed and a blacksmith shop

Best Season to View House: Late
spring-summer

Number of Yearly Visitors: 2,500

Number of Rooms: 9

Style of Architecture: Early Folk Victorian
farmhouse

Year House Built: 1861, addition 1900

On-Site Parking: Yes **Wheelchair Access:** No

Description of House

Harrison Brunk built this farmhouse in 1861 and today it stands as one of the oldest houses in all of Polk County. The Brunks were legendary for their hospitality—it is said that they never turned away anyone in need—and their house quickly became a stopping-off place for early travelers and circuit riders. In its heyday, their farm totaled over 1,000 acres. Here Brunk grew grain and fruit trees, and raised cattle and hogs. In addition to being a successful farmer, Brunk was deeply involved in state politics and judged international livestock shows, traveling to Chicago and San Francisco in that capacity.

This early Victorian home is a side-gabled, two-story structure built on a rock and brick foundation. There is a full front porch and a balcony on the second floor. All of the walls in the house are built of staggered one-inch thick planks which, standing back to back, form two-inch thick walls. The floorboards are joined with a six-inch tongue-and-groove; the wood is covered with hand-woven rugs in all rooms for warmth. As is true of many early homes, the kitchen and dining were in a separate structure at the rear of the main house. This was a precaution against fire. Many of the furnishings on display here belonged to the Brunk family.

Notable Collections on Exhibit

Early utensils used by the family are displayed on the kitchen wall and over the mantel is a gun rack with the first gun to be used on the Oregon State Prison towers. In the parlor is a pump organ which still plays beautifully.

Additional Information

The Brunk House is listed on the National Register of Historic Places.

Hoover-Minthorn House

115 South River Street
Newberg, OR 97132
(503) 538-6629

Contact: State of Oregon, National Society
of Colonial Dames in America

Open: Mar.-Nov., Wed.-Sun. 1–4 p.m.;
Dec.and Feb., Sat. and Sun. 1–4 p.m.;
closed month of January

Admission: Donations

Activities: Group tours by appointment

Suggested Time to View House: 40 minutes

Description of Grounds: Gardens located
across the street from the Herbert
Hoover Park

Best Season to View House: Spring-fall

Number of Yearly Visitors: 2,000

Year House Built: 1881

Number of Rooms: 10

Style of Architecture: National, frame

On-Site Parking: Yes **Wheelchair Access:** No

Description of House

The Hoover-Minthorn House was the boyhood home of President Herbert Hoover, who lived here from 1884 to 1889. Dr. and Mrs. Henry Minthorn and their three children moved into this house in 1884, three years after it was built and the year Minthorn was appointed superintendent of the Friends Pacific Academy. Shortly after moving in, one of the Minthorn sons died, and the doctor wrote to his young orphaned nephew, Herbert Hoover, to invite him to join their family. Hoover eventually became Henry Minthorn's foster son and was deeply influenced both by the affectionate nature and the Quaker beliefs of his adopted family. In 1889 Henry Minthorn moved his family to Salem and there Hoover served as his uncle's office clerk. He decided to enter college and became a member of Stanford University's first freshman class in 1891—he had begun the long road which would someday take him to the White House.

The Hoover-Minthorn House was purchased and restored with funds donated by friends of Herbert Hoover. It is a plain L-shaped frame house. Some of the furnishings in the home are original to the years when Hoover was living here; these include his bedroom set and a cast-iron stove. The original wallcoverings were so completely papered over that entirely new wallpaper had to be hung when the house was restored. The Hoover-Minthorn House is the oldest house still standing in Newberg.

Additional Information

The yard surrounding the Hoover-Minthorn features a beautiful 19th-century garden in which one can see the pear tree that a young Herbert Hoover climbed.

Burrows House Museum

545 Southwest Ninth Street
Newport, OR 97365
(503) 265-7509

Contact: Lincoln County Historical Society

Open: Summer, Tues.-Sun. 10 a.m.–5 p.m.; winter, Tues.-Sun. 11 a.m.–4 p.m.; closed major holidays

Admission: Free

Activities: Guided tours, slide programs, workshops

Suggested Time to View House: 30–45 minutes

Facilities on Premises: Museum shop, research library

Description of Grounds: Victorian-style flower beds

Best Season to View House: Spring and summer

Year House Built: 1895, remodeled 1919, additions 1982

Number of Yearly Visitors: 13,000

Number of Rooms: 11, 7 open to the public

Style of Architecture: Victorian Queen Anne

On-Site Parking: Yes **Wheelchair Access:** Yes

Description of House

In 1883 John Burrows brought his family from South Norwood in London, England to Portland, Oregon and came to settle first in the Corvallis area. When John went to work for the Oregon & Pacific Railroad Company, he had to move to Yaquina and eventually his family joined him there. Papers show that he married a woman named Susan in Yaquina in 1894 but there is no record of the death of his first wife, or of a divorce. A year later, he built this house in Newport, where he had become a general contractor and his sons had established themselves in various trades. In 1898, the mysterious second wife, Susan, divorced John and turned their home into a boarding house. So it remained until 1918; then, for the next fifty-eight years, it served as a funeral home. In 1976, the Burrows House was presented to the Lincoln Historical Society by the Bank of Newport and relocated to its present site.

This two-story asymmetrical Victorian-style structure features a flared roof line, front gables with decorative scallop-shaped vergeboards, alternating yellow and brown shingle bands, a tower with a small porthole window, and a dramatic turret. The original windows have all been replaced. Because the house served as a funeral home, the ground floor rooms have been altered for that purpose and not been restored to the period when the Burrows lived in it. The upstairs, though, is much the same as when it was built and two rooms are completely restored to the period of the 1890s: the parlor and the bedroom. The furnishings are all donated pieces, including a square grand piano.

Additional Information

The Burrows House Museum also serves as the headquarters for the Lincoln County Historical Society.

McLoughlin House National Historic Site

713 Center Street
Oregon City, OR 97045
(503) 656-5146

Contact: McLoughlin Memorial Association
Open: Tues.-Sat. 10 a.m.–4 p.m.; closed
holidays, month of January
Admission: Adults $3.00; seniors $2.50;
students (6-17) $1.00; groups of 12 or
more $2.00 each
Activities: Guided tours, slide programs
available to school groups
Suggested Time to View House:
45–50 minutes
Facilities on Premises: Gift shop
Description of Grounds: City park
Best Season to View House: Year round
Number of Yearly Visitors: 12,750
Year House Built: 1845
Number of Rooms: 12

Style of Architecture: Modified Georgian
On-Site Parking: Yes **Wheelchair Access:** Yes

Description of House

Dr. John McLoughlin moved to Oregon City in 1846. He took over the leadership of the Hudson Bay Company at Fort Vancouver on the Columbia River and became known as the "Father of Oregon" for helping settlers and early missionaries who had come West.

The McLoughlin House is a two-story mansion, approximately thirty feet by fifty feet, built near the Willamette River. In addition to the period furnishings which fill the house is a portrait of Dr. McLoughlin painted in the late 1880s.

Additional Information

Also part of the McLoughlin Memorial Association is the Barclay House, the former residence of Dr. Forbes Barclay, a physician who practiced at Fort Vancouver in the 1840s and moved to Oregon City in 1850. This house, built in 1849, is a fine example of the Early Classical Revival style.

Stevens-Crawford Museum

603 Sixth Street
Oregon City, OR 97045
(503) 655-2866

Contact: Clackamas County Historical Society

Open: Tues.-Sat. 10 a.m.–4 p.m., Sun. 1–4 p.m.; closed national holidays, month of January

Admission: Adults $1.50; seniors $1.25; children (5-12) $.50

Activities: Guided tours, groups by reservation

Suggested Time to View House: 45 minutes

Description of Grounds: Lawn and flowers

Best Season to View House: Summer

Number of Yearly Visitors: 3,000

Year House Built: 1908

Style of Architecture: Eclectic Colonial Revival, four-square

Number of Rooms: 14

On-Site Parking: No **Wheelchair Access:** No

Description of House

Harley Stevens was a railroad depot agent and entrepeneur who moved to Oregon in 1860 and married Mary Elizabeth Crawford. They built this Colonial Revival-style house in 1908.

This two-story structure features a hipped roof, a central dormer, broad overhanging eaves with brackets, a porch supported by simple Doric columns, and classical frieze details. The Vondereh Brothers, local builders with a reputation for superior workmanship, were responsible for the fine woodwork and detailing. The house, which still stands on its original site, was one of the first in the area to be hooked up to the city water and sewer systems; it also boasts light fixtures that can take either gas or electric lamps. The kitchen is in full working condition and features a wood-burning stove and oven in which bread was baked.

Notable Collections on Exhibit

The Stevens' furnishings, which date from 1908, reflect their lives at the turn of the century. In addition to the family's possessions, there is a collection of Native American artifacts on display, including numerous baskets collected by Harley Stevens.

William L. Holmes House

536 Holmes Lane at Rilance Lane
Oregon City, OR 97045
(503) 656-5146

Contact: Rose Farm Museum
Open: Mar.-Nov., Sun. 1–4 p.m.
Admission: Adults $1.50; students $.50
Activities: Guided tours
Suggested Time to View House: 1 hour
Description of Grounds: 2 acre lot with
heritage rose garden
Best Season to View House: Summer
Number of Yearly Visitors: 500
Year House Built: 1847
Style of Architecture: National, frame
Number of Rooms: 8
On-Site Parking: No **Wheelchair Access:** No

Description of House

The William L. Holmes House is notable for two reasons: first, it is the oldest American house in Oregon City; and, second, it is thought to be the only building in which both Oregon's Provisional and Territorial Legislatures met. Joseph Lane, when he was Territorial Governor of Oregon, delivered his first official address from the balcony of this house to a crowd gathered on the lawn.

In 1843, William and Louisa Holmes, and their four children, came to Oregon from Missouri and settled on a 640 acre land grant here in the shadow of Mt. Hood. They lived in a log cabin for the first four years on the farm, until their permanent house was completed. It was later named the Rose Farm because of Louisa's love of roses—the early mission roses she cultivated on this property are said to have been especially lovely.

The simple frame farmhouse was completed in 1847 when its windows and doors arrived from New England. The basic structure, however, was made of timbers cut and hewn from trees growing on the farm. The house features a second floor overhang supported by simple columns, two separate entry doors, a mid-section balcony, and a ballroom on the second floor. It is smartly furnished with early Oregon pieces except for the piano, which was transported West in 1858 by ship.

Additional Information

The William L. Holmes House is listed on the National Register of Historic Places.

Pittock Mansion

3229 Northwest Pittock Drive
Portland, OR 97210
(503) 823-3623

Contact: City of Portland Bureau of Parks and Pittock Mansion Society

Open: Mon.-Sun. Noon–4 p.m.

Admission: Adults $3.50; seniors $3.00; children (6-18) $1.50

Activities: Guided tours, dinners and receptions in the evening, interpretive materials in Japanese

Suggested Time to View House: 30–60 minutes

Facilities on Premises: Gift shop, restaurant

Description of Grounds: 46 acre landscaped grounds suitable for strolling and picnicking and wooded trails for hiking

Best Season to View House: Summer and early fall

Number of Yearly Visitors: 100,000

Year House Built: 1914

Style of Architecture: Eclectic Period Revival, French Renaissance-Chateauesque

Number of Rooms: 22

On-Site Parking: Yes **Wheelchair Access:** No

Description of House

Henry Louis Pittock once said, "The man who sits down never reaches the top". Pittock spoke from experience—he was a member of the first party credited with having reached the summit of Mt. Hood. He also built this mansion on a hill a thousand feet above downtown Portland; from here he could look at the city he helped build and continued to dominate. His holdings—newspapers, real estate, banking, railroads, steamboats, a sheep ranch, silver mining, and pulp and paper making—were extensive enough to be called a financial empire. But the Pittocks, Henry and his wife Georgiana, were equally well-known for their community service. Georgiana helped found the Ladies' Relief Society in 1867, worked with both the Women's Union and the Marsha Washington Home, and helped organize the annual Portland Rose Festival.

The couple built their mansion when they were enjoying their greatest success, but they only lived here briefly. Georgiana died in 1918 at the age of seventy-three and Henry a year later at eighty-three. The house remained in the family until 1958, when Peter Gantenbein, a grandson, put it up for sale. Concerned citizens banded together to raise funds which would enable them to preserve the house and finally the City of Portland purchased the estate in 1964 for $225,000.

This magnificent twenty-two room Chateauesque structure was designed by a young architect from San Francisco named Edward T. Foulkes. In it he incorporated all the latest in household technology: a central vacuum system, intercoms, indirect lighting, a walk-in refrigerator, and an elevator. Local craftsmen used native Pacific Northwest materials in building much of the house; the exterior walls are of Tenino stone from Washington, the roof is terra cotta tile, and the main hallway is made of Columbia marble from California. The house, particularly its roof, suffered severe damage during the infamous Columbus Day storm of 1962.

Notable Collections on Exhibit

Though the interiors are largely in the French Renaissance style, there are also Turkish and English elements as well. Furnishings include pieces which date from the 17th century up to the 1920s and include Kirk sterling holloware, Chinese Coromandel screens, an Aubusson-style handmade rug, a superb hand-carved bedroom set in the south bedroom, and elaborate parquetry in the "Turkish Smoking Room."

Additional Information

The Pittock Mansion is listed on the National Register of Historic Places.

Historic Bush House

600 Mission Street Southeast
Salem, OR 97302
(503) 363-4714

Contact: Salem Art Association

Open: Oct.-May, Tues.-Sun. 2–5 p.m.;
June-Sept., Tues.-Sun. Noon–5 p.m.

Admission: Adults $2.00; seniors and
students $1.50; children (6-12) $.75

Activities: Guided tours, special events
including annual Open House

Suggested Time to View House: 30 minutes

Facilities on Premises: Greenhouse and
art center

Description of Grounds: 90 acres of park
with community art center

Best Season to View House: Spring and
summer

Number of Yearly Visitors: 10,000

Number of Rooms: 19

Year House Built: Started 1877, completed
1878

Style of Architecture: Italianate

On-Site Parking: Yes **Wheelchair Access:** Yes

Description of House

When Asahel Bush II went West in 1850, he was a young lawyer looking to establish himself in a career. By the time he died in 1913, his estate was the largest to have come under provision of the state's inheritance tax laws. Bush began his professional life in Oregon as the founder of the *Oregon Statesman*, a newspaper which served as the voice of the Democratic Party in the territory. He became more and more involved in politics and in 1859 was named the State Printer. After he sold his paper in 1861, Bush went into banking with a partner, W. S. Ladd. The two founded a bank in Salem bearing their names, which would become one of the largest in the Pacific Northwest.

Asahel Bush completed this magnificent house in 1878 and his descendants lived here until the 1950s. The mistress of the Bush House was Sally, Asahel's second daughter; her mother, the former Eugenia Zieber, had died in 1863 of consumption and left her husband with four children to raise. Sally Bush was responsible for furnishing much of the house, for expanding the gardens, and for maintaining the character of the estate through the years. The house was part of an estate that included a barn, a greenhouse—the oldest in Oregon, and pasturelands; now, the barn is used as the community art center and the grounds have become a municipal park.

The richly detailed nineteen-room Italianate-style mansion reflects a winning combination of the then-latest advances in household technology with a very European sense of beauty and craftsmanship. Each of the ten fireplaces is cut in a distinct style from imported Italian marble; and yet, we see a central heating system, hot and cold running water, and gas lighting made possible by the installation of a gas pump shipped from the Eastern United States. One still sees much of the original French wallpaper here and the furnishings, over half of which belonged to the Bushes, reflect the period of High Victorian style. The Historic Bush House is listed on the National Register of Historic Places.

Jason Lee House and John D. Boon House at Mission Mill Village

1313 Mill Street Southeast
Salem, OR 97301
(503) 585-7012

Jason Lee House

John D. Boon House

Contact: Mission Mill Village Association

Open: Oct.-May, Tues.-Sat. 10 a.m.–4:30 p.m.; June-Sept., also Sun. 1–4:30 p.m.

Admission: Admision includes tour of historic houses and the Woolen Mill: adults $4.00; seniors and students $3.00; children $2.00

Activities: Guided tours, groups by reservation, speaker series, special events such as the Sheep to Shawl Festival, Quilt Show, Textile Festival

Suggested Time to View House: 50 minutes per house

Facilities on Premises: Museum, gift shops and a restaurant

Description of Grounds: 5½ acres includes the Thomas Kay Woolen Mill Museum, the Jason Lee House, the John D. Boon House, the 1841 Methodist Parsonage, the 1858 Pleasant Grove Presbyterian Church and the Mentzer Machine Shop

Best Season to View House: Summer and fall

Number of Yearly Visitors: 20,000+

Year House Built: Lee-1841, Boon-1847

Style of Architecture: National-Folk with New England-style influences

Number of Rooms: Lee-6, Boon-5

On-Site Parking: Yes **Wheelchair Access:** Yes

Description of House

Visiting Mission Hill Village is taking a journey back in time to the days when the Thomas Kay Woolen Mill was the center of life in Oregon's Willamette River Valley. Here one can see the process by which fleece was turned into fabric (until man-made fibers put the mill out of business in the late 1950s). Thomas Kay, the founder of the original mill, trained as a millworker in England, then emigrated to Oregon where he was instrumental in the development of a wool industry in the fledgling Territory. Three generations of the Kay family ran the mills after Thomas' death; today, his descendants are owners of the Pendleton Mills of Oregon.

At the Village, we can also visit two historic houses, the Jason Lee House, built in 1841, and the John D. Boon House, built in 1847. Both houses interpret the lives of the early missionaries who came to the Oregon Territory in the period from the 1830s to the 1850s. The 1841 Methodist Parsonage and the 1858 Grave Presbyterian Church provide a look at the religious foundations of the early settlements.

Jason Lee was the person most responsible for the existence of the Methodist mission in the Pacific Northwest. He first arrived in the area in 1834 on horseback after a grueling trek across the country. Reverend Lee ministered to the needs of the Kalapooian Indians as well as to the few white settlers in the region. The Jason Lee House is the oldest known surviving frame house in the Pacific Northwest, and it is furnished with artifacts from the early missionary period. The John D. Boon house is a historic interpretation of Oregon's pioneer families in the years between 1847 and 1880. It is named after the man who was the first state treasurer.

Additional Information

Both the Jason Lee House and the John D. Boon House are listed on the National Register of Historic Places.

Historic Hughes House

91814 Cape Blanco Road, P.O. Box 285
Sixes, OR 97476
(503) 332-6774

Contact: Friends of Cape Blanco State Park
Open: May-Sept., Thurs.-Mon.
10 a.m.–5 p.m., Sun. Noon–5 p.m.
Admission: Donations accepted
Activities: Self-guided tour with volunteer
on-duty
Suggested Time to View House:
30–60 minutes
Facilities on Premises: Small gift area

Description of Grounds: Located at the
mouth of the Sixes River and the Pacific
Ocean
Best Season to View House: Spring
Number of Yearly Visitors: 8,000-10,000
Year House Built: 1898
Style of Architecture: Late Victorian Queen
Anne-Eastlake
Number of Rooms: 11
On-Site Parking: Yes **Wheelchair Access:** Yes

Description of House

The story of the Irish immigrant Patrick Hughes—his struggles and eventual success—begins in County Tyrone and ends here, on this magnificent site on the north side of Cape Blanco with views in all directions: the distant hills, the Pacific Ocean, the Sixes River, and the fields which once constituted the Hughes dairy ranch. Before moving into this splendid Queen Anne-style house in 1898 at the age of sixty-eight, Hughes traveled a hard road. In 1850, he emigrated to Boston where he married Jane O'Neil; five years later he sailed alone to California in search of gold. In 1857, she finally joined him and they went north to Langlois, Oregon where Patrick got a job on a ranch owned by A. H. Thrift. After nearly three years, he was able to trade his hard labor for 80 acres of farmland. By 1868, he was able to buy "Sullivan's Mine," a black sand gold mine on the south side of Cape Blanco (the Hughes family would work this mine until 1940). Patrick Hughes was a progressive dairyman whose quality products had a reputation as far south as San Francisco; he became very prosperous and his ranch increased in size to almost 2,000 acres. In 1893, he built a small church on his property called "Mary, Star of the Sea." The youngest of the seven Hughes children,

Francis, and his bride, Rosanna Doyle, moved into the house in 1905; "Annie" would be the last of the family to live here.

This T-shaped, two-story structure was built out of Port Oxford cedar by the builder P. J. Lindberg. It contains some 3,000 square feet of living space broken up into the public rooms—formal guest parlor, men's parlor, dining room, kitchen, pantry, and chapel—and master bedroom on the first floor and the other bedrooms upstairs. Outside, the house features decorative cross-bracing, variegated roof shingles, patterned roof tiles, and one-story bay extensions with multiple window arrangements. Notable details inside the house include a beautiful mahogany banister leading upstairs, the painted ceiling in the chapel, and a rose-colored chandelier.

Additional Information

This 1,800 acre park contains a cemetery, a campground, and a horse camp in addition to the Hughes House. Nearby is the 1870 Cape Blanco Lighthouse, Oregon's oldest continuously operated light; Patrick Hughes' son, James, became the lightkeeper here upon his retirement from ranching. The Historic Hughes House is listed on the National Register of Historic Places.

Texas

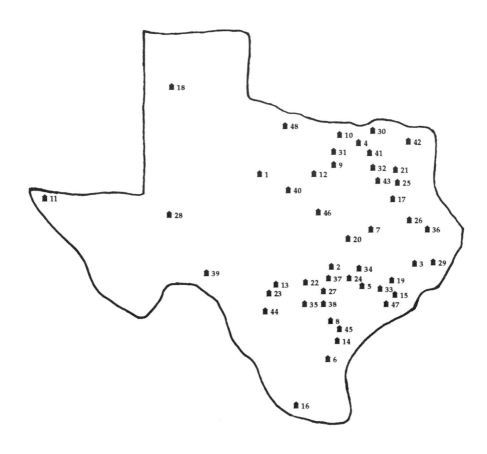

1. Albany
   Ledbetter Picket House

2. Austin
   Carrington-Covert House
   Neill-Cochran House
   O. Henry House
   Texas Governor's Mansion

3. Beaumont
   John Jay French House Museum
     and Trading Post
   McFaddin-Ward House

4. Bonham
   Sam Rayburn House

5. Columbus
   Alley Log Cabin
   Dilue Rose Harris House
     Museum
   Keith-Traylor House, "Lura"
   Senftenberg-Brandon House
     Museum

6. **Corpus Christi**
   Galvan House of Heritage Park
   Sidbury House

7. **Crockett**
   Downes-Aldrich House

8. **Cuero**
   Bates-Sheppard House

9. **Dallas**
   DeGolyer House
   George House at Old City Park
   "Millermore" at Old City Park

10. **Denison**
    Eisenhower Birthplace State
    Historical Place

11. **El Paso**
    Magoffin Home State Historic
    Site

12. **Fort Worth**
    Eddleman-McFarland House

13. **Fredericksburg**
    Kammlah House at the Pioneer
    Memorial Museum Complex

14. **Fulton**
    Fulton Mansion, "Oakhurst"

15. **Galveston**
    1839 Samuel May Williams
    Home
    1859 Ashton Villa
    Moody Mansion

16. **Harlingen**
    Lon C. Hill Home

17. **Henderson**
    Howard-Dickinson House

18. **Hereford**
    E. B. Black House

19. **Houston**
    Kellum-Noble House at Sam
    Houston Historical Park
    Nichols-Rice-Cherry House at
    Sam Houston Historical Park
    Old Place at Sam Houston
    Historical Park
    Pillot House at Sam Houston
    Historical Park
    San Felipe Cottage at Sam
    Houston Historical Park
    Staiti House at Sam Houston
    Historical Park

20. **Huntsville**
    Woodland Home and the
    Steamboat House

21. **Jefferson**
    Beard House
    Historic Freeman Plantation
    "House of the Seasons"

22. **Johnson City**
    Lyndon B. Johnson Birthplace
    Lyndon B. Johnson Boyhood
    Home

23. **Kerrville**
    Captain Charles Schreiner
    Mansion

24. **La Grange**
    Kreische Homestead and Brewery

25. **Marshall**
    "Maplecroft"—Starr Family
    State Historical Park,

26. **Nacogdoches**
    Sterne-Hoya House

27. **New Braunfels**
    Carl Baetge House

28. **Odessa**
    White-Pool House

29. Orange
   W. H. Stark House

30. Paris
   Sam Bell Maxey House State
   Historical Park

31. Plano
   Farrell-Wilson Farmstead

32. Quitman
   Stinson Home

33. Richmond
   A. P. George Ranch Home
   J.H.P. Davis Mansion

34. Round Top
   Lewis-Wagner Farmstead
   and House
   McGregor-Grimm House

35. San Antonio
   José Antonio Navarro House
   Spanish Governor's Palace
   Steves Homestead
   Yturri-Edmunds Historic Site

36. San Augustine
   Ezekiel Cullen House

37. San Marcos
   Charles L. McGehee, Jr. Cabin
   Charles S. Cock Museum

38. Seguin
   Sebastopol House

39. Sonora
   Miers Home Museum

40. Stephenville
   J. D. Berry Cottage

41. Sulphur Springs
   Atkins House

42. Texarkana
   Draughon-Moore, The Ace of
   Clubs House

43. Tyler
   Bonner-Whitaker-McClendon
   House

44. Uvalde
   John Nance Garner House–
   Ettie R. Garner Building

45. Victoria
   McNamara House Museum

46. Waco
   Earle-Harrison House and
   Gardens
   Earle-Napier-Kinnard House
   Fort House Museum
   John Wesley Mann House,
   East Terrace Museum
   McCulloch House Museum

47. West Columbia
   Plantation House Museum

48. Wichita Falls
   Kell House Museum

Ledbetter Picket House

Bank Park, P.O. Box 185
Albany, TX 76430
(915) 762-2525

Contact: Albany Chamber of Commerce
Open: Mon.-Fri. 9 a.m.–Noon and 1–4 p.m.
Admission: Free
Activities: Guided tours
Suggested Time to View House: 15 minutes
Description of Grounds: Located in park
   surroundings

Style of Architecture: National,
   "picket-style" with "dog-trot"
Best Season to View House: Late spring
Number of Yearly Visitors: 2,000
Year House Built: Between 1874 and 1877
Number of Rooms: 2
On-Site Parking: Yes **Wheelchair Access:** No

Description of House

The story of the Ledbetter Picket House is the story of the settlement of an inhospitable land by a tough and resourceful Southerner backed by the weight of the U.S. Cavalry. William Henry Ledbetter, who, after being elected county judge in 1876, would be forever known as Judge Ledbetter, was born in 1833 in Georgia, moved to Mississippi for a spell where he met and married Miss M. E. Allison, and came to Texas in 1858. A year later, the couple settled on the Clear Fork of the Brazos River just down from Camp Cooper, a U.S. Army outpost. Here he discovered a salt spring. Salt was a scarce commodity and therefore worth a great deal, not only to the locals, but especially to the Confederate Government which needed to keep its troops fed, primarily on cured meat. Soon the Ledbetter Salt Works was supplying that army tons of salt crystals.

Unfortunately for the Judge, and his family and workers, the salt works got in the way of the Comanches, who harassed the settlement mercilessly. In 1865, a worker was killed and around the same time one of Ledbetter's sons was kidnapped. The boy was never found, but years later when a white Comanche warrior bearing scars identical to the child's showed up at Fort Griffin, most folks figured he was the young Ledbetter come back, even though he didn't stay long with the family. These Comanche attacks finally drove the Judge to move his family to Fort Griffin where, after living temporarily in a buffalo hide shelter, he built this house in the "picket" style common to military barracks of the era. It was here at Fort Griffin that Ledbetter was appointed Justice of the Peace and later elected Judge. He died in his picket home in 1884.

Built of readily available small oak timbers, like most of Fort Griffin itself, the house that the Judge designed comprises two rooms with a dog run between them. The whole is covered with a simple hipped roof and each room has a stone fireplace and chimney. The small rock cellar under the west room was used for storing provisions. In the 1920s, when the picket house was moved to the town of Albany, an iron roof was added and the dog run was enclosed. Other than that, no changes have been made to the original structure. In 1953, Albany acquired the house from the Judge's heirs, moved it again, and restored it to its 1870s appearance.

Notable Collections on Exhibit

In addition to the collected furnishings on display, there are two remaining iron evaporation pots from the Ledbetter Salt Works and the boiler from the Army's saw mill which was used to prepare the timber seen in the fort and the house.

Carrington-Covert House

1511 Colorado Avenue
Austin, TX 78711
(512) 463-6100

Contact: Texas Historical Commission

Open: Mon.-Fri. 8 a.m.–5 p.m.

Admission: Free

Activities: Special receptions, book signings, Preservation Day Celebration

Suggested Time to View House: 1 hour

Facilities on Premises: Publications for sale, picnic grounds

Best Season to View House: Spring and summer

Description of Grounds: Restored gardens based on 1850 residential landscape plans with herb and bulb gardens, large pecan trees and cast iron ornamentation

Number of Yearly Visitors: 6,250

Year House Built: 1857

Style of Architecture: Greek Revival

Number of Rooms: 19

On-Site Parking: Yes **Wheelchair Access:** Yes

Description of House

Leonidas Davis Carrington, originally a resident of Columbus, Mississippi, settled in Austin with his wife and children where he owned a large and successful general store on Congress Avenue. In 1857, he commissioned master builder John Brandon to construct this Greek Revival house; it was meant to reflect his elevated stature, for he had been elected alderman, taken part in Governor Sam Houston's inauguration, and began to publish a newspaper, the *Texas Sentinel*. Unfortunately, his wife died in 1859 and, by 1870, Carrington had to sell the house to settle the family estate. Thirty-three years later, the house was bought by F. M. Covert, one of Austin's earliest car dealers. The Covert family, some of whom are still in the automobile business, lived here until 1935. By 1968, when the house was acquired by Texas, it had been converted into an apartment building. It was fully restored in 1971 and now serves as the executive office of the Texas Historical Commission.

The two-story house is built of locally quarried white limestone with long leaf pine floors—the timber came from nearby Bastrop County—featuring a five bay facade with six-over-six fenestration and paired doors at the main entry leading into the main hall. At the rear ell there is a two-story porch and exterior staircase; the double porch allows cooling breezes into both floors of the house. In the 1890s, the house served as the

Texas Eye, Ear and Throat Hospital and the rear ell underwent significant alteration.

Downstairs on the inside, the restored house features a parlor—looking much the way it would have during the Carrington occupancy—a library, a kitchen fashioned out of the main hall, and offices. Bedrooms are upstairs. All of the furnishings on display are appropriate to the period and were donated to the Texas Historical Commission.

Notable Collections on Exhibit

The American Empire furniture in the parlor is particularly noteworthy, as are the two large hand-tinted photographs of L. D. Carrington set in their original frames.

Additional Information

The Carrington-Covert House is listed on the National Register of Historic Places.

Neill-Cochran House

**2310 San Gabriel Street
Austin, TX 78705
(512) 478-2335**

Contact: National Society of Colonial
Dames of America

Open: Wed.-Sat. 2–5 p.m.; closed holidays

Admission: Adults $2.00;
children (under 6) free

Activities: Guided tours

Suggested Time to View House: 45 minutes

Facilities on Premises: Gift shop

Description of Grounds: Large yard with
shrubs and trees surrounded by
decorative fence

Best Season to View House: Spring and fall

Number of Yearly Visitors: 600

Year House Built: 1855

Number of Rooms: 10

Style of Architecture: Greek Revival

On-Site Parking: Yes **Wheelchair Access:** No

Description of House

The Neill-Cochran House was built in 1855 and initially used as the First Institute for the Blind in Texas. During Reconstruction, when the United States Army was conducting a campaign of enforcing the peace, especially in what had been the western theater, troops under the command of General Custer garrisoned here. In 1876, it was purchased by Colonel Neill, a prominent lawyer and state legislator. He lived here until 1893 but there are those who claim that his ghost has stayed on and haunted the place. Judge Cochran, an entirely practical man, bought the house immediately after Neill's death and lived in it until 1958.

The splendid Greek Revival residence with beautiful classical-style fluted columns has been restored to its mid-19th-century appearance but contains furnishings from a number of different periods, although most are Victorian.

Additional Information

The Neill-Cochran House is listed on the National Register of Historic Places.

O. Henry House

409 East Fifth Street
Austin, TX 78701
(512) 472-1903

Contact: City of Austin Parks and Recreation Department and O. Henry Museum

Open: Wed.-Sun. Noon–5 p.m.; closed Thanksgiving, Christmas, New Year's Day

Admission: Donations appreciated

Activities: Guided tours on request, special theme events including the O. Henry Birthday Party

Suggested Time to View House: 30 minutes

Description of Grounds: Located on Brush Square, one of the four early Austin parks developed in 1839 as part of the Waller City plan

Best Season to View House: Spring

Number of Yearly Visitors: 15,000

Year House Built: 1891

Style of Architecture: Folk Victorian, cottage

Number of Rooms: 7

On-Site Parking: Yes **Wheelchair Access:** No

Description of House

From 1893 to 1895, this Folk Victorian-style cottage served as the home of William Sidney Porter and his family—wife Athol and daughter Margaret—while he was working at the First National Bank of Austin and starting up a weekly newspaper called *The Rolling Stone*. A few years later, the world would know him as O. Henry, master of the short story.

Porter was born in North Carolina in 1862, apprenticed as a pharmacist there, was sent to Texas at the age of twenty to cure his lingering cough, and, while living there on a ranch owned by Dr. James Hall, formed a friendship with the doctor's son, Robert. Robert took Will to Austin, where the young man held a number of jobs—pharmacist, draftsman, bank teller, and reporter—and met his darling Athol, who married him despite her mother's objections. The couple's first child died shortly after birth; their second, born in 1889, survived and was named Margaret. In 1891, Will took a position as teller at the First National Bank after his political aspirations were foiled; the family moved into this house two years later. 1895 was a year of tremendous strain; first, Will lost his job because of cash shortages at the bank, was charged with embezzlement, and had to flee to Honduras; second, his dear wife fell ill. Two years later she would be dead. When Will returned to be with her he was made to stand trial, and, in February 1898, was found guilty and sentenced to five years in prison. During the winter he published his first short story in a national magazine. After serving a little over three years of his sentence, he was released. He moved to New York City, and in the eight years before his death in 1910, Will, who now called himself O. Henry, published over three hundred and fifty stories.

This box frame, single-wall cottage shows a number of details typical to a folk interpretation of the Victorian style: clapboard siding, exterior shutters, covered front porch with railing, "cut-out" trim, and decorative trusses in the front gable. The interior layout is asymmetrical, with the public rooms off to the left of the entry hall and two bedrooms located to the right. The back porch hall is fully enclosed.

Notable Collections on Exhibit

Artifacts and memorabilia relating to O. Henry's life and work are on display.

Additional Information

The O. Henry House will undergo extensive exterior restoration in the spring of 1994. The restoration is expected to take six months and the house will be closed for that period. The O. Henry Museum offices will relocate to the Dougherty Arts Center; the phone number is (512) 397-1468. This house is listed on the National Register of Historic Places.

Texas Governor's Mansion

1010 Colorado Street
Austin, TX 78711
(512) 474-9960

Contact: Friends of the Governor's Mansion
Open: Mon.-Fri. 10–11:40 a.m.; closed some holidays and at the discretion of the Governor
Admission: Free
Activities: Guided tours
Suggested Time to View House: 20 minutes
Best Season to View House: Year round

Description of Grounds: Large yard with shrubs and trees surrounded by decorative wrought iron fence
Number of Yearly Visitors: 35,000
Year House Built: 1856, additions 1859 and 1914
Style of Architecture: Greek Revival
Number of Rooms: 25, 6 open to the public
On-Site Parking: No **Wheelchair Access:** Yes

Description of House

This splendid Greek Revival mansion, built in 1856, has been home to thirty-seven Texas Governors and is one of the oldest continually occupied executive residences in the United States. During its dramatic first fifty-eight years of existence, before the 1914 renovation and addition, the house survived numerous threats of abandonment by the state legislature, the ravages of natural deterioration, a fire, a suicide, its unwanted occupancy by Federal troops during Reconstruction, and the haunting of a ghost! In 1979, the mansion was completely restored.

The Texas Governor's Mansion was designed and built by Abner Cook who had done his apprenticeship in the Greek Revival style in Tennessee and Georgia. His floor plan is based on the square, with four rooms upstairs and four down lying on either side of a wide central hall which served as a sitting room. A spiral staircase leads to the second floor. In 1859, a partition was built between the upstairs north bedrooms to create another room, most likely for one of Sam Houston's eight children. Of particular note are the Sam Houston Bedroom and the Gov. Elisha M. Pease Bedroom. The exterior features a full-facade porch with twenty-nine-foot-tall fluted columns topped with Ionic capitals, a five-part door framed by Doric pilasters, and large eighteen-pane sash windows with shutters. A two-story wing containing the kitchen is connected to the house by a covered walkway.

Notable Collections on Exhibit

The mansion contains a museum-quality collection of American Federal and Empire furniture, including pieces by Duncan Phyfe, Samuel McIntire, and Charles Honore Lannuier, which belonged to its various occupants. In addition, one can view Robert Onderdonk's 1903 painting, "The Fall of the Alamo," long considered one of the most accurate depictions of the 1836 siege.

Additional Information

The Texas Governor's Mansion is listed on the National Register of Historic Places.

John Jay French House Museum and Trading Post

2985 French Road
Beaumont, TX 77706
(409) 898-0348

Contact: Beaumont Heritage Society

Open: Tues.-Sat. 10 a.m.–4 p.m., Sun. 1–4 p.m.; closed major holidays

Admission: Adults $2.00; students $.50

Activities: Guided tours, special seasonal events including Spring Heritage Days, and Christmas Candlelight Tour

Suggested Time to View House: 60–90 minutes

Facilities on Premises: Gift shop

Description of Grounds: "Swept yard" of dust and few shrubs

Best Season to View House: Spring-fall

Number of Yearly Visitors: 7,000

Year House Built: 1845

Style of Architecture: Greek Revival

Number of Rooms: 8

On-Site Parking: Yes **Wheelchair Access:** Yes

Description of House

Born in 1799, John Jay French was a partner in a Connecticut tannery and a trader who had traveled to the territories of Texas and Louisiana three times peddling assorted goods before finally settling near Beaumont in 1838. On this last trip west to the Republic of Texas, he brought his wife, Sally Caleb Munson, and their children. By 1845, when Texas achieved statehood, the French family had established a trading post, tannery, and distillery and built their home on this site. The home is the only structure that remains of their settlement. Beaumont was a thriving mill town and John and Sally French became wealthy landowners by the time of the Civil War. During that conflict, the tannery, now owned by his sons, supplied the Confederate Army with leather goods. In 1884, the elderly couple got the wanderlust again and headed west, ultimately settling on a piece of land near Merkel, Texas. There they both died, Sally in 1885 and John four years later.

The John Jay French House is the oldest surviving house in Beaumont and one of the oldest on the whole of the Gulf Coast prairie. A vernacular interpretation of the Greek Revival, the house exhibits some of the typical details of that style: a full-facade porch, low pitched roof, plain lintel with full transom, and a hint of boxed cornice returns. Inside, four rooms and a kitchen wing flank a central hall in an unusual asymmetrical floor plan. The second floor consists of one large room. Most of the interior is done in pine boards painted the original brilliant blue though some pink and white areas were uncovered during the restoration. The house was built on a rise so it would catch whatever breezes came along to cool its occupants. The yard has been swept clean and cleared of all vegetation—to prevent snakes and other pests from surprising anyone by their approach.

Most of the furniture was contributed by descendants of the French family; many pieces are locally made and authentic to the period 1850 to 1860.

Notable Collections on Exhibit

Exceptional items on display include an English music box c.1850, the French family Bible, a pillared Seth Thomas Clock, and a hand-loomed wool coverlet done in a Double Rose pattern dated 1856.

Additional Information

The John Jay French House Museum and Trading Post are listed on the National Register of Historic Places.

McFaddin-Ward House

1906 McFaddin Avenue
Beaumont, TX 77701
(409) 832-1906

Contact: McFaddin-Ward House, Inc.

Open: Tues.-Sat. 10 a.m.–3 p.m., Sun.
1–3 p.m.; closed major holidays

Admission: $3.00 ; no children under 8

Activities: Guided tours by reservation,
video orientation, annual lecture series

Suggested Time to View House: 1 hour

Facilities on Premises: Visitor center, small
gift shop

Best Season to View House: Spring

Description of Grounds: Restored
landscaped grounds with rose gardens,
original garden ornaments and two one-
hundred-year-old twin giant oaks

Number of Yearly Visitors: 8,500

Year House Built: 1906

Style of Architecture: Eclectic Neoclassical
with some Colonial Revival elements

Number of Rooms: 17

On-Site Parking: Yes **Wheelchair Access:** Yes

Description of House

In the 1820s, James McFaddin of Tennessee was a awarded a pioneer land grant and moved west to the Texas Republic with his family. His son, William, took the land and developed a huge cattle-raising and rice-growing enterprise. In turn, William's son, W. P. H. (Perry) McFaddin, inherited the land and titles in 1897, three years after his marriage to Ida Caldwell. Shortly thereafter, in 1901, Beaumont gained international notoriety as the place where oil was discovered at the Spindletop blow and W. P. H. became one of the wealthiest men in all of Texas. In 1907, he purchased the house which had originally been built for his sister; upon his death, it fell to his daughter, Mamie McFaddin Ward.

The McFaddin-Ward House was designed by Henry Conrad Mauer, Beaumont's first formally trained architect. Though he employed many stylish elements on the exterior, including a hipped roof, prominent cornice moldings, and classical detailing, one's attention is immediately drawn to the massive two-story Ionic columns, spacious porches, and smaller flanking columns at the main entrance. Interior details include a pink parlor showing rose and vine highlights, elaborate leaded glass in the front doors, decorative marquetry panels, newel posts crowned with crystal lamps, and beautiful Art Nouveau stained glass windows.

All furnishings in the house are original and include many fine pieces in the Late Victorian and Colonial Revival styles, as well as a Victor talking machine c.1911, gilt parlor suite, Mannerist Revival sofa with carved griffin arm supports made by Robert Mitchell of Cincinnati, French Rococo New Orleans-style chiffonier, and a Mission-style bed and dresser. All of the rugs on display were hand-woven in Persia specially for the house.

Notable Collections on Exhibit

The McFaddin-Ward House is essentially a museum interpretative of the first half of this century and, as such, it includes a wide range of objects, from the homely to the exotic, which belonged to the various family members who lived here.

Additional Information

The two giant oaks on the property are registered with the Louisiana Live Oak Society; they are said to have grown from acorns found at the site of the Battle of San Jacinto by William McFaddin, who had been a guard there. The McFaddin-Ward House is listed on the National Register of Historic Places.

Sam Rayburn House

Route 82, 1 mile west of town
Bonham, TX 75418
(903) 583-5558

Contact: Texas Historical Commission
Open: Tues.-Fri. 10 a.m.–5 p.m., Sat.
1–5 p.m., Sun. 2–5 p.m.; closed on
Thanksgiving, Christmas, New
Year's Day
Admission: Free
Activities: Guided tours, introductory slide
program
Suggested Time to View House: 30 minutes
Facilities on Premises: Small gift shop
Description of Grounds: Grounds include
several outbuildings and garden
Best Season to View House: Year round
Number of Yearly Visitors: 4,000 - 5,000
Year House Built: 1916, remodeled c.1930
Number of Rooms: 15

Style of Architecture: Modified Neoclassical
On-Site Parking: Yes **Wheelchair Access:** Yes

Description of House

Though Sam Rayburn lived here for much of his adult life, it may be said that it was really only his second home. His first home was, of course, the United States House of Representatives, where he served for twenty-five terms, from 1912 to 1960. In his heyday as Speaker of that body—his seventeen years as Speaker is far and away the longest that anyone has ever served in that capacity—Rayburn was perhaps the second most powerful man in America. He, and his protégé Lyndon Johnson, were responsible for many pieces of legislation still in effect today.

Rayburn was born in Tennessee in 1882, but his family moved to Texas well before his tenth birthday. He built this house for his parents in 1916 and used it for himself whenever he was back home from Washington. He died here in 1961.

This two-story house features an entry porch running its full width. In the 1930s, it underwent a number of major changes: a bedroom and a two-story screened porch were added, and, on the facade, an additional column was built. These alterations have made the home look more like a typical Southern plantation than the more modest Neoclassical structure built twenty years earlier. All of the furnishings on display are original and belonged to the Rayburns.

Additional Information

The Sam Rayburn House is listed on the National Register of Historic Places.

Alley Log Cabin

1224 Bowie Street
Columbus, TX 78934
(409) 732-8385

Contact: Magnolia Homes Tour, Inc.

Open: First and third Thursday of each
month 10 a.m.–4 p.m.; other times for
groups of 25 or more by appointment

Admission: Adults $2.00; children (12 and
under) $1.00; special group rates available

Activities: Guided tours, annual May
Magnolia Homes Walking Tours

Suggested Time to View House: 15–30 minutes

Description of Grounds: Unadorned yard
with indigenous plants and oak trees
surrounded by a split rail fence

Style of Architecture: Folk, square notch
oak log cabin

Best Season to View House: Year round

Number of Rooms: 2

Year House Built: 1836, addition 1855
On-Site Parking: Yes **Wheelchair Access:** No

Description of House

The Alley brothers, descendants of three French Huguenot brothers named
Allees who emigrated to the American colonies in the mid-18th century, were
all members of Stephen Austin's famous "Old Three Hundred." Rawson Alley
served as Austin's surveyor on the Colorado River in 1821 and his brothers
Abram, Thomas, and John joined him a year later when they arrived at his land
grant from Ste. Genevieve, Missouri. Another brother, William, arrived in 1824.
By 1833, only two of the five brothers were still alive: John was killed by Indians,
Thomas drowned in the Brazos River, and Rawson died in the early part of that
year. In 1835, Abram married Nancy Millar, the daughter of an Alabaman
who'd settled on the western bank of the Colorado near Atacosita Crossing.

During the revolution in Texas, Abram and his wife led a group of
women and children out of the way of the advancing Mexican Army, leaving
behind them burnt homes and scattered possessions. After Santa Anna's
defeat, the Alleys returned to their land and rebuilt the cabin. Here they
farmed, raised cattle, and got involved in local politics. In 1837, Alley was
appointed President of the Board of Land Commissioners of Colorado
County by Sam Houston. He died in 1863 and his wife thirty-one years later;
some of their land is still owned by their descendants.

Built in a typical Midwestern square notch design, this oak log cabin
has two rooms, each with a stone chimney on its end gable. The exterior
features three front entrances, nine-over-six windows, hand-split shutters,
and an outside door which leads directly to the upper level. The front porch
runs to the full width of the cabin but the back porch is only half that size.
All of the logs are roughly finished both out and in, and the interior is
interpreted to reflect the early years of the house when the walls had no
coverings or paint. The furnishings on display were found locally; they are
all typical of the period and include some early Texas "primitive" pieces.

Dilue Rose Harris House Museum

602 Washington Street
Columbus, TX 78934
(409) 732-8385

Contact: Magnolia Homes Tour, Inc.

Open: First and third Thursday of each month 10 a.m.–4 p.m.; open other times for groups of 25 or more by appointment

Admission: Adults $2.00; children (12 and under) $1.00; special group rates available

Activities: Guided tours; annual May Magnolia Homes Walking Tours

Suggested Time to View House: 30–60 minutes

Description of Grounds: Small yard with several oak trees and rose gardens surrounded by a white picket fence

Best Season to View House: Year round

Year House Built: 1858

Style of Architecture: Greek Revival-style cottage with "tabby" construction

Number of Rooms: 7

On-Site Parking: Yes **Wheelchair Access:** No

Description of House

Dilue Rose Harris, who moved with her family from Missouri to Texas in 1833, when she was only eight years old, lived here for nine of her eighty-nine years, from 1860 to 1869. Her husband, Ira, was sheriff of Colorado County during those years and it was here that the couple built their house and raised seven children before Ira died in 1869. That's when Dilue sold the house to the Brune family and moved to Eagle Lake where she herself died in 1914. Dilue was an inveterate diarist and her memoirs are considered one of the best primary sources on the history of the Lone Star State. This house, which was first turned into a museum in 1968, underwent full restoration in 1977 by Laura Ann Dick Rau. A decade later saw it re-open as a museum dedicated to its first occupant.

The Dilue Harris House is a fine example of the locally important method of construction called "tabby." "Tabby" is a mixture of gravel, sand, and lime combined with water and poured to form large building blocks. These blocks, when fitted together, formed walls 12" to 14" thick. Outside, these walls were scored so it would look as though they'd been built of stone, and inside they were plastered. The front door has a typical segmented transom—many small homes had these so as to get some air circulating during the hot, humid summers. The dirt-floor basement comprises two rooms and is accessible by step ladder. The door frames down there are fashioned out of cedar to discourage termites. A number of exterior details are typical of the Greek Revival: the entry porch with its Doric columns, the six-over-six fenestration, and the hipped roof with its tin ridge line. The woodwork, including the doors and fireplace mantels, is all original to the house.

The furnishings are a combination of Texas "primitive" c.1840-1850 and some later Victorian-style pieces. An original walnut plantation-style desk made by slaves on the Stafford's Point Plantation may also be seen.

Notable Collections on Exhibit

In the kitchen, one may see numerous items which were unearthed when the basement was excavated.

Additional Information

Located next door at 604 Washington Street is the Mary Elizabeth Hopkins Santa Claus Museum, which features a collection of over 2,000 Santas, including the first one that Mrs. Hopkins ever purchased.

Keith-Traylor House, "Lura"

808 Live Oak
Columbus, TX 78934
(409) 732-8385

Contact: Magnolia Homes Tour, Inc.

Open: First and third Thursday of each month 10 a.m.–4 p.m.; open other times for groups of 25 or more by appointment

Admission: Adults $2.00; children (12 and under) $1.00; special group rates available

Activities: Guided tours, audiovisual presentation, annual May Magnolia Homes Walking Tours

Suggested Time to View House: 30–60 minutes

Description of Grounds: Yard with huge indigenous trees of cedar, hackberry and myrtle, largest of their kind in Columbus

Best Season to View House: Year round

Year House Built: 1872

Style of Architecture: Folk Victorian, cottage

Number of Rooms: 7

On-Site Parking: Yes **Wheelchair Access:** No

Description of House

This superb Victorian cottage was built in 1872 by a local lumber merchant, John Keith, who sold it three years later to Charles Traylor, who bought it for his new bride, Lura Perry. The couple raised three daughters here. Oddly enough, one of their daughters married the son of John Keith and thereafter the house remained in the family's possession until "Lura" was presented as a gift to Columbus' Magnolia Homes Tour by John Keith's grandson, James.

The cottage, one of the only examples of its kind to escape later alteration, is a relatively simple one-story structure with a small front gable. This gable features ornate vergeboards with crossbracing whereas the side gables show incised trim details. There is the typical full-width porch with elaborate bracketing. Inside, the floor plan consists of four rooms lying on either side of a wide center hall. The attached kitchen and dining room were probably added to the house in 1881. The Victorian trim and the fine redheart pine wainscotting in the hall and parlor were added in the 1890s. The interior is in the process of being restored to its original appearance. Most of the furnishings on display date from the last third of the 19th century; they belonged to the Keith and Traylor families and feature a wonderful "golden oak" bedroom set, an ebonized upright piano, walnut and pine food safes, an early cast iron wood stove, and locally-manufactured walnut tables.

Notable Collections on Exhibit

The collection of vintage clothing worn by the Traylor girls is superb; also of interest are the several chromolithographs in period frames and two oils c.1890.

Additional Information

When visiting Columbus, a town of historic riches, one should take note of several fine bed-and-breakfasts which offer accommodations as well as further examples of the area's history and architecture. Three such are: the Greek Revival-style 1887 Ilse Home, "Raumonda," the 1870 German vernacular-style Gant House with its original stenciling, and the 1890 Magnolia Oaks Victorian Cottage featuring many Queen Anne Eastlake-style details.

Senftenberg-Brandon House Museum

616 Walnut Street
Columbus, TX 78934
(409) 732-8385

Contact: Magnolia Homes Tour, Inc.

Open: First and third Thursday of each month 10 a.m.–4 p.m.; open other times for groups of 25 or more by appointment

Admission: Adults $2.00; children (12 and under) $1.00; special group rates available

Activities: Guided tours; annual May Magnolia Homes Walking Tours

Suggested Time to View House: 30 minutes

Facilities on Premises: Gift shop

Description of Grounds: Town yard with pecan and magnolia trees

Best Season to View House: Year round

Year House Built: c.1860, remodeled c.1890

Style of Architecture: Greek Revival

Number of Rooms: 10

On-Site Parking: Yes **Wheelchair Access:** No

Description of House

The house which now serves as a museum depicting life in small town America a century ago, and also as the headquarters for the Magnolia Homes Tour, was originally built just prior to the Civil War by the Tates. Mr. Tate was later elected mayor of Dallas. At that time, the house was a relatively simple Greek Revival-style home. In 1890, it was purchased by the Senftenbergs, local merchants who operated a general store on the first floor of the Stafford Bank and Opera House Building. They added all the "gingerbread" trim of the Gothic Revival, thus giving the house a decidedly Victorian appearance. The Senftenbergs also altered the floor plan and redecorated the interior. Five years later, the Brandon family bought the house and made their own changes, primarily by enlarging the northeast bedrooms, both upstairs and downstairs, at the expense of the porches on that face of the building.

Despite the changes wrought by the home's various owners, its off-center design exhibits a remarkable unity and creates some unique effects, most particularly in the way the full-width, full-height porches swing around the right side of the building forcing a surprising asymmetry upon the viewer who has just turned the corner from the reflected front facade. The two-story house also features a hipped roof covered in fishscale shingles, an "Oriental" motif in the porch and balcony railings, double front gables, and plain elongated windows with green shutters. The original structure built by the Tates had wood frame walls covered in wood lathe and plaster, a possible adaptation of the East Texas or Louisiana style of construction. The exterior colors are purely Victorian, the light yellow with red trim as was added by the Senftenbergs; these colors, and the ubiquitous brown which can be seen on the Ilse Home mentioned above, were typical of the Victorian period.

Inside, much of the original woodwork—done in solid redheart burl pine—and flooring can be seen downstairs. The basement shows hand-made brick and glazed doors with sidelights can be found on both floors.

Notable Collections on Exhibit

The house is a treasure trove of period furniture, some pieces of which came from the first capitol building in Austin. The styles represented include Eastlake, Renaissance Revival, and American Empire. Amid all the marvelous decorative objects and furniture, one notices a more homely artifact—the citizenship papers of Mr. Golger, the Austrian cabinet maker who carved the main staircase.

Additional Information

When touring Columbus, take time to visit its other historical treasures, especially the Opera House, the Court House, and the Confederate Memorial.

Galvan House of Heritage Park

1581 North Chaparral Street
Corpus Christi, TX 78401
(512) 883-0639

Contact: City of Corpus Christi Parks and Recreation Department

Open: Mon.-Fri. 10 a.m.–4 p.m., Sat. 10 a.m.–2 p.m.; closed Sunday and national holidays

Admission: Adults $2.00; seniors and children $1.00; group rates available

Activities: Guided tours available by appointment, self-guided tours, monthly exhibits, ethnic craft demonstrations

Suggested Time to View House: 30 minutes

Description of Grounds: Located in the center of Heritage Park, a district consisting of nine historic houses built between 1851 and 1908

Style of Architecture: Eclectic Colonial Revival

Best Season to View House: Year round

Number of Yearly Visitors: 50,000+

Number of Rooms: 10

Year House Built: 1908

On-Site Parking: Yes **Wheelchair Access:** Yes

Description of House

In 1908, A. M. French and his wife built this Colonial Revival-style house on Chaparall Street. French was a surveyor for the Texas-Mexico Railroad and the first person to start a title and abstract company in Corpus Christi. In 1942, the house was bought by Rafael Galvan, the first Hispanic policeman on the Corpus Christi force, who lived here with his family until 1982. In addition to his twenty years on the force, Galvan also owned and operated a number of local businesses and ranches.

The Galvan House is a two-and-a-half-story structure built mostly of yellow pine. The exterior features a full wrap-around porch with classical supports, a hipped roof accented with balustrades, and a center attic dormer with a small Palladian-style window. Inside, the ceilings are twelve feet high and the transoms and sidelights have their original leaded glass; much of the stripped-style brass hardware is also original. A particularly graceful hand-carved newel post crowned with a globe light can be seen on the central staircase. Though the interior woodwork has been restored, much of it is painted white for exhibition purposes.

Notable Collections on Exhibit

The Galvan House serves as a museum featuring different monthly exhibits and ethnic craft demonstrations. The furniture display is on loan from area residents.

Sidbury House

**1609 North Chapparal Street
Corpus Christi, TX 78401
(512) 883-9352**

Contact: Junior League of Corpus Christi
Open: Tues., Wed., Sat. 10 a.m.–1 p.m.;
   special tours by prior arrangement
Admission: Donations welcome
Activities: Guided tours, participate in
   Heritage Park activities
Suggested Time to View House: 30 minutes
Description of Grounds: Small sitting area
   with benches and gazebo
Best Season to View House: Year round
Number of Yearly Visitors: 50,000
Year House Built: 1893
Style of Architecture: High Victorian
   Queen Anne
Number of Rooms: 9

On-Site Parking: Yes **Wheelchair Access:** No

Description of House

The Sidbury House is the last remaining example of the high Victorian-style left in Corpus Christi. Originally built as a rental property by Charlotte Cook Scott Sidbury, local civic leader, rancher, and lumber company manager, it was fully restored by the Junior League of Corpus Christi in 1975 and now stands as a monument to historic preservation.

The two-story house features characteristic first and second floor wrap-around porches and balconies accented with elaborate Eastlake-style spindlework. Other exterior details include an extended open bay, multiple cross gables, and wrought iron roof cresting. Inside, one is compelled to note the wallpapers especially: they have been restored by a local company which hand-printed them from the original pear-wood blocks that were used a hundred years ago. Those in the entry hall and parlor are done in the green and white "Pugein Trellis" and the green, white, gold, and rose "Pugein Rose" patterns. The house is fully furnished, with most pieces done in the popular Eastlake style. Upstairs, one can find a five-piece oak bedroom set which is advertised in the open Sears, Roebuck Catalogue for $16.95, including shipping and handling.

Notable Collections on Exhibit

In addition to the furniture mentioned above, two items of note are the 1885 Bible displayed on the library desk and the 1893 Steinway piano.

Additional Information

In 1979, the Sidbury House was given the President's Award by the National Trust for Historic Preservation. The house has also received the San Antonio Conservation Society Award and the Historic Preservation Award from the Texas Historical Commission. It is listed on the National Register of Historic Places.

Downes-Aldrich House

206 North Seventh Street
Crockett, TX 75835
(409) 544-4804

Contact: Historical and Cultural Activities
Center of Houston County, Texas, Inc.

Open: Mar.-Dec.,Wed., Sat., Sun. 2–4 p.m.;
closed months of January and February

Admission: Adults $2.00; students $1.00;
children (under 10) $.50

Activities: Guided tours by appointment

Suggested Time to View House: 1 hour

Facilities on Premises: Gift shop

Description of Grounds: Small yard with
trees and shrubs

Style of Architecture: Victorian Queen
Anne with elaborate Eastlake spindlework

Best Season to View House: Spring

Number of Yearly Visitors: 300

Number of Rooms: 15

Year House Built: 1893

On-Site Parking: No **Wheelchair Access:** No

Description of House

In 1893, Colonel James A. Downes, a Confederate veteran of the Civil War, built this magnificent Queen Anne-style house and lived here until 1910. At that time, he sold it to Judge Armstead Aldrich. Judge Aldrich was a local historian of some note, in addition to being a lawyer and community leader. The house remained in his family until 1977 when it was deeded to the State of Texas by the last surviving Aldrich daughter. Stewardship of the property was subsequently given over to the Historical and Cultural Activities Center of Texas.

The Downes-Aldrich house is a charming two-story structure featuring many of the characteristic elements of the late Victorian Queen Anne style: gables finished with decorative vergeboards, a shingled roof showing wrought iron cresting and finials, trusses with "lace" brackets, a full width wrap-around porch, and elaborate Eastlake spindlework. The wonderful half-moon porch brackets re-appear as a motif in the transoms and sidelights found on one of the main floor window treatments. On the second floor, above the main entry, one comes upon a "surprise" recessed porch. The exterior also features a turret with an S-curved roof. Inside, the details include five fireplaces, walk-through windows, curly pine paneling, stained glass windows, and an unusual summer kitchen. All of the interior doors have transoms. The period reproduction wallpapers in the double parlors and dining room were done by Bradbury & Bradbury of California. All pieces on display have been donated to the Center and are authentic to the period of the 1890s. Most of the furnishings in the living room and bedrooms are done in the Eastlake style.

Additional Information

The Downes-Aldrich House is listed on the National Register of Historic Places.

Bates-Sheppard House

312 East Broadway, P.O. Box 745
Cuero, TX 77954
(512) 275-6322

Contact: DeWitt County Historical Museum
Open: Thurs., Fri. 9 a.m.–4:30 p.m.,
Sun. 2–5 p.m.; closed Thanksgiving,
Christmas, New Year's Day
Admission: Free
Activities: Guided tours, annual Wildflower
Show
Suggested Time to View House:
30–60 minutes

Facilities on Premises: Bookstore
Description of Grounds: Yard with flower
garden and several outbuildings
including a "dog-trot" log cabin
Best Season to View House: Year round
Number of Yearly Visitors: 1,100
Year House Built: 1886, remodeled 1925
Style of Architecture: Folk Victorian, frame
Number of Rooms: 9
On-Site Parking: No **Wheelchair Access:** Yes

Description of House

It was on land purchased from the Cuero Land and Immigration Company that F. W. Bates and two of his wife's younger brothers built this house in October 1886. The boys, Joseph and Henry Sheppard, had been left homeless and motherless when the great Hurricane of '86 swept through their hometown of Indianola the previous August. So Bates and the boys gathered up any usable lumber, transported it to Cuero, and began work on the new home. The house remained in the Bates family until 1968; it now serves as the DeWitt County Museum.

The original two-story structure consisted of a dining room, living room, and several bedrooms. It features a symmetrical design wherein two identical side wings and gables lie on either side of the center-gabled body of the house. In 1925, the house was substantially remodeled; additions included an upstairs bedroom, the present kitchen, and two indoor bathrooms. The wallpaper was stripped, the walls were painted cream color, and the wood trim brown. On the outside, the house displays very few decorative elements; there is only a diminutive one-story porch with its square supports and the brown shutters which highlight the buff-colored exterior. The donated Victorian furnishings are all appropriate to the period and include a four-poster bed, couches, chairs, and a sideboard.

Additional Information

The Bates-Sheppard House is listed on the National Register of Historic Places.

DeGolyer House

Contact: Dallas Arboretum

Open: Mar.-Oct., daily 10 a.m.–6 p.m.;
Nov.-Feb., daily 10 a.m.–5 p.m.; closed
Thanksgiving, Christmas, New Year's Day

Admission: Adult $6.00; seniors $5.00;
children (6-12) $3.00; group rates available

Activities: Guided tours

Suggested Time to View House: 30 minutes

Facilities on Premises: Gift shop

Best Season to View House: Year round

Description of Grounds: Located on the
magnificent 66 acre Dallas Arboretum
which lies on the eastern shore of White
Rock Lake. The historic Camp House now
serves as the Dallas Arboretum's offices.

Style of Architecture: Spanish Eclectic or
Spanish Colonial Revival

Number of Yearly Visitors: 500,000

Year House Built: 1939

Number of Rooms: 13

On-Site Parking: Yes **Wheelchair Access:** Yes

Description of House

The history of modern Texas is often a tale of the fantastic transformation of lives and landscape by the fortunes that grew of the discovery of oil. Few individual lives illustrate the process as well as that of Everette L. DeGolyer who was born in a sod hut in Kansas in 1886. DeGolyer is widely recognized as the founder of the field of applied petroleum geophysics; a geologist by training, he made his first big oil strike in Mexico in 1910 and then built Amerada-Hess into the largest independent oil company in the country. Later, he invested in the company which would become Texas Instruments, funded J. C. Karcher's seismographic research, founded Core Laboratories and his own consulting company, and even owned the magazine *Saturday Review*. The splendid library he amassed is now housed at Southern Methodist University but his acquisitions in art and antiques may be seen in this house, which he built in 1939. He and his family set up the DeGolyer Foundation for the express purpose of maintaining this property as a cultural and educational center for the city of Dallas. Everette died in 1956, his wife sixteen years later; it was after her death that the house was transferred to SMU which then sold it to the city.

The house was built on a White Rock Lake dairy farm called "Rancho Encinal." The DeGolyers hired the California architects Denman Scott and Burton Schutt to design it, then traveled with them throughout California to study the Spanish Mission-style architecture seen in the old haciendas that the DeGolyers so admired. They then hired Harvard-educated landscape architect Arthur Berger and his wife to site the house and design its elaborate gardens. The plan they got is an extended "X" laid across a long center axis featuring two inner courtyards, one in the south wing where the family lived, and the other in the northern servants' wing, which also includes a splendid greenhouse. The interior walls are made of plaster over wood lathing, the floors are finished with random oak planks, and the ceilings encompass many different treatments; they range from the barrel-vaulted ceiling in the dining room to the Indian Room's wood-beamed ceiling with vigas.

The stone exterior with its massive arches is mainly in the Spanish Colonial Revival style, featuring 22" thick walls, a tile roof, and wrought iron grilled French windows, but many other styles are in evidence as well. Despite this eclectic mix of occasionally disparate elements, the whole retains a unity reinforced by the geography of the site.

Additional Information

The DeGrolyer House is listed on the National Register of Historic Places.

George House at Old City Park

1717 Gano Street
Dallas, TX 75215
(214) 421-5141

Contact: Dallas County Heritage
Society, Inc.

Open: Tues.-Sat. 10 a.m.–4 p.m.,
Sun. Noon–4 p.m.

Admission: Adults $5.00; seniors $4.00;
children (3-12) $2.00; group rates available

Activities: Self-guided tours, introductory
slide presentation, special seasonal
events including Holiday Candlelight
and Texas Heritage Day

Facilities on Premises: Gift and print shop

Description of Grounds: 13 acre park with
thirty-five historic houses and commercial
buildings. Located in Dallas' first park.

Best Season to View House: Year round

Suggested Time to View House:
House-30 minutes, park-4 hours

Number of Yearly Visitors: 180,000

Number of Rooms: 10

Style of Architecture: Victorian Queen
Anne-Eastlake

Year House Built: 1900

On-Site Parking: Yes **Wheelchair Access:** Yes

Description of House

The Old City Park Museum in Dallas consists of several historical structures which are meant to represent the major historical and cultural aspects of the city's development from 1840 to 1910, from the Gano Log House built in 1846 to the General Store built in 1907. In this park, the George House typifies the Victorian residential architecture of the middle class at the turn of the century. It was built in 1900 by the hardware merchant David C. George as wedding present for his wife. The original site of the George House was in Plano, Texas, where the couple, their children, and George's mother all lived.

This two-story Queen Anne-style structure features a symmetrical floor plan, bay windows, jig-saw trim under the eaves, a many-gabled roof, a turret, and decorative siding—all elements typical to this High Victorian style. There is also an partial wrap-around porch with very fine lace bracketing. Inside, the house is interpreted to the first years of the family's occupancy, around 1900. The electric light fixtures are original, as is the linoleum and cast iron stove in the kitchen, and the metal shingle roof. Wallpapers include floral and Oriental design motifs. The built-in china cabinet in the dining room is a rarity for any home in Texas at the turn of the century. The furnishings consist entirely of collected pieces, predominantly in the Eastlake style.

Additional Information

In addition to the George House, and the Gano Log House and General Store mentioned above, the Old City Park Museum also contains the Missouri-Kansas-Texas railroad depot built in 1886, a mansion called "Millermore" c.1860 (which is also listed in this guide), and the Pilot Grove Church built in the 1890s. The complex is definitely worth a visit.

"Millermore" at Old City Park

1717 Gano Street
Dallas, TX 75215
(214) 421-5141

Contact: Dallas County Heritage Society, Inc.

Open: Tues.-Sat. 10 a.m.–4 p.m., Sun. Noon–4 p.m.

Admission: Adults $5.00; seniors $4.00; children (3-12) $2.00; group rates available

Activities: Self-guided tours, introductory slide presentation, special seasonal events including Holiday Candlelight and Texas Heritage Day

Suggested Time to View House: House-30 minutes, park-4 hours

Facilities on Premises: Gift and print shop

Description of Grounds: 13 acre park with thirty-five historic houses and commercial buildings. Located in Dallas' first park.

Best Season to View House: Year round

Number of Yearly Visitors: 180,000

Year House Built: Between 1855 and 1862

Style of Architecture: Greek Revival

Number of Rooms: 8

On-Site Parking: Yes **Wheelchair Access:** Yes

Description of House

In 1847 William Brown Miller moved his family from Missouri to Texas and settled on 1280 acres southwest of the Trinity River in what is now the Oak Cliff area of Dallas. With the slaves he brought with him, Miller farmed and raised cattle here. Miller constructed a simple log house as temporary shelter until the permanent house, "Millermore," was completed in 1862. This modest building also served as one of the first schools in the area when Miller, who had twelve children, brought a teacher to his ranch from Kentucky to teach his five daughters as well as seven girls from neighboring farms. By 1880, Miller had become the largest landowner in Dallas County. The house stayed in the Miller family until 1962. "Millermore" is now part of Dallas' Old City Park Museum, along with the George House listed above.

Construction of this antebellum Greek Revival-style house was begun in 1855 and completed seven years later. The symmetrical main part of the two-story structure is composed of a center hall flanked on both floors by square rooms; in the rear is an ell which consists of an office and dining room downstairs and a bedroom and dressing room up. In the early 20th century, a kitchen was added, as was the full-facade front porch and four supporting columns. The exterior also features double-hung windows in the typical six-over-six pane arrangement. Two doors—the main entry and the second-floor balcony door—are both glazed and feature a segmented transom light. The interior walls are all painted in pastel colors appropriate to the 1870s, except for the music room which features French reproduction wallpaper. The late Empire-style furniture includes five pieces which belonged to the Millers; the rest are donated pieces.

Additional Information

For more information about the Old City Park Museum, see the entry for the George House.

Eisenhower Birthplace State Historical Place

**208 East Day Street
Denison, TX 75020
(903) 465-8908**

Contact: Texas Parks and Wildlife
Department
Open: Daily 10 a.m.–5 p.m.; closed
Christmas and New Year's Day
Admission: Adults $2.00; children
(under 12) $1.00; children (under 6) free
Activities: Guided tours
Suggested Time to View House: 20 minutes
Description of Grounds: 6 acre city park
Best Season to View House: Spring and fall
Number of Yearly Visitors: 71,000
Year House Built: c. 1885
Number of Rooms: 6, 4 open to the public

Style of Architecture: Late Gothic Revival
On-Site Parking: Yes **Wheelchair Access:** Yes

Description of House

On October 14, 1890, in this modest house, Dwight David Eisenhower, future five-star General of the Army and thirty-fourth President of the United States, was born to David Jacob Eisenhower and Ida Elizabeth Stover. The family lived here for a total of three years while the father worked on the Missouri, Kansas and Texas Railroad as an engine wiper. Less than a year after Eisenhower's birth, the family moved to Abilene, Kansas.

The white frame house with green shutters has six rooms comprising a little less than 1,700 square feet. The exterior has been fully restored to its appearance in 1890 and a railed upstairs porch thought to be part of the house when it was built around 1880 has also been reconstructed. Although the hand-made quilt in the bedroom where Ike was born is the only authenticated family possession in the house, the donated pieces are all representative of the period and provide a good interpretation of what the home looked like a hundred years ago. Some of these pieces include a calendar clock c.1891, a porcelain plate from Ireland, an 1890s Morris rocker-recliner, an 1890s wood-coal stove, and a hand-crafted German silver coffee server.

Notable Collections on Exhibit

On display is a painting of an American Indian—one of the first paintings done by Eisenhower himself.

Additional Information

In addition to the Eisenhower Birthplace, Dennison is home to the Grayson County Frontier Village, a superb collection of seventeen relocated and restored buildings which includes three houses that should not be missed: the Bullock-Bass House, the first house in the village and the first house in the county to have glass windows, an Early Classical Revival structure built in 1858; the Bradley-Bodkin House, built by Thomas Bradley in 1847; and the Thompson House, built by Grayson County's first judge in the 1840s. The Village is located at New Highway 75 and Loy Lake Road and their phone number is (903) 463-2487.

Magoffin Home State Historic Site

1120 Magoffin Avenue
El Paso, TX 79901
(915) 533-5147

Contact: Texas Parks and Wildlife Department

Open: Wed.-Sun. 9 a.m.–4 p.m.; closed Thanksgiving, Christmas, New Year's Day

Admission: Adults $2.00; children (6-12) $1.00; school groups $.50 per person

Activities: Guided tours, outreach programs, special seasonal events including El Paso History Day and Hispanic Heritage Month

Suggested Time to View House: 60–90 minutes

Facilities on Premises: Gift and book shop

Description of Grounds: 1½ acre restored landscaped area with some original plantings

Best Season to View House: Spring-fall

Number of Yearly Visitors: 10,000

Year House Built: 1875

Style of Architecture: Anglo-Territorial Adobe with extensive Greek Revival characteristics

Number of Rooms: 19

On-Site Parking: No **Wheelchair Access:** Yes

Description of House

In 1840, Kentuckian James Wiley Magoffin settled on the Rio Grande opposite the ancient Mexican town of Paso del Norte and built an adobe home, a store, and a warehouse; soon his little settlement came to be known as Magoffinville. When U.S. Boundary Commissioner John Russell Bartlett was surveying the U.S.-Mexican border in the 1850s he used Magoffinville as his headquarters. In 1854 Fort Bliss was built here. Then, in 1868, the Rio Grande flooded and the fort and most of the surrounding buildings were completely washed away. Magoffinville was abandoned.

Some years later, Magoffin's second son, James, would return to this site, now called El Paso instead of Magoffinville, across from Juarez, not Paso del Norte, and make his mark in business and politics. He built the present structure in 1875; after his death, it was occupied by his daughter, Josephine, and her husband, the Brigadier General William Glasgow, then by their daughter Octavia Magoffin Glasgow, who lived here until her death in 1986. The house had been purchased by the City of El Paso and the State of Texas some ten years earlier.

The house features elements typical of the Territorial Adobe style: a flat roof with parapet and viga supports, decorative lintels, and an asymmetrical design featuring multiple entrances and windows. However, some of the details, most notably the scoring of the plaster on the facade so it resembles cut stone, the pediments above the doors and windows, and the painted shutters, owe more to the Greek Revival style than the adobe style. The uneven wings of the U-shaped floor plan surround a courtyard. The interior of the house, unlike the exterior, has been only partially restored; even so, it is furnished with many original family items, including a unique bedroom set featuring a thirteen-foot-tall canopied bed, a full-length mirrored wardrobe, and a marble-topped chest and washstand.

Notable Collections on Exhibit

Especially noteworthy is the collection of personal letters and other documents (c.1820 to c.1920) which chronicle the Magoffin family history. This collection includes a letter dated 1866 from Mexican President Benito Juarez to "Don Santiago Magoffin."

Additional Information

This site is listed on the National Register of Historic Places.

Eddleman-McFarland House

1110 Penn Street
Fort Worth, TX 76102
(817) 332-5875

Contact: Historic Fort Worth, Inc.

Open: Mon., Wed., Fri. 9 a.m.–Noon; closed New Year's Day, Fourth of July, Labor Day, Thanksgiving, Christmas

Admission: $2.00 per person

Activities: Guided tours

Suggested Time to View House: 30–45 minutes

Description of Grounds: Victorian plantings and rose garden

Best Season to View House: Spring and winter

Number of Yearly Visitors: 500

Year House Built: Started 1899, completed 1900

Number of Rooms: 15, 7 open to the public

Style of Architecture: Late Victorian Queen Anne, patterned masonry

On-Site Parking: Yes **Wheelchair Access:** No

Description of House

The Eddleman-McFarland House, built on a high bluff overlooking the Trinity River, is one of only three remaining examples of Ft. Worth's opulent "cattle baron" homes. Originally built for Mrs. Sarah Ball of Galveston by the English architect Howard Messer of the firm Sanguinet & Sanguinet, it was purchased by W. H. Eddleman in 1904. Eddleman made his fortune driving cattle from Texas to Colorado, then went into banking: he owned the Farmer's and Merchant's Bank of Weatherford outright and had a controlling interest in twenty-six other institutions. His daughter, Carrie, married the Tennessee-born rancher Frank McFarland. After Eddleman's wife died in 1921, he lived here with his daughter and son-in-law; Carrie lived here until her death in 1978 at the age of 100.

This Queen Anne gem has over three thousand square feet of living space; its exterior features include 22" thick walls built of Pennsylvania pressed brick with sandstone trim, a Neoclassical wrap-around porch with Ionic grouped supports and a floor of pink Georgian marble, a steep pitched roof with flared gables, patterned masonry chimneys, copper finials, bas-relief keystone insets, and tap design bracketed window surrounds. Inside, one finds a wide array of wood molding and paneling, all of it ordered from a pattern book and hand-finished on site. The rim lights around the coffered ceiling are all electric and original to the house; the silver plated wall sconces probably are as well.

Additional Information

The Eddleman-McFarland House is listed on the National Register of Historic Places.

Kammlah House at the Pioneer Memorial Museum Complex

309 West Main Street
Fredericksburg, TX 78624
(512) 997-2835

Contact: Gillespie County Historical Society

Open: March 1-Dec. 15, Mon.-Fri.
10 a.m.–5 p.m., Sun. 1–5 p.m.; closed
Christmas Eve, Christmas Day, New
Year's Day

Admission: Adults $2.00; students (first
grade-high school) $.50

Activities: Guided tours

Suggested Time to View House:
45–60 minutes

Facilities on Premises: Book and gift shop

Description of Grounds: Grounds include
several historic buildings: the 1860 Log
Cabin, a one-room school house and a
blacksmith shop

Style of Architecture: Folk, "Fachwerk"
frame with half-timber and native rock

Best Season to View House: Spring

Number of Yearly Visitors: 20,000

Number of Rooms: 8

Year House Built: Between 1847 and 1849
On-Site Parking: Yes **Wheelchair Access:** No

Description of House

During the middle of the 19th century, German immigrants, attracted by the prospect of homesteading free land in the gently rolling hill country of central Texas, came to settle that area of the young state in large numbers. One hundred and twenty of these immigrants pioneered the town of Fredericksburg. One of these was Henry Kammlah, who arrived in Fredericksburg with his wife and young children and built this "Fachwerk" house in the late 1840s. His son, Henry Kammlah II, was attracted to the merchant trade and opened a store in the front part of the house in 1870; the store stayed in operation for the next fifty-four years. Three generations of Kammlahs were born and raised in this house before it was vacated around the time of World War II. In 1955, it was bought by the Gillespie County Historical Society who turned it into the Pioneer Memorial Museum.

The "Fachwerk" (German for "framework") is constructed of hand-cut native oak timbers filled in with limestone and mortar; pegs are used instead of nails. The house grew as the family grew—the first three rooms were built over three years, one each year—but the original walls are still standing. In 1870, it underwent a major alteration when the front room was turned into a general store. The interior also features three kitchens, fully outfitted with utensils appropriate to the period. The floors are made of rock and there is a ten-foot-wide cooking fireplace inside.

Notable Collections on Exhibit

In addition to the various domestic and commercial items on display, one may view a painting of the signing of the Comanche peace treaty.

Fulton Mansion, "Oakhurst"

Henderson Street and
Fulton Beach Road
Fulton, TX 78358
(512) 729-0386

Contact: Texas Parks and Wildlife
Department and Fulton Mansion State
Historical Park

Open: Wed.-Sat. 9–11:30 a.m., 1–3:30 p.m.;
closed Christmas Day

Admission: Adults $3.00; children (6-12)
$1.50; bus group rates available

Activities: Guided tours, special seasonal
events, outreach programs

Suggested Time to View House: 1 hour

Description of Grounds: 2½ acre park
with large Prairie Oak and picnic tables

Best Season to View House: Year round

Number of Yearly Visitors: 33,000

Year House Built: 1877

Style of Architecture: Victorian Second
Empire

Number of Rooms: 28, 10 open to the
public

On-Site Parking: Yes **Wheelchair Access:** Yes

Description of House

Although Colonel George Ware Fulton got to Texas too late to fight for her independence, he did find a job in the Republic's General Land Office. He also met Henry Smith, the former provincial governor, and the two became partners in locating and patenting land claims on Live Oak Peninsula in Refugio County. In Brazoria he met Smith's eldest daughter and the two got married in 1840. For the next twenty-eight years, the Fultons lived in Baltimore, Maryland where the Colonel worked on the *Baltimore Sun*, superintended railroad and bridge construction, and worked with the famous bridge-builder John Roebling. After his wife became principal heir to the Smith land holdings, Fulton moved back to Texas where he joined two sets of brothers, the Colemans and the Mathises, in a ranching partnership. Soon he and the Colemans bought out the Mathises and incorporated the Coleman-Fulton Pasture Company, controlling over 165,000 acres of land. Thereafter, Colonel Fulton would get involved in railroading, developing Coastal Bend, and founding the town which bears his name.

The Fulton Mansion, "Oakhurst," is an unusual house for rural South Texas in its opulence, its stack-and-stagger method of building, its solid foot-thick wood walls, and Fulton's inclusion of some genuine innovations in his design: a central heating system and central gas lighting system, indoor plumbing with both hot and cold running water, an attached kitchen, and a laundry room in the basement. The four-story French Second Empire-style house features a mansard roof and was built of cypress, long-leaf pine, and black walnut. The floor plan puts the public rooms—dining room, parlor, conservatory, library—on the main floor (which also had a bathroom, a rarity), reserves the two middle floors for bedrooms, bathrooms, and a sitting room, and features a "growlery" on the fourth and final floor. This was Fulton's office. In the restored house, only the first two floors are open to the public. Because of the solidity of the construction, and the level of craftsmanship throughout, "Oakhurst" is one of the few 19th-century Gulf Coast homes still standing.

Notable Collections on Exhibit

The mansion houses one of the most extensive collections of late 19th-century decorative artifacts in Texas.

Additional Information

The Fulton Mansion is listed on the National Register of Historic Places.

1839 Samuel May Williams Home

3601 Bernardo de Galvez
and Avenue P
Galveston, TX 77550
(409) 765-1839

Contact: Galveston Historical Foundation

Open: Daily Noon–4 p.m.; closed
Thanksgiving, Christmas Eve and Day,
New Year's Day

Admission: Adults $3.00; seniors and
students $2.50; children (under 6) free

Activities: Audiovisual presentations on the
life and times of Samuel May Williams

Suggested Time to View House: 45 minutes

Facilities on Premises: Museum shop
featuring Texas and early American crafts

Description of Grounds: Sited on a ¼ acre
of the original Williams farm outside
Galveston

Style of Architecture: Greek Revival with
French Colonial-Louisiana Creole
influence

Best Season to View House: Year round

Number of Yearly Visitors: 10,000

Number of Rooms: 9 open to the public

Year House Built: 1839

On-Site Parking: Yes **Wheelchair Access:** No

Description of House

This wonderful modified Greek Revival home, the oldest restored house
on Galveston Island, was framed out in Maine and shipped by schooner to
the Texas coast in 1839 for Samuel May Williams. Williams, who had made
his fortune in the Republic of Texas as a planter, merchant, and banker, won
wide renown and his fellow citizens' gratitude for having personally
financed the acquisition of a fleet for the fledgling Texas Navy during their
war for independence. He also served as Stephen Austin's private secretary.

When the house was completed, it was one of the largest and finest on
the whole of the western frontier, in keeping with the stature of its owner.
The one-and-a-half-story structure features a full-width wrap-around
verandah, French-style doors, and a low hipped roof. Visitors may ascend
a winding staircase to the widow's walk and lantern (cupola). Inside, the
walls are whitewashed plaster; although there are gilded valences and some
black horsehair pieces, no particular color scheme predominates. The floor-
to-ceiling windows and segmented transoms with sidelights allow both
light and air free circulation throughout the house.

The furnishings include some pieces which belonged to the Williams
family, including a piano and an early recliner. The rest are a mix of early
Victorian style; one noteworthy piece is the the Greek Revival-style tester
bed in the master bedroom.

Notable Collections on Exhibit

On display is an extensive collection of antique 19th-century toys.

1859 Ashton Villa

2328 Broadway
Galveston, TX 77550
(409) 762-3933

Contact: Galveston Historical Foundation

Open: Year-round, daily 10 a.m.–3 p.m.; closed Thanksgiving, Christmas Eve and Day

Admission: Adults $4.00; seniors and students $3.50, children (under 6) free

Activities: Guided tours, Victorian Christmas Celebration

Suggested Time to View House: 1 hour

Facilities on Premises: Museum shop specializing in Victoriana

Description of Grounds: Located on the main thoroughfare of town, the house and garden of palms and native flowers are surrounded by an ornate cast iron fence

Best Season to View House: Spring

Number of Yearly Visitors: 45,000

Year House Built: 1859, remodeled 1880s

Style of Architecture: Italianate Villa

Number of Rooms: 11 open to the public

On-Site Parking: Yes **Wheelchair Access:** Yes

Description of House

Colonel James Moreau Brown, a native New Yorker who made a fortune in the hardware business, built this Italianate mansion in 1859. It was the first of Galveston's great Broadway mansions and perhaps the first brick house in all of Texas. After Brown's death, the house was taken over by his unmarried daughter, Miss Bettie. Miss Bettie was a Galveston "character," an amateur artist and world-traveler who lived here until 1926; when she died, Ashton Villa became a Shrine Temple. It remained such until it was bought by the City of Galveston in 1969 and converted to a museum.

Ashton Villa features the wide, overhanging eaves, extended roof line pediments, and oversized brackets characteristic of the Italianate style. The exterior achieves a marvelous harmony through the fenestration: floor-to-ceiling windows on the front of the first two floors, six-over-six side windows, and the smaller arched windows on the third floor, all of which are shuttered. The striking two-story cast-iron verandah was manufactured in Philadelphia. The interiors are done in the High Victorian style of the 1880s, when both Galveston and the Browns were at their peak of wealth. Some of the rooms are dazzling: the gilded Rococo Revival-style parlor called, appropriately enough, the Gold Room; the Gothic Revival-style dining room filled with Eastlake furniture; and the inlaid Empire-style bedroom. Most of the pieces on display belonged to the Brown family.

Notable Collections on Exhibit

There is an outstanding collection of silverware and china belonging to the family as well as a rich sampling of the paintings done by Miss Bettie after her return from a Viennese art school. In the carriage house, there is an exhibit of artifacts discovered in an archaeological dig conducted near the servants' wing; this exhibit also relates the destruction done to Galveston by the 1900 hurricane and the island's subsequent recovery.

Additional Information

As fine as the Ashton Villa is, it is only one of Galveston's restored treasures. A visit to this Gulf Coast city really should include all three landmark districts: the East End National Historic Landmark District, the Strand National Historic Landmark District, and the Silk Stocking Historic District. The Ashton Villa is listed on the National Register of Historic Places.

Moody Mansion

2618 Broadway, P.O. Box 1300
Galveston, TX 77553
(409) 762-7668

Contact: Moody Mansion and Museum
Open: Mon.-Sat. 10 a.m.–4 p.m.,
   Sun. 1–4:30 p.m.; closed Easter,
   Thanksgiving, Christmas
Admission: Adults $6.00; seniors $5.00;
   children $3.00; children (under 6) free
Activities: Guided tours, orientation film
Suggested Time to View House: 60–90 minutes
Facilities on Premises: Gift shop, food
   service for groups
Description of Grounds: City yard with
   native plantings not accessible to the public
Style of Architecture: Richardsonian
   Romanesque
Best Season to View House: Year round
Number of Yearly Visitors: 72,000
Year House Built: Between 1893 and 1895
Number of Rooms: 31

On-Site Parking: Yes **Wheelchair Access:** Yes

Description of House

Narcissa Willis, the widow of a successful Galveston merchant, hired the English architect William Tyndall to design and build this house in 1893. Five years after its completion, it was purchased by W. L. Moody, Jr. who had made his fortune as a banker and chief executive of the American National Insurance Company. On December 12, 1911, his daughter, Mary, had her debut; for some time the house was interpreted to that year. At the Moody Mansion, the interpretations change approximately every three years. Over the next half century, the prominent family had interests ranging from ranching to the hotel industry and a voice in politics at every level. When Moody died in 1954, ownership of the house fell to Mary, who had been widowed by then. The restoration of the house, and its conversion into a museum, was executed according to her wishes.

The imposing three-story mansion is done in the Richardsonian Romanesque style over an English basement. The exterior is built of brick set on a steel frame with Bolton limestone and terra cotta roof tiles. The interiors were done by the New York design firm of Pottier & Stymus who cleverly executed each room in a different revival style. The museum's archives include the fascinating detailed correspondence of the designers. All furnishings are original to the house.

Notable Collections on Exhibit

The museum is still in the process of developing the exhibition space necessary to exhibit some of the thousands of items currently held in their archive. These items include over 10,000 photographs and negatives, 1,500 cubic feet of family papers, and a 2,000 volume reference library primarily concerning Texas history and the decorative arts.

Lon C. Hill Home

Corner of Boxwood and Raintree Streets
Harlingen, TX 78550
(512) 423-3979

Contact: Rio Grande Valley Museum
Open: Year-round, Wed.-Sat.
10 a.m.–4 p.m., Sun. 1–4 p.m.;
closed month of June
Admission: Free
Activities: Guided tours, museum
presentations, lectures
Suggested Time to View House:
15–45 minutes
Facilities on Premises: Museum shop
Description of Grounds: Native plantings,
shrubs and palms
Best Season to View House: Spring and
late fall
Number of Yearly Visitors: 4,000+
Year House Built: 1905
Number of Rooms: 5 open to the public

Style of Architecture: National, brick
On-Site Parking: Yes **Wheelchair Access:** Yes

Description of House

Harlingen was settled and developed as agriculture followed irrigation in the Rio Grande Valley and Lon C. Hill was one of those who pioneered the area. In 1905, he built the first house in town—the house has since been relocated—of bricks fired in his own kiln. Upon close inspection, one notices the letter "K" impressed on the bricks; "K" was Hill's brand. This part of Texas was still wild country during the first part of the century; during the 'teens, bandit raids were not uncommon and the chimney served as a perfect hiding place for the children.

The simple brick house has porches on the outside and includes an office, a living room, a kitchen, a parlor and one bedroom. Some of the furnishings belonged to the Hill family and rest are appropriate to the period. One particularly noteworthy piece is the bathtub.

Additional Information

In addition to the Lon C. Hill House, the Rio Grande Valley Museum complex includes a modern museum with traveling historical exhibits and permanent collections relating to the development of this part of Texas.

Howard-Dickinson House

501 South Main Street
Henderson, TX 75652
(214) 657-6925

Contact: Rusk County Heritage Association
Open: Mon.-Fri. 1–5 p.m.; closed all major holidays
Admission: Adults $2.00; children $1.00
Activities: Guided tours, annual Christmas Candlelight Tour
Suggested Time to View House: 30 minutes
Best Season to View House: Early spring

Description of Grounds: Small yard with "gazebo"-type well house
Number of Yearly Visitors: 5,000
Year House Built: 1855, addition 1905
Style of Architecture: Transitional Greek Revival with elements of the Italianate
Number of Rooms: 10
On-Site Parking: No **Wheelchair Access:** No

Description of House

Dave and Logan Howard, two brothers from Richmond, Virginia, came to Rusk County in the 1850s with the right skills to make their mark in the frontier community: brick masonry and carpentry. They built this house in 1855—the first brick structure in Rusk County—and would go on to build a least seven buildings in downtown Henderson. The brick industry that they started was one of the earliest in the county; it wasn't long before folks from all of the surrounding area came to the kiln and brick machine for their building materials. Dave married a cousin of Sam Houston's, Martha Ann, and they had nine children. Because the house had only two bedrooms at the time, all of the boys had to sleep with their uncle Logan, more familiarly called "Loge." The Howards lived here until 1905 when the Dickinsons moved in. During their forty-five years here, they converted part of the structure into a boarding house and built a rear addition. From 1950 to 1964, the house lay vacant and was severely vandalized; then it was purchased by Homer Bryce who sold it, in turn, to the Rusk County Heritage Association for one dollar with the following condition: the Association would have to restore it.

The main part of this two-story structure was built by the Howards in brick with hand-planed woodwork, whereas all the wood in the Dickinsons' addition is milled. The interior features six fireplaces, a dining room showing its original plaster despite the high humidity in this part of the state, and bedrooms without closets because closets could be taxed. All of the restored rooms are named after well-known and popular citizens of Henderson. Outside, one sees evidence of the Greek Revival style: doors with transoms and sidelights, six-over-six fenestration, a hipped roof with overhanging eaves, and a full-height porch and balcony.

The period furnishing include some fascinating pieces: the first pump organ seen in Henderson (a Mason & Hamlin), an American Empire-style sofa made by Duncan Phyfe c.1840, and a desk belonging to William Hays, a veteran of the battle of San Jacinto and local Justice of the Peace.

Notable Collections on Exhibit

Among the many charming and historical artifacts on display, two are especially interesting: a leather trunk which belonged to Sam Houston and served as his campaign trunk during the Battle of San Jacinto, and a "postage-stamp" quilt, made up of 8,730 hand-sewn pieces, called "Hailstorm."

E. B. Black House

508 West Third Street
Hereford, TX 79045
(806) 364-4338

Contact: Deaf Smith County Historical
Museum
Open: By appointment only
Admission: Donations accepted
Activities: Guided tours
Suggested Time to View House:
45–60 minutes
Description of Grounds: Gazebo
surrounded by an English garden
Best Season to View House: Early
Spring-late fall
Style of Architecture: Eclectic mix of late
Victorian Queen Anne, Neoclassical and
Period Revival styles
Number of Yearly Visitors: 1,500
Number of Rooms: 11

Year House Built: 1909
On-Site Parking: Yes **Wheelchair Access:** No

Description of House

This lovely Victorian house was built in 1909 by Mr. and Mrs. E. B. Black who had moved to Hereford from Cleburne some eight years earlier. Here Mr. Black established the furniture company bearing his name which was to operate continuously under the family's ownership until 1977. As the business thrived, the couple became leaders in the community's religious, educational, and cultural institutions. In 1977, the house was given to the Deaf Smith County Historical Society by Prudia Prichard Black, who specified that it was to used for the benefit of Hereford.

The two-story house features a porch which wraps around both the southern and eastern facades, a balcony on the second floor facing south, and much of its original fenestration. Over the years, some minor renovations were made to the house, but the basic structure has remained fully intact. Inside, the furnishings are all appropriate to the period when the Blacks first began to live here, though the majority of the pieces did not actually belong to the family.

Additional Information

The E. B. Black House is listed on the National Register of Historic Places.

Kellum-Noble House at Sam Houston Historical Park

1100 Bagby Street at Lamar Street
Houston, TX 77002
(713) 655-1912

Contact: Harris County Heritage Society
Open: Mon.-Sat. 10 a.m.–4 p.m., Sun. 1–5 p.m.
Admission: Adults $4.00; seniors and students $2.00
Activities: Guided tours, audiovisual presentations
Suggested Time to View House: 30 minutes
Facilities on Premises: Gift shop and tea room

Description of Grounds: Park and museum complex with several historic buildings
Best Season to View House: Late fall–early summer
Year House Built: 1847
Number of Yearly Visitors: 492,750 park visitors
Style of Architecture: Greek Revival with characteristics of "The Louisiana Style"
Number of Rooms: 9
On-Site Parking: Yes **Wheelchair Access:** Yes

Description of House

The Kellum-Noble House is the oldest brick house and residential structure of any sort still standing on its original site in the city of Houston. It has served as a model of the Greek Revival "Louisiana style" for generations of Houston architects and is the only house in Sam Houston Historical Park which wasn't relocated here. The property on which it stands has a history which predates the founding of the city.

The house was built in 1847 by Nathaniel Kelly Kellum, a Virginian who came to Texas in 1939, married Elmyra Cotton of Mississippi, started up a business manufacturing bricks, then made his fortune as a builder. He became a friend to many prominent Texans, Sam Houston among them. The house has had a number of owners down through the years, most notably Abram W. Noble, Houston's first banker, whose wife started one of the city's first private schools in the house.

A prime example of a typical plantation house of the mid-19th century, this two-story home features a full-height wrap-around porch, a second floor balcony, shuttered windows, brick walls, high-ceilinged rooms, and an exterior staircase leading to the second floor. The first floor consists of an entry hall, a school room, parlor, dining room, and an office. Upstairs, bedrooms lie on either side of a center hall. The house is furnished appropriately to the period; special pieces include a sofa in the school room said to be purchased by Sam Houston's mother-in-law and a Sinumbra Solar Lamp c.1840 in the parlor.

Additional Information

On the grounds of the nearby University of St. Thomas, at 3800 Montrose Blvd., one may visit the Link-Lee Mansion. This eclectic Beaux Arts and Mission-style mansion was built for the founder of the Houston Land Corporation and later owned by oilman T. P. Lee. The three-story, fourteen-room home was designed by the firm Sanguinet, Stoates & Barnes and features an ornate interior well worth viewing.The Kellum-Noble House is listed on the National Register of Historic Places.

Nichols-Rice-Cherry House at Sam Houston Historical Park

1100 Bagby Street
at Lamar Street
Houston, TX 77002
(713) 655-1912

Contact: Harris County Heritage Society
Open: Year-round, Mon.-Sat. 10 a.m.–4 p.m., Sun. 1–5 p.m.
Admission: Adults $4.00; seniors and students $2.00
Activities: Guided tours, audiovisual presentations
Suggested Time to View House: 30 minutes
Facilities on Premises: Gift shop and tea room

Description of Grounds: Park and museum complex with several historic buildings
Best Season to View House: Late fall-early summer
Number of Yearly Visitors: 492,750 park visitors
Year House Built: 1850
Style of Architecture: Greek Revival
Number of Rooms: 8
On-Site Parking: Yes **Wheelchair Access:** Yes

Description of House

In 1850, the early Houston shipping magnate Ebenezer Nichols, who'd come to Texas from Cooperstown, New York, built this splendid home—a prime example of the style pursued by the upper classes of the antebellum Gulf Coast. After Nichols, the house served as residence for a number of Houston's most famous citizens, notably William Marsh Rice, Nichols' business partner who founded the university which bears his name, John Finnegan, father of the suffragette, and Emma Richardson Cherry, Houston's first professional artist who established the Houston Museum of Fine Arts. During the Civil War, the house was used as both a hospital and hotel for Confederate officers. It has been moved five times since being built; the last time was in 1959 when it became the first house to be relocated to the Sam Houston Historical Park.

The two-story Greek Revival structure features verandas supported by characteristic Doric columns. The windows, all of which are shuttered, include a number of the "ship-lap" type, two of which were converted into doorways leading onto the verandas; these were used especially during the frequent social gatherings which took place at the house. Take note also of the pocket doors which slide into the walls between the formal parlor and dining rooms—these created a dance floor large enough for William Rice's extravagant parties. Other features include an elaborately carved front door and an ornate turkey-quilled entry hall. As typical of homes built then, the kitchen is in a separate building connected to the main house by a breezeway. The furnishings are appropriate to the period and include a set of six side chairs manufactured in Baltimore c.1820 and a superb walnut and cedar bookcase desk in the Empire style. This piece was made in Austin c.1850.

Notable Collections on Exhibit

A number of items which belonged to William Rice are displayed, among them a collection of leather fire buckets c.1820s. They remind the viewer that Rice had served as a volunteer on the Liberty Fire Company.

Old Place at Sam Houston Historical Park

**1100 Bagby Street at Lamar Street
Houston, TX 77002
(713) 655-1912**

Contact: Harris County Heritage Society

Open: Mon.-Sat. 10 a.m.–4 p.m.,
Sun. 1–5 p.m.

Admission: Adults $4.00; seniors and
students $2.00

Activities: Guided tours, audiovisual
presentations

Suggested Time to View House: 30 minutes

Facilities on Premises: Gift shop and
tea room

Description of Grounds: Park and
museum complex with several historic
buildings

Best Season to View House: Late fall-
early summer

Number of Yearly Visitors: 492,750 park
visitors

Year House Built: c. 1823

Number of Rooms: 1

Style of Architecture: Folk, hewn-log cabin

On-Site Parking: Yes **Wheelchair Access:** No

Description of House

By the time the Davises named this cabin the "Old Place" in 1871, it had been home to at least five different families and already come to represent the history of the development of Texas itself. Thought to be the oldest standing building in Harris County, the Old Place was built in 1824 by the squatter John C. Williams on the 177 acres he had been granted by the Mexican Government as one of Stephen Austin's "Old Three Hundred." After Williams, residents included the Vince brothers, ranchers who bought it for 100 pesos; the Duerrs of Houston; Robert Waters who died in Matamoros, Mexico, as a soldier during the Mexican-American War; and John and Jane Owens whose daughter, Harriet Alice, was the first person known to be born in the cabin. The Davis family, members of which lived here from 1871 to 1970, incorporated the simple one-room structure into a much larger plantation home. Here at the Sam Houston Historical Park, it stands restored to interpret the period of the Texas Republic and the frontier life of its first occupants.

The Old Place is a one-story, one-room unpainted clapboard cabin framed out of hand-hewn cedar logs. It has two doors, one front and one back, and top windows; the wooden doors currently seen are reproductions of the originals. A number of the boards were either added or replaced during the 19th century. The interior reflects the life of the Anglo-American frontier and features many items common to all pioneer life; the furnishings are utilitarian, simple, and usually cheap. Some were imported, others were manufactured locally; the visitor will be struck by the ingenuity and frugality that these artifacts attest to.

Pillot House at
Sam Houston Historical Park

1100 Bagby Street
at Lamar Street
Houston, TX 77002
(713) 655-1912

Contact: Harris County Heritage Society

Open: Mon.-Sat. 10 a.m.–4 p.m.,
Sun. 1–5 p.m.

Admission: Adults $4.00; seniors and
students $2.00

Activities: Guided tours, audiovisual
presentations

Suggested Time to View House: 30 minutes

Facilities on Premises: Gift shop and
tea room

Description of Grounds: Park and museum
complex with several historic buildings

Style of Architecture: Victorian Queen
Anne-style cottage with spindlework
detailing

Year House Built: 1868

Best Season to View House: Late fall-
early summer

Number of Rooms: 8

Number of Yearly Visitors: 492,750 park
visitors

On-Site Parking: Yes **Wheelchair Access:** Yes

Description of House

The Pillot House was built as a retirement home 1868 for Eugene Pillot,
the eldest son of Claude Pillot, who had emigrated to the Republic of Texas
from France in 1832. Claude built a sawmill and the family prospered as
Houston grew; Eugene followed his father's example and became a builder
and carpenter. He and his wife, Zeolie Sellers of Louisiana, had twelve
children, only six of whom survived to adulthood. In addition to his trade,
Eugene also sat on the board of the fledgling Houston Gas Company—he
was thus able to install gas lighting in his house—and served on the city
council. In later years, he took on the role of theatrical impresario.

Though this one-story cottage shows a modest exterior, the spacious-
ness of its rooms indicates that its owners had money. The floor plan
includes an entry hall, three parlors—one French, one "oriental," and the
last for smoking—a dining room, one bedroom done in the Colonial Revival
style, another done in bamboo, and a kitchen which is thought to be the first
attached kitchen in Houston. The exterior of the house features a large
decorated front door, a front porch and veranda, and large elongated windows; here one can view the iron fence which originally stood outside the
home and the two sculptured dogs standing guard.

The interior is interpreted to the post-antebellum period; furnishings
include a set of Rococo Revival pieces in the French parlor and a four-sided
velvet "Turkish" chair c.1880 in the oriental parlor.

San Felipe Cottage at
Sam Houston Historical Park

1100 Bagby Street
at Lamar Street
Houston, TX 77002
(713) 655-1912

Contact: Harris County Heritage Society

Open: Mon.-Sat. 10 a.m.–4 p.m.,
Sun. 1–5 p.m.

Admission: Adults $4.00; seniors and
students $2.00

Activities: Guided tours, audiovisual
presentations

Suggested Time to View House: 30 minutes

Facilities on Premises: Gift shop and
tea room

Description of Grounds: Park and
museum complex with several historic
buildings

Best Season to View House: Late fall-
early summer

Number of Yearly Visitors: 492,750 park
visitors

Year House Built: 1868, remodeled 1870
and 1880

Number of Rooms: 6

Style of Architecture: National, described as
a "European dog trot" cottage

On-Site Parking: Yes **Wheelchair Access:** Yes

Description of House

Built on property which once belonged to the pioneer landowner Obedience Fort Smith by an unprepossessing German immigrant couple named Ruppersburg, the San Felipe Cottage bears the name of the road on which it first stood—the San Felipe Road which ran from the colonial capital of San Felipe de Austin to Harrisburg. The Ruppersburgs built their modest home sometime in the late 1860s out of their savings; ownership then passed through a number of families, but those who held it longest were the Meyers. During their sixty years here, they did considerable renovation and remodeling and the cottage is now restored to the period of the 1870s, when they first took possession.

The two-story balloon frame structure was originally quite small; the 1870 and 1880 remodelings significantly increased its size. The downstairs now consists of an entry hall, parlor, dining room, back porch, kitchen, and passageway. The second floor has two bedrooms—one for adults, the other for the children—flanking a central hall. The wood framing is visible on the exterior; the windows are shuttered. The difficult period following the Civil War saw the rise of Houston's German community and two of the items on display here attest to their new status: the New York-manufactured sewing machine c.1886 seen in the bedroom and the Boston-built reed organ c.1880 located in the parlor.

Staiti House at Sam Houston Historical Park

1100 Bagby Street
at Lamar Street
Houston, TX 77002
(713) 655-1912

Contact: Harris County Heritage Society

Open: Mon.-Sat. 10 a.m.–4 p.m.,
Sun. 1–5 p.m.

Admission: Adults $4.00; seniors and
students $2.00

Activities: Guided tours, audiovisual
presentations

Suggested Time to View House: 30 minutes

Facilities on Premises: Gift shop and
tea room

Description of Grounds: Park and
museum complex with several historic
buildings

Best Season to View House: Late fall-
early summer

Year House Built: 1905, remodeled 1915

Number of Rooms: 17

Number of Yearly Visitors: 492,750 park
visitors

Style of Architecture: Modified Prairie
School

On-Site Parking: Yes **Wheelchair Access:** Yes

Description of House

The Staiti House is a fine example of the kind of Prairie-School home which was built for Houston's upper middle class during the first decades of the 20th century. Unlike the other homes on display at the Sam Houston Historical Park, this house was built speculatively; during the Southeast Texas oil boom, such homes were sure to sell. The buyer of this house was Henry Thomas Staiti, a native Texan who accurately predicted the discovery of oil in the area known as Spindletop—when the Lucas gusher blew he gained worldwide fame—and went on to own fields in four states. His wife, Odelia Reisner, was a music teacher and patron of the arts; though the couple had no children, their extended family often filled the house. The house sustained a good deal of damage in the hurricane of 1915 and underwent a thorough remodeling after that storm under the direction of Alfred Finn's architectural firm.

The three-story structure features high ceilings, large windows, broad verandas, and spacious rooms; the first floor includes the public rooms and kitchen and the second floor consists of the bedrooms and an office. Both floors have two porches—downstairs for eating, upstairs for sleeping. The third floor, which is closed to the public, contained Mr. Staiti's workshop. The exterior features an attached porte-cochere and a teahouse with a connecting pergola. The Staiti House was one of the first in Houston to have electricity.

Notable Collections on Exhibit

The painting in the main hall is by Emma Richardson Cherry, a resident of the Nichols-Rice-Cherry House and frequenter of the Staiti garden, where she liked to paint.

Woodland Home and the Steamboat House

1836 Sam Houston Avenue
Huntsville, TX 77341
(409) 294-1832

Contact: Sam Houston Memorial Museum

Open: Tues.-Sun. 9 a.m.–5 p.m.; closed
Thanksgiving, Christmas, New Year's Day

Admission: Donation

Activities: Guided group tours by
reservation, craft demonstrations

Suggested Time to View House: 2 hours

Facilities on Premises: Gift shop with books

Description of Grounds: 15 acre park on
the site of the original homestead of
Texas leader Sam Houston

Best Season to View House: Spring and
late fall

Style of Architecture: National-Folk,
described as "dogtrot" cottage,
Folk-Eclectic, described as a
"steamboat" house

Number of Yearly Visitors: 64,000

Number of Rooms: 7

Year House Built: c.1848

On-Site Parking: Yes **Wheelchair Access:** Yes

Description of House

The American soldier and statesman Sam Houston moved to Huntsville and lived with his family in the Woodland Home during the period he served in the United States Senate, from 1847 to 1859. In that year, he was elected Governor of Texas but did not serve long in that office. Because Houston stood counter to prevailing public opinion and opposed secession for Texas at the outset of the Civil War, he was deposed in 1861 and forced to return to private life in Huntsville. Here he rented the Steamboat House. In this house Houston, commander-in-chief of the Texas Army during the war for independence, victor over Santa Anna at the Battle of San Jacinto, and former President of the Republic of Texas, died in 1863.

The Woodland Home is a simple wooden house, a National frame cottage, restored to the period of the Houston family's occupancy. The Steamboat House is far more elaborate and interesting architecturally; it is a variant of the Spanish Colonial style whereupon two verandas flank the central part of the structure and the front gables have been made to look like steamboat stacks; hence the name. Both houses are furnished with period pieces and contain some of Sam Houston's personal artifacts. The Sam Houston Museum is listed on the National Register of Historic Places.

Notable Collections on Exhibit

Among the Sam Houston artifacts on display are his leopard-skin vest, pistols and sword, and some correspondence. In addition, one may view the saddle which once belonged to the defeated Mexican general, Santa Anna.

Beard House

212 Vale Street
Jefferson, TX 75657
(903) 665-2606

Contact: Beard House

Open: Daily except Wed. and
   Sat. 10 a.m. and 1:30 p.m.;
   other times by appointment

Admission: Free

Activities: Guided tours

Suggested Time to View House: 45 minutes

Description of Grounds: Small yard with
   shrubs and trees surrounded by ornate
   wrought iron fence.

Best Season to View House: Spring and
   summer

Year House Built: 1860

Number of Rooms: 6

Style of Architecture: Greek Revival

On-Site Parking: No **Wheelchair Access:** No

Description of House

The Beard House was built by Noble Birge, a prominent local merchant, during the period when Jefferson was a thriving river port. It is named for its second owner, who lived here until 1895. In 1960, the house was acquired by the DeWare family, descendants of Jefferson pioneers; they have completed its restoration to the period just after the Civil War.

The one-story structure sits on a foundation made of hand-hewn cypress sills. Inside, the rooms feature pine flooring and fourteen foot ceilings; the library is an enclosed porch which once housed the brick well. The original kitchen sits on the property some way from the main house, but a new kitchen, made of brick and native cypress, has been added inside. The house shows some details typical to the Greek Revival: a traditional segmented transom and sidelights at the front door, a full-height entry porch, pilasters at the building's corners, and traditional shuttered windows. The bracketing under the roof line is quite unusual. The period furniture has been acquired for display by the DeWares.

Notable Collections on Exhibit

The library contains an extensive collection of leather bound volumes on the history of the Civil War which were published shortly after the end of that conflict.

Additional Information

The Beard House is listed on the National Register of Historic Places.

Historic Freeman Plantation

**Highway 49 West, P.O. Box 668
Jefferson, TX 75657
(903) 665-2320**

Contact: Historic Freeman Plantation
Open: Daily except Wed., guided tours at
3:00 p.m. and 3:30 p.m.; closed Easter,
Thanksgiving, Christmas
Admission: Adults $4.00; children $1.00;
group rates available
Activities: Guided tours
Suggested Time to View House: 45 minutes
Description of Grounds: Plantation with
carriage house situated in wooded area
with creek and pond
Best Season to View House: Spring and
summer
Year House Built: 1850
Number of Rooms: 8

Style of Architecture: Greek Revival
On-Site Parking: Yes **Wheelchair Access:** No

Description of House

Parts of East Texas, especially the area around Jefferson, are largely indistinguishable from Louisiana. Thus, the Freeman Plantation appears to be a typical Southern plantation in every way: the crops grown here were cotton and sugar cane, the Freemans were slaveholders, the house was built of cypress found in the nearby bayou, and the family suffered mightily during and after the Civil War. The Freemans came to Jefferson from Georgia by way of New Orleans and the Red River. They owned a small steamboat and hauled freight on the Big Cypress Bayou before establishing their thousand acre plantation in 1850. Devoutly religious, the Freemans were responsible for establishing the First Baptist Church of Jefferson. During the war, after three daughters died of disease, and his wife of worry and fatigue, Williamson Freeman retreated into his grief, stopped eating, and also died in January 1866. The next seventy years saw the decline of the plantation; it was in a terrible state of disrepair when purchased in 1937 by Longview oilman Lawrence Flannery. He and his wife completely restored the house, adding a wing and protective window bars. The house is presently owned by Mr. and Mrs. Jesse DeWare.

The Freeman house is a good example of the Louisiana raised-cottage style variant of the Greek Revival, with its brick main floor and wooden second floor. This construction enabled these houses to survive the seasonal flooding of the bayous. The materials used in building the house, including the brick, are all native to the plantation. The floor plan consists of a library, a dining area, and three children's bedrooms downstairs, where the ceilings were only seven feet high, and two parlors, the master bedroom, a smaller bedroom, a large hall, and the formal dining room upstairs under fourteen foot ceilings. The front facade features four large brick columns covered in stucco and white paint. All of the furnishings are authentic Empire and Victorian-style antiques but none actually belonged to the Freemans. The Historic Freeman Plantation is listed on the National Register of Historic Places.

"House of the Seasons"

409 South Alley Street, P.O. Box 686
Jefferson, TX 75657
(903) 665-1218

Contact: House of the Seasons

Open: Daily schedule posted; closed
  Thanksgiving and Christmas

Admission: Adults $5.00; students $4.00;
  children $2.00

Activities: Guided tours scheduled on a
  daily basis; annual Christmas tours

Suggested Time to View House:
  45–60 minutes

Facilities on Premises: Carriage house
  guest accommodations

Description of Grounds: Large landscaped
  yard with gazebo area, flower and herb
  gardens and some of the largest
  magnolia trees in the state

Style of Architecture: Transitional late
  Greek Revival with some Italianate-style
  characteristics

Best Season to View House: Spring and fall

Number of Rooms: 15

Year House Built: 1872

On-Site Parking: Yes **Wheelchair Access:** No

Description of House

At one time Jefferson was the largest and most prosperous inland port in Texas and this house, built in 1872 at the height of the town's preeminence, fully illustrates that fact. The builder, Benjamin H. Epperson, was a prominent lawyer, politician, entrepreneur, and confidant of Sam Houston.

This two-story house is a superb specimen of the Greek Revival style to which a few Italianate details have been added. The fenestration is nine-over-six on the first floor and the typical six-over-six on the second. The rear wing door shows a segmented transom and sidelights topped with a classical pediment, whereas the front door is of a double glazed design showing small sidelights and a unique curved transom with an oval glass inset. The full-width porch has simple supports and the two-story bay on the left of the house has window treatments which echo that of the facade. The whole effect is one of surpassing grace.

The House of the Seasons boasts two extraordinary features: a dome, the interior of which is covered in frescoes of allegorical female figures, visible from the first floor through a well-like opening in the second floor hallway; and a cupola surrounded by a widow's walk. This cupola features multi-colored glazing—red, green, and blue—which causes the light it throws to change as the daylight changes, thus creating some stunning effects on the interior walls. It is said that these two details taken together give the house its name.

Additional Information

The House of the Seasons is listed on the National Register of Historic Places.

Lyndon B. Johnson Birthplace

Johnson City Sites
south of the LBJ Ranch
Johnson City, TX 78636
(512) 868-7128

Contact: National Park Service and Lyndon
B. Johnson National Historical Park

Open: Daily 9 a.m.–5 p.m.

Admission: Free

Activities: Self-guided tours

Suggested Time to View House: 90 minutes

Facilities on Premises: Visitor center
bookshop

Description of Grounds: 200 acre state park
with a number of structures integral to the
history of the Johnson family

Best Season to View House: Spring and fall

Number of Yearly Visitors: 200,000

Year House Built: Original c.1880,
reconstructed 1964

Number of Rooms: 7

Style of Architecture: National, "dog-trot"
farmhouse

On-Site Parking: No **Wheelchair Access:** Yes

Description of House

This farmhouse is a 1964 replica of the original house built by Lyndon
Johnson's father, Sam Ealy Johnson, sometime between 1882 and 1890. Here,
in this modest structure among the rolling hills of central Texas on the
Pedernales River, the thirty-sixth President of the United States was born in
1908. Johnson, proud to be the first Texan ever to attain the highest office in
America, never forget his roots—the poverty, the rough-and-tumble politics,
and the boundless optimism—which this house represents so well.

The Johnson Birthplace is a typical National-style frame farmhouse of
the "dog-trot" variant. It features a cedar shingle roof on a frame structure
built on a stone foundation. The painted plank flooring, beaded wood
ceilings, and front-and-back porches are all typical. The house was built
from photographs and other documentary evidence, some of which seems
contradictory. The kitchen, for instance, which is now thought to have been
one large room, was originally reconstructed with a separate dining room.
Some of the building materials used for the reconstruction were salvaged
from the original house.

Notable Collections on Exhibit

The house is furnished with antiques from both sides of the Johnson
family. In addition, some of the President's personal items are on display.

Additional Information

Lyndon Johnson's Birthplace is only one of the sites which make up the
Lyndon Johnson National Historical Park.

Lyndon B. Johnson Boyhood Home

Johnson City Sites
south of the LBJ Ranch
Johnson City, TX 78636
(512) 868-7128

Contact: National Park Service and Lyndon
B. Johnson National Historical Park

Open: Daily 9 a.m.–5 p.m.

Admission: Free

Activities: Self-guided tours

Suggested Time to View House: 30 minutes

Facilities on Premises: Visitor center
bookshop

Description of Grounds: 200 acre state park
with a number of structures integral to the
history of the Johnson family

Style of Architecture: Folk Victorian
farmhouse

Best Season to View House: Spring and fall

Number of Yearly Visitors: 200,000

Number of Rooms: 7

Year House Built: 1900

On-Site Parking: Yes **Wheelchair Access:** Yes

Description of House

In 1913, when Lyndon Baines Johnson was only five years old, his family moved into this six-room farmhouse just a short distance from the house in which he was born. His father, Sam, was a Texas state legislator; his mother was the former Rebekah Baines. It was in this house that the future President began to form an idea of who he must make himself into; perhaps it was here, even before college and his brief teaching career, that the boy showed the first signs of that vaulting ambition which drove him to seek elected office and the applause of his fellows. The house has been fully restored to appear as it did in 1920.

The single-wall, wood framed house sits on a foundation of stone rubble, its lapped siding painted white. The cedar shake roof is painted grey-green and features white metal cresting at the ridge. The floor plan consists of a living room, dining room, and kitchen surrounding a large stone fireplace in the center of the house, and two wings extending to the east and west which hold the bedrooms and Sam Johnson's office. In addition, there are two sleeping porches off to the south. The house is surrounded by a decorative white fence. The interior construction of this home is similar to that of the reconstructed Lyndon Johnson Birthplace. Few of the furnishings actually belonged to the Johnsons; most are collected and are appropriate to the period of the 1920s.

Additional Information

This house, and the LBJ Birthplace, are two of the attractions in the Lyndon B. Johnson National Historical Park. The well-known LBJ Ranch also falls within the park's boundaries but remains closed to the public since Ladybird Johnson stills resides there. This entire site is listed on the National Register of Historic Places.

Captain Charles Schreiner Mansion

226 Earl Garrett Street
P.O. Box 107
Kerrville, TX 78029
(210) 896-8633

Contact: Hill Country Preservation Society, Inc.

Open: Mon.-Sat. 9 a.m.–5 p.m.; closed
Thanksgiving, Christmas, New Year's Day

Admission: Adult $3.00; seniors $2.50;
students $1.50

Activities: Guided tours, occasional special
exhibits

Suggested Time to View House:
30–60 minutes

Facilities on Premises: Gift shop with books

Description of Grounds: Rear courtyard
with formal rose garden

Best Season to View House: Spring and
summer

Number of Yearly Visitors: 15,000

Year House Built: 1874, remodeled 1879
and 1897

Number of Rooms: 15

Style of Architecture: Early Richardsonian
Romanesque

On-Site Parking: Yes **Wheelchair Access:** No

Description of House

Captain Charles Schreiner, a native of Alsace who emigrated to Texas in 1852 at the age of fourteen, served as one of the Texas Rangers during the Civil War years, then made his fortune in cattle. At one time he owned some 600,000 acres of ranch land and organized the Southwestern Cattleman's Association, and the Texas Sheep and Goat Raisers Association. He founded Schreiner College and served as its treasurer for thirty years.

Captain Schreiner hired San Antonio architect Alfred Giles to build a house which would recall those turreted castles which he had seen or imagined during his childhood in Europe. This three-story fantasy in stone features multiple turrets and gables with parapets, limestone arches hand-carved by German artisans, an imported iron grill-work fence, oversized windows and doors, and two long front verandas. The rooms are voluminous. Interior details include three original fireplaces, an elaborate curved walnut staircase, fourteen foot ceilings on the first floor and twelve foot ceilings upstairs, and the original parquet flooring. It is a bit of a shock to come upon this "castle" in the midst of the Texas hill country, particularly since the whole is somewhat less than sum of its parts. The furnishings are mostly done in the French style of the turn of the century, but few of them are original to the house. The Captain Charles Schreiner Mansion is listed on the National Register of Historic Places.

Notable Collections on Exhibit

The Schreiner Mansion contains an impressive collection of Civil War memorabilia, as well as vintage clothing and antique quilts and coverlets. Look for Kerrville's first telephone switchboards on display here.

Kreische Homestead and Brewery

Highway 77 South to Spur 92
P.O. Box 699
La Grange, TX 78945
(409) 968-5858

Contact: Monument Hill and Kreische
Brewery State Historical Park

Open: Park, daily, 8 a.m.–5 p.m.; Kreische
House, Sun. afternoons; other times by
reservation

Admission: Adults $2.00; students $1.00;
seniors and children (under 5) free

Activities: Guided tours, special seasonal
programs, Pioneer Camp for youngsters

Suggested Time to View House: 1 hour

Description of Grounds: 5 manicured acres
with historic marker commemorating the
fallen heroes of the 1842 Battle of Salado
Creek and the ill-fated 1843 Mier
Expedition. The Kreische House, and
Brewery ruins are sited on 15 scenic acres.

Best Season to View House: Year round

Facilities on Premises: Visitor center and
museum, interpretative nature trail

Number of Yearly Visitors: 70,000

Number of Rooms: 12

Style of Architecture: Folk, German
"fachwerk" style, board-and-batten

Year House Built: Between 1855 and 1857

On-Site Parking: Yes **Wheelchair Access:** Yes

Description of House

In 1846, the stonemason Heinrich L. Kreische emigrated from Saxony to Texas, where he settled on a bluff overlooking the Colorado River just south of the town of La Grange. He chose this site because it was a natural limestone quarry. By 1870, he had switched from stonemasonry to brewing—the brewery, which was one of the first commercial breweries in the state, was built just down the hill from the house. Kreische's beer was sold at a beer garden built on the bluff and in a beer hall down in La Grange. After his death in 1882, the business faltered and the brewery fell into ruin, despite the fact that his descendants continued to live here until 1952.

This large two-story house stands about a hundred feet back from the bluff; it is built mainly of sandstone, with "fachwerk" (framework) and board-and-batten elements. The exterior features very little ornament, but does have an almost Spanish Colonial-style full-length veranda. The windows are nine-over-six; the exposed rubble front facade is rather formal, while the rear is plastered and all three floors are visible there. The house has been restored to the period of the 1860s and 1870s. Inside, the whitewashed walls are highlighted with black trim and wainscotting, and here one may see the vents which were used to heat and cool the house. Some of the furniture on display belonged to the Kreisches; these pieces are mainly in the Texas "primitive" style. The Kreische Homestead and Brewery are listed on the National Register of Historic Places.

"Maplecroft"—
Starr Family State Historical Park

407 West Travis Street
Marshall, TX 75670
(903) 935-3044

Contact: Texas Parks and Wildlife Department

Open: Fri., Sat., Mon. 9 a.m.–5 p.m., Sun. 1–5 p.m.; group tours available seven days a week; closed Christmas, New Year's Day

Admission: Adults $2.00; children (6-12) $1.00

Activities: Guided tour, introductory slide show, annual "Festival of Lights"

Suggested Time to View House: 45 minutes

Description of Grounds: 4 acre flower and vegetable gardens and orchard in a park setting

Best Season to View House: Spring

Number of Yearly Visitors: 12,000

Year House Built: 1871, addition 1875, remodeled c.1930

Style of Architecture: Original-Italianate, remodel-Eclectic Colonial Revival

Number of Rooms: 13

On-Site Parking: Yes **Wheelchair Access:** No

Description of House

"Maplecroft" was built by Frank Starr in 1871 on the southwest quadrant of his father's recently acquired property in Marshall. Frank's father was Dr. James Harper Starr, who, with his brother Capt. Franklin J. Starr, settled in Nagadoches in the 1830s and became actively involved in the affairs of the young republic. Frank and his brother, Amory Reilly, both served in the Confederate Army during the Civil War. After the war, he attended the University of Virginia and, upon his return to Texas, joined his father in the land business. By 1873, he was managing a significant portion of the family investments. At the time Marshall was one of the larger cities in Texas, well served by the telegraph and railroads, thus making it a magnet for businessmen. The Starrs moved here in 1870.

The Starr house was designed by Frank with the assistance of his father-in-law, George L. Clapp, a builder from Jefferson named Witkorn, the New Orleans architect Charles Lewis Hillger, and, finally, one Mr. Miller, an eccentric draftsman who actually drew the final plans. The wonder is that the design of the house is as unified as it is! Before the 1875 remodeling, which added an east wing for the residence of Frank's mother-in-law, the house consisted of eight rooms, four up and four down, and a separate kitchen and servants' room connected to the main structure by a covered breezeway. The house, which took six months to build, is framed and sided in native pine and oak; the foundation and fireplaces are made of locally fired brick. Virtually all of the other materials used, from the cypress in the sashes and doors to the hardware and carpeting, were shipped here from New Orleans. A feature of particular note is the "deafening"—a mixture of lime, sand, and straw—used as insulation ad soundproofing between floors. In the 1930s, Ruth Starr Blake remodeled the house to reflect the Colonial Revival style. "Maplecroft" is listed on the National Register of Historic Places.

Notable Collections on Exhibit

The furnishings, which include both Victorian and Renaissance Revival-style pieces, are original to the house.

Sterne-Hoya House

211 South Lanana Street
Nacogdoches, TX 75961
(409) 560-5426

Contact: Sterne-Hoya House Library and Museum

Open: Mon.-Sat. 9 a.m.–Noon and 2–5 p.m.; closed major holidays

Admission: Free

Activities: Guided group tours

Suggested Time to View House: 45 minutes

Facilities on Premises: Library

Description of Grounds: Small rose garden in the front of the house

Best Season to View House: Spring and summer

Number of Yearly Visitors: 8,000

Year House Built: c.1830

Style of Architecture: Greek Revival

Number of Rooms: 8

On-Site Parking: Yes **Wheelchair Access:** Yes

Description of House

The Sterne-Hoya House is the oldest residence in Nagadoches and the oldest structure of any sort to predate the Texas Revolution still standing in this town. It was built in the late 1820s by Nicholas Adolphus Sterne, a German immigrant who settled here in 1826 after a brief stay in New Orleans. He worked on behalf of the Republic of Texas and later served as State Representative and Senator. It is said that Davey Crockett spent a fortnight here in 1836. It was also the site of the signing of the Cherokee peace treaty, whereby Chief Bowles promised that his nation would not fight on the side of Mexico during the revolution. In 1869, Sterne's widow sold the the house to Joseph von der Hoya, another German immigrant who had made his success in farming and land speculation. It was given to the city of Nagadoches in 1958 by von der Hoya's granddaughters.

The Sterne-Hoya House is a fine early example of the Greek Revival style which was to become so popular in this part of Texas during the middle part of the 19th century. It features the symmetrical facade with columns and pilasters, central hall, and painted white exterior characteristic of that style. One of the parlors has been restored to the period of the Sternes' occupancy and another features the Victorian decorations of the Hoyas' years.

Notable Collections on Exhibit

Among the items on display, there are a pair of earrings and brooch given by Sam Houston to one of Sterne's daughters and a signed C. F. Albrecht pianoforte dated 1825.

Additional Information

The Sterne-Hoya House is listed on the National Register of Historic Places. Nagadoches is also home to Millard's Crossing, a complex of several homes and commercial buildings which reflect a typical 19th-century small town in East Texas. All of the structures—including the Millard-Lee House (1837), the Millard-Burrows House (1840), the Watkins Homestead (1895), and the Methodist Parsonage (1900)—have been meticulously restored and most are furnished with period antiques.

Carl Baetge House

1300 Church Hill Drive
New Braunfels, TX 78130
(210) 625-8766

Contact: New Braunfels Conservation Society

Open: Tues.-Fri. 10 a.m.–3 p.m., Sat. and Sun. 2–5 p.m.; closed Thanksgiving, Christmas, New Year's Day

Admission: Adults $2.00; children (6-18) $.50

Activities: Guided tours, special annual events including the May Folkfest and Holiday Candlelight Tour

Suggested Time to View House: 45–60 minutes

Facilities on Premises: Gift counter

Best Season to View House: Year round

Description of Grounds: 3½ acre village site with eight outbuildings and antique rose conservatory

Number of Yearly Visitors: 3,800

Number of Rooms: 9

Style of Architecture: Folk, German "fachwerk" with some Georgian-style modifications

Year House Built: 1852

On-Site Parking: Yes **Wheelchair Access:** Yes

Description of House

Carl Baetge, a German civil engineer who counted the building of the Moscow-St. Petersburg railroad line as one of his professional accomplishments and had married one of the Russian Czarina's ladies-in-waiting, emigrated to Texas in 1850. Here Baetge and his fellow German immigrants settled in the hilly central part of the state near San Antonio, and founded the town of New Braunfels.

The house that Baetge built in 1852 is a two-story "fachwerk" structure consisting of six rooms on the first floor and three rooms upstairs. These upstairs rooms, originally used as bedrooms, were left unfinished during the restoration—this allows the visitor to examine the structural materials which constitute this German-style "framework" residential architecture. The interior also features two center fireplaces downstairs—a rarity in a house of this type. The exterior of the house remains largely unadorned; it has a small second-floor balcony but no porch. The roof line is flat and the windows are of the nine-over-six sash type. The furnishings on display include both locally hand-crafted and imported German Biedermeier pieces, just a few of which belonged to the Baetge family.

Notable Collections on Exhibit

Copies of Carl Baetge's drawings of his Russian engineering projects are on display.

White-Pool House

112 East Murphy
Odessa, TX 79761
(915) 333-4072

Contact: Ector County Historical
Commission

Open: Tues.-Sat. 10 a.m.–5 p.m.,
Sun. 2–5 p.m.; groups of twelve
or more call for appointment

Admission: Free

Activities: Guided tours

Suggested Time to View House:
60–90 minutes

Description of Grounds: Grounds are not
accessible to the public

Best Season to View House: Spring and fall

Number of Yearly Visitors: 2,000

Year House Built: 1887

Number of Rooms: 7

Style of Architecture: Folk Victorian, red brick
On-Site Parking: Yes **Wheelchair Access:** Yes

Description of House

The history of the White-Pool House mirrors the development of Odessa and surrounding Ector County, from its beginnings as an agricultural community to the boom days after oil was discovered here. Having lost almost everything during the Civil War, the Quaker couple Charles and Lucy White came to Odessa with their two sons. Charles was a prime mover behind the organized agriculture of Ector County and opened a general store; his wife was active in the Sunday school which preceded the building of the first church in Odessa. Their sons left by the turn of the century, Charles died in 1905, and Mary moved to Mineral Wells. The house underwent a number of changes in ownership until Oso Pool arrived in Odessa looking for work and bought the house. After oil was found, workers descended upon the town, and Pool converted the house into a five unit apartment building.

This two-story red brick structure is the oldest building in Ector County. The exterior features two porches, one at the front and the other around the south side of the rear. Inside, the construction is of plaster over wooden lattice boards; there are hardwood floors, beaded ceilings, and molded woodwork. The floor plan consists of four high-ceilinged rooms downstairs and three bedrooms and a hallway upstairs. These rooms are decorated to reflect the two periods when the families for whom the house is named lived here—the late Victorian and the 1920s.

Notable Collections on Exhibit

Among the items on display is a silver fruit platter—a White family heirloom dated 1822—and fifteen pieces of Wedgwood china that was carried by the Whites to Odessa in 1887.

Additional Information

The White-Pool House is listed on the National Register of Historic Places.

W. H. Stark House

610 West Main Street
Orange, TX 77630
(409) 883-0871

Contact: Nelda C. and H.J. Lutcher Stark
Foundation
Open: Tues.-Sat. 10 a.m.–3 p.m.
Admission: $2.00 per person
Activities: Guided tours reservations
requested
Suggested Time to View House: 45 minutes
Best Season to View House: Fall-spring

Description of Grounds: Complex
consisting of museum, theater, church
and park located in downtown Orange
Number of Yearly Visitors: 3,500
Year House Built: 1894
Style of Architecture: Victorian Queen
Anne-Eastlake
Number of Rooms: 15
On-Site Parking: Yes **Wheelchair Access:** No

Description of House

After the Civil War, the young William Henry Stark was delivering mail
between the East Texas towns of Orange and Burkesville when he decided
that Orange was a place of opportunity and aimed to settle in the town,
getting himself started in the lumber industry by taking a position with the
firm of J. B. Russell & Son, sawmill operators. In 1881, he married Miriam
Lutcher, a native Pennsylvanian who had come to Texas in the 1870s with
her family. Stark's youthful optimism was justified, for he rose in
prominence to become one of the most influential citizens of Texas, having
added to his lumber fortune with investments in oil, rice, insurance, and
banking. In 1894, the wealthy and distinguished Stark built this impressive
home out of yellow pine milled by a lumber company—The Lutcher &
Moore Lumber Company—in which he was a partner.

The W. H. Stark House is done primarily in the Queen Anne-Eastlake
style; its three story exterior exhibits such characteristic features as curved
and carved brackets, bay windows, gables, fish-scale shingles, and a
hexagonal turret. The asymmetrical floor plan is highlighted by variegated
exterior finishes—horizontal bands of different siding materials and styles.
The entryway features a stained glass key-hole window and longleaf yellow
pine inset panels. The house is filled with original furnishings and many
personal items and artifacts which belonged to the Starks.

Additional Information

The W. H. Stark House was designated a Recorded Texas Historic
Landmark in 1976 and entered on the National Register of Historic Places
that same year.

Sam Bell Maxey House State Historical Park

812 South Church Street
Paris, TX 75460
(903) 785-5716

Contact: Texas Parks and Wildlife Department

Open: Wed.-Sun. 10 a.m.–12:00 p.m., 1–4:30 p.m.; closed Christmas and New Year's Day

Admission: Adults $2.00; children $1.00

Activities: Daily guided tours, annual Holiday Open House

Suggested Time to View House: 30–45 minutes

Description of Grounds: 2½ acres of public park land with two outbuildings

Best Season to View House: Spring , summer, and winter holidays

Number of Yearly Visitors: 27,000

Year House Built: 1867, remodeled 1911

Number of Rooms: 11

Style of Architecture: Italianate

On-Site Parking: Yes **Wheelchair Access:** Yes

Description of House

Samuel Bell Maxey was a graduate of West Point—he'd been a classmate of Ulysses S. Grant there—who served as a General in the Confederate Army, got pardoned after the war, and returned to Paris to practice law and involve himself in politics. He and his wife moved into this house in 1868. Maxey was elected to the United States Senate in 1874 for the first of two terms. In that same year, his only child, Dora, married Henry Lightfoot; they would have two children, Sallie Lee and Thomas Chenoworth. After Samuel Bell Maxey died in 1895, and his wife in 1908, possession of the house fell to Sam Bell Maxey Long, Long's wife, and cousin Sallie Lee Lightfoot. When Sallie Lee died in 1966, the house was given to the Lamar County Historical Society. It is now operated by the Texas Parks and Wildlife Department.

The main part of the Maxey House is a superb example of the Italianate style of architecture. The two-story plan is square, with each floor consisting of four rooms divided by a central hall. The east facade of the house is particularly noteworthy: it features a two-story portico with elaborate Corinthian capitals topping its twelve columns, decorative hoods and curved brackets over the first floor windows, and large carved brackets under the eaves; these details all subservient to a symmetrical, well-proportioned whole. The house is painted white with black shutters. The rear wing, a later addition, was intended as a service wing and does not reflect the high style of the original structure. In 1911, the Longs did some remodeling, adding bathrooms, a second floor over the rear wing, maple and oak flooring, and they converted the south porch into a breakfast room. The furnishings on display were collected over the years by the Maxey, Lightfoot, and Long families. The Sam Bell Maxey House is listed on the National Register of Historic Places.

Farrell-Wilson Farmstead

**1900 West Fifteenth Street
Plano, TX 75075
(214) 424-7874**

Contact: Heritage Farmstead Association
Open: June 1-Aug. 31, Tues.-Sat.
  10 a.m.–1 p.m., Sun. 1–4 p.m.;
  Sept. 1-May 30, Thur. and Fri.
  10 a.m.–4 p.m., Sat. 10 a.m.–1 p.m.,
  Sun. 1–4 p.m.
Admission: Adults $3.00; seniors and
  children $2.00
Activities: Guided tour, audiovisual
  presentations, seasonal events
Suggested Time to View House: 75 minutes
Facilities on Premises: Country store
  gift shop
Description of Grounds: Four acre site
  with twelve original farm outbuildings
  including foreman's cottage, root
  cellars, vegetable gardens and orchards
Style of Architecture: Folk Victorian
  farmhouse with eclectic mix of
  Carpenter Gothic and Shingle Style
Best Season to View House: Spring and fall
Number of Rooms: 14

Year House Built: 1891, remodeled 1900
On-Site Parking: Yes **Wheelchair Access:** Yes

Description of House

The Farrell-Wilson Homestead is a highly regarded interpretation of a typical Northeast Texas family farm at the turn of the century. The original owners of the farm were Hunter F. Farrell, a native Virginian who had come to Texas and worked at a number of jobs before marrying, and his wife, Mary Alice Lanham, who was born in Weston, Texas. Their farm was quite successful and Hunter began to get involved in outside businesses which took him away from home for long periods of time. Finally the couple divorced and Mary Alice got possession of the farm. Her daughter by a previous marriage, Ammie Estelle, whose fine education included finishing school in Nashville, Tennessee, married Dr. Woods Lynch in 1901. Their son and his wife lived here until 1933; Ammie Wilson was a nationally known breeder of registered Hampshire sheep.

The shingled farmhouse is an excellent example of the late Victorian style and features its original exterior colors of green and mauve. Other exterior features include some Carpenter's Gothic details, an elaborate wrap-around porch which may have been added in the early 1900s, and jig-saw trim over the windows and doors. Though the exterior trim was probably cut on site, the interior trim may have been ordered out of the 1895 edition of the Montgomery Ward catalog. Inside, the house consists of fourteen rooms, all of which have been painted and wallpapered more than once over the years. The furnishings are mostly collected, but all are authentic to the period 1890-1925 and reflect the rather typical lives of the occupants. The Farrell-Wilson Homestead is listed on the National Register of Historic Places.

Stinson Home

518 South Main Street
Route 3 on Park Road 45
Quitman, TX 75783
(214) 763-2701

Contact: Governor Hogg Shrine State Historical Park

Open: Year-round, Fri. 1–5 p.m., Sat. 8 a.m.–5 p.m., Sun. 1–5 p.m.; closed Christmas, New Year's Day

Admission: Adult $2.00; children (6-12) $1.00; school sponsored event all $.50 each

Activities: Guided tours, audiovisual program, Summer Youth Volunteer Program, on-site programs for the disabled

Suggested Time to View House: 45–75 minutes

Style of Architecture: National, frame with elements of late Colonial and Greek Revival styles

Best Season to View House: Year round

Facilities on Premises: Visitor center, picnic area, nature trails

Number of Yearly Visitors: 3,000

Number of Rooms: 9

Description of Grounds: Park area with more than four hundred old oak trees

Year House Built: 1869

On-Site Parking: Yes **Wheelchair Access:** Yes

Description of House

James Stephen Hogg was the first native-born Texan to become Governor of his state. His father was Colonel James A. Stinson. Colonel Stinson, a part-time Methodist minister born of Irish parents, was one of the first settlers in Texas to apply scientific techniques to agriculture and be successful at it. He also got a post office established in Spear and served in the Texas State Legislature. Although the timber in the Stinson house is almost entirely original, the house itself has been moved some thirteen miles from its original site. It is a two-and-a-half-story structure with a full-width front porch, a veranda and porch in the rear, and a U-shaped "dogtrot" which runs from the main house to the kitchen and dining areas. The original construction was done with hardly any nails; wooden pegs and joints were used instead. The front elevation features an asymmetrically placed gable and a main entrance door with a segmented transom and sidelights. There is a second, smaller entrance at the wing. Other exterior details include a one-story bay extension with long, narrow windows and three gabled dormers featuring small six-over-six sash windows. The rooms are filled with Victorian-style furniture of the late 19th and early 20th centuries, as befits the period when the house was occupied.

Notable Collections on Exhibit

Among the items on display are some Currier & Ives prints and English ironstone china in the Anthony Shaw pattern.

A. P. George Ranch Home

10215 FM 762
twenty miles southwest of Houston
Richmond, TX 77469
(713) 545-9212

Contact: George Ranch Historical Park
Open: Call for seasonal schedules
Admission: Adults $5.00; children (5-12) $2.00; children (under 5) free
Activities: Guided tours, special seasonal events
Suggested Time to View House: 30–45 minutes
Facilities on Premises: Gift shop
Best Season to View House: Spring-winter

Description of Grounds: 474 acre living history complex including the A. P. George Ranch Home, the J. H. P. Davis Mansion and several outbuildings such as a blacksmith shop and a smokehouse.
Number of Yearly Visitors: 11,000
Year House Built: 1900 remodeled 1911
Style of Architecture: Folk Victorian, frame
Number of Rooms: 10
On-Site Parking: Yes **Wheelchair Access:** Yes

Description of House

Albert Peyton George went to work for J. H. P. "Judge" Davis in 1892 and married the Judge's daughter, Mamie, four years later. They had one child who died in infancy. George's chief interest was in raising cattle; he'd gone and spent some time studying the breeding methods used on the famous King Ranch, bought his first herd of Brahmans in 1897, and later raised Shorthorns. By 1937, he had developed his own breed of cattle, which was called "Brahorn." By that time, oil had been discovered on the ranch and George was a wealthy man.

In 1900, the already successful cattleman A. P. George hired Galveston architect Nicholas Clayton to design a ranch house which would be built on the site where his wife's grandparents' log cabin had burned down. The Victorian "cottage" which Clayton designed was a one-and-a-half-story frame structure which underwent major remodeling in 1911. At that time, the house was expanded to a full second floor. It has now been restored to the period of the 1930s and 1940s, when the Georges were at their most successful. Many of the furnishings on display belonged to the family.

Additional Information

In addition to the house, the George Ranch Historical Park also includes several restored outbuildings and an oak tree planted in 1824 by Susan Davis's maternal grandmother, Nancy Jones.

J. H. P. Davis Mansion

10215 FM 762
twenty miles southwest of Houston
Richmond, TX 77469
(713) 545-9212

Contact: George Ranch Historical Park
Open: Call for seasonal schedules
Admission: Adults $5.00; children (5-12) $2.00; children (under 5) free
Activities: Guided tours, special seasonal events
Suggested Time to View House: 30–45 minutes
Facilities on Premises: Gift shop
Best Season to View House: Spring-winter

Description of Grounds: 474 acre living history complex including the A. P. George Ranch Home, the J. H. P. Davis Mansion and several outbuildings such as a blacksmith shop and a smokehouse
Number of Yearly Visitors: 11,000
Year House Built: c. 1880
Style of Architecture: Victorian Queen Anne
Number of Rooms: 9 plus servants quarters
On-Site Parking: Yes **Wheelchair Access:** Yes

Description of House

J. H. P. "Judge" Davis was one of the wealthiest and most influential men in Fort Bend County in the late 19th and early 20th centuries. He was married to Susan E. Ryon, whose mother had created the Ryon Farm and Pasture Company out of ranch lands settled by her parents in 1824 during the "colonization" of the territory. It was by managing this ranch, then taking the wealth so derived and going into banking, that the Judge attained his preeminent status. Unfortunately, in the early 1920s his banks failed and it shook the family's finances. The Judge died in 1927.

The house was built shortly after Judge Davis married Susan Ryon in 1875. It has been moved from its original site in Richmond to the George Ranch—A. P. George was the Davises' son-in-law—and restored to the period when Mamie Davis George was growing up here. This well-proportioned house is a two-story Queen Anne-style structure featuring an asymmetrical design with large covered porches and balconies that wrap halfway around the house. Inside, the high-ceilinged rooms allow for maximum ventilation during the hot summer months. The furnishings reflect the Victorian period; some of the pieces belonged to the Davis family, the rest have been purchased.

Notable Collections on Exhibit

In addition to the period Eastlake-style furniture and family portraits on display, there is a substantial collection of Victorian decorative arts found in 1880s Texas.

Lewis-Wagner Farmstead and House

FM 1457 off FM 2714
Round Top, TX 78954
(409) 278-3530

Contact: University of Texas at
Austin-Winedale Historical Center

Open: Sat. 9 a.m.–5 p.m., Sun.
Noon–5 p.m.; Mon.-Fri.by appointment

Admission: Adults $2.00; students $.50

Activities: Guided tours

Suggested Time to View House: 90 minutes

Facilities on Premises: Picnic area and
nature trail

Description of Grounds: Site of several
restored historic buildings including the
Lewis-Wagner House, the McGregor-
Grimm House, the Lauderdale House and
Hazel's Lone Oak Cottage

Style of Architecture: Folk, German "dog
trot" farmhouse

Best Season to View House: Spring

Number of Yearly Visitors: 10,000

Number of Rooms: 9

Year House Built: 1834, addition 1850

On-Site Parking: Yes **Wheelchair Access:** Yes

Description of House

Many early Texas residences were architectural hybrids because of the divergent influences brought to bear on their construction—many settlers had to make do with found materials and expedient plans, while honoring their immigrant backgrounds. The Lewis-Wagner Farmhouse is just such a structure. In 1831, the Mexican Government granted the land on which the house was built to one William Townsend from Austin. He built the oldest part of the house in 1834. Then Samuel Lewis, a South Carolinian, expanded the holdings into a thousand acre cotton and livestock plantation and also expanded the house to its present size. During the 1850s, when the the main road from Brenham to La Grange ran by the farm, the house became a stagecoach stopping place. Fifteen years after Lewis died in 1869, the house was bought by Joseph George Wagner, a German immigrant who had come to Round Top in the 1850s.

The house is a simple two-story affair with eight rooms, two rooms on either side of a central passage on both the first and second floors. The front rooms are larger than those at the rear and feature fireplaces. Though the design is plain, the craftsmanship evident in some of the details is of a very high order. The timbers, for instance, are joined in an almost medieval fashion, with mortises, tenons, notches, and pegs. The window and door frames are also skillfully cut and fitted. All of the cedar used in the frame, the siding, the floors, and for the shingles was cut on the farm. The furnishings, some of which belonged to the occupants, are all appropriate to the period of the mid-19th century.

Notable Collections on Exhibit

The fine painted ceilings were done by the German artist, Rudolph Melchior.

McGregor-Grimm House

FM 1457 off FM 2714, P.O. Box 11
Round Top, TX 78954
(409) 278-3530

Contact: University of Texas at
Austin-Winedale Historical Center

Open: Sat. 9 a.m.–5 p.m., Sun.
Noon–5 p.m.; Mon.-Fri. by appointment

Admission: Adults $2.00; students $.50

Activities: Guided tours

Suggested Time to View House: 90 minutes

Facilities on Premises: Picnic area and
nature trail

Description of Grounds: Site of several
restored historic buildings including the
Lewis-Wagner House, the McGregor-
Grimm House, the Lauderdale House
and Hazel's Lone Oak Cottage and other
farm outbuildings.

Style of Architecture: Greek Revival-style
farmhouse

Best Season to View House: Spring

Number of Yearly Visitors: 10,000

Number of Rooms: 7

Year House Built: 1861

On-Site Parking: Yes **Wheelchair Access:** No

Description of House

When one thinks of Texas wealth, one inevitably connects it to oil or perhaps cattle; but the area around Round Top, halfway between Houston and Austin near the Colorado River, saw a cotton boom in the 1850s and it created some good-sized fortunes for some growers. This luxurious house was built in 1861 by Dr. Gregor McGregor, a Washington County cotton planter and land speculator, for his beloved wife, Anna Portia Fordtran. Though it now stands reconstructed at the Winedale Historical Center, it was originally built in Wesley, some fifteen miles to the east.

The house is in the Greek Revival style which epitomized elegance and luxury for the wealthy landowners of the 1840s and 1850s in Texas. It has the full-height entry porch and wide-trimmed gable characteristic of the style. Inside, a number of the rooms feature wonderful decorative wall paintings done by Rudolph Melchior, a German artist responsible for decorating a few homes in the area.

José Antonio Navarro House

**228 South Laredo Street
San Antonio, TX 78207
(210) 226-4801**

Contact: José Antonio Navarro State
Historical Park

Open: Tues. and Wed. 1–4 p.m., Fri.
and Sat. 10 a.m.–4 p.m.

Admission: Adults $2.00;
children (6-12) $1.00

Activities: Guided tours

Suggested Time to View House:
30–45 minutes

Description of Grounds: Three historic
19th-century houses located on a
⁶⁄₁₀ acre lot in downtown San Antonio

Style of Architecture: Territoral Adobe
with later German-Alsatian influences

Best Season to View House: Spring and fall

Number of Yearly Visitors: 4,000

Number of Rooms: 5

Year House Built: c.1850, refaced 1856

On-Site Parking: No **Wheelchair Access:** Yes

Description of House

José Antonio Navarro (1795-1871), a successful Mexican-American rancher, is famous for having been a signer of the Texas Declaration of Independence. In so doing, he declared his own intention to stay and live with his fellow Mexican-Americans in San Antonio. He and his wife, Margarita, built this home around 1850; it is one of only two adobe structures in city of San Antonio known to have survived from that period.

The house that Navarro originally built was a simple two-room adobe structure; subsequently, three rooms built of limestone were added and the house was plastered inside and out with lime and whitewashed. Three of the rooms have fireplaces and the floors and thirteen foot ceilings are made of wood. Also of wood are the shingles which make up the roof. No original Navarro family items have been discovered, but all the furnishings are antiques which match the interpretation to the period of 1856 to 1871. Pieces include a square grand piano, two day beds, a simple desk, and a bedroom set. Everything has been restored to the modest scale called for in Navarro's own descriptive writings.

Additional Information

The José Antonio Navarro House is listed on the National Register of Historic Places.

Spanish Governor's Palace

105 Plaza De Armas
San Antonio, TX 78265
(210) 224-0601

Contact: City of San Antonio Department of
  Parks and Recreation
Open: Mon.-Sat. 9 a.m.–5 p.m., Sun.
  10 a.m.–5 p.m.; closed Christmas Eve and
  Day, New Year's Eve and Day, last two
  weeks of April-Fiesta Jacinta
Admission: Adults $1.00;
  children (7-13) $.50
Activities: Self-guided tour
Best Season to View House: Spring and fall

Suggested Time to View House:
  20–30 minutes
Facilities on Premises: Gift shop
Description of Grounds: Courtyard with
  native plants
Number of Yearly Visitors: 45,000
Year House Built: 1749
Style of Architecture: Spanish Colonial
Number of Rooms: 10
On-Site Parking: No **Wheelchair Access:** Yes

Description of House

The Spanish Governor's Palace, built in 1749 as the Commandancia (Commander's Residence) of the Presidio de San Antonio de Bajar by Fernando Perez de Alamazon, is the only Spanish Colonial Mansion left in Texas. The Presidio was built to protect the Mission San Antonio de Valero and its surrounding colony. The Mission, which has come to be known as the Alamo—Spanish for "cottonwood"—still stands a few blocks away. The settlement was founded in 1718 by missionaries who had come to convert the Indians of the Papaya tribe under direct orders of Spain's King Philip V. In 1772, when San Antonio was declared the capital of the Spanish Province of Texas, the Commandancia became the Governor's Palace. In 1804, the Palace was bought by José Ignacio Perez of Spain for 800 pesos. After 1822, the building ceased being a residence; instead, it served as a second-hand clothing store, a tailor's shop, a bar, a restaurant, and a schoolhouse! Finally, it was purchased by the city of San Antonio in 1928 which restored it the following year at a cost of over $29,000.

The restored Spanish Governor's Palace is authentic to the last detail; it features three-foot-thick rock walls painted white, a floor of native flagstone, hand-carved walnut doors, and brick ovens. A keystone above the door bearing a modified Hapsburg coat-of-arms is inscribed with the words, "año 1749-se acabó," proclaiming the date of the Palace's completion. The floor plan is an enclosed square featuring the terrace and courtyard typical to the Spanish Colonial style. Rooms include a front entry hall, two bedrooms, living and dining rooms, a ballroom, the chapel, the office of the governor, and a kitchen with its own terrace. The furnishings are all 16th and 17th century colonial pieces appropriate to the period when the Palace was built. The Spanish Governor's Palace is listed on the National Register of Historic Places.

Notable Collections on Exhibit

The collection of Spanish Colonial antiques is extensive; some noteworthy items include handmade samplers, two portraits of King Philip V and his wife, 16th-century brass stirrups, and a 300-year-old hand-carved brazier.

Steves Homestead

509 King William Street
San Antonio, TX 78204
(210) 225-5924

Contact: San Antonio Conservation Society

Open: Daily 10 a.m.–4:15 p.m.

Admission: Adults $2.00;
children (under 12) free

Activities: Docent guided tours

Suggested Time to View House: 35 minutes

Facilities on Premises: Visitor center and
gift shop

Description of Grounds: 1½ acres with
laurel and herb gardens, and with native
trees as pecan, palm and black walnut.
A carriage house with an antique
carriage display, and a laundry building
are also located on the property which is
enclosed by a pegged fence.

Best Season to View House: Year round

Number of Yearly Visitors: 28,000

Year House Built: 1876

Style of Architecture: Eclectic mix of
Italiante and Second Empire

Number of Rooms: 11

On-Site Parking: Yes

Wheelchair Access: Yes

Description of House

The King William Historic District in San Antonio may have one of the finest concentrations of worthy historical homes in Texas—a visitor should plan at least half a day to wander the streets here—and, of these, the Steves Homestead ranks at the very head. Edward Steves emigrated to Texas in 1848, made his fortune in lumber, and built this house in 1876. His wife, who outlived him by some forty years, died here in 1930. The Steves Homestead was donated to the San Antonio Conservation Society in 1952 by Edna Steves Vaughn, granddaughter of the original owners.

The mostly Second Empire-style mansion is said to have been designed by the prominent architect Alfred Giles. It is built of ashlar limestone and features a slate-covered mansard roof with splendid wrought iron cresting. The two-story floor plan has two rooms on either side of a center hall stairway and an ell in the rear. Most of the elaborate trim and architectural detailing on both the exterior and inside the house was copied from pattern books, or, like the pocket doors in the parlor, ordered from these catalogs. The decorative artwork and stenciling on the walls and ceilings was done around 1912 by an unknown artist. There are four bedrooms; each of them features the rare luxury of built-in closets and wash basins. The Steves house was the first in San Antonio to have electricity installed and was converted early to a steam heating system. In 1910 Mrs. Steves built a natatorium (a River Haus for swimming) on the property; it has since been converted into meeting rooms for the Conservation Society. The house has been restored to the period of 1876 to 1930.

Most of the furniture is in the styles of the late Victorian era, primarily Renaissance and Rococo Revival; most of the pieces were purchased from mail-order catalogs or acquired on European trips.

Notable Collections on Exhibit

Among the furnishings is a rare Chickering piano and a superb inlaid mosaic table. The bronze fountain in the garden was bought by Steves while he was attending the Centennial Exposition in Philadelphia.

Additional Information

Native San Antonians are justifiably proud of the King William District, named after Prussia's King Wilhelm I, and the fact that it was the first historic district in the United States to be listed on the National Register of Historic Places. The Steves Homestead is also listed on the National Register of Historic Places.

Yturri-Edmunds Historic Site

257 Yellowstone at Mission Trail
San Antonio, TX 78204
(210) 224-6163

Contact: San Antonio Conservation Society

Open: Year-round, Mon.-Sat.
10 a.m.–4 p.m., Sun. Noon–4 p.m.

Admission: Adults $2.00;
children (under 12) free

Activities: Guided tours

Suggested Time to View House:
30–45 minutes

Facilities on Premises: Visitor center with
wheelchair accessibility

Best Season to View House: Year round

Description of Grounds: Gardens
featuring pecan trees, shrubs and
seasonal flowers

Number of Yearly Visitors: 5,000

Number of Rooms: 6

Style of Architecture: Territorial Adobe
with Spanish Colonial and Anglo
influences

Year House Built: c.1860

On-Site Parking: Yes **Wheelchair Access:** No

Description of House

In 1824, when the San Antonio Missions were secularized and their lands were meted out to those Native Americans and settlers who had been tenants, Manuel Yturri-Castillo was granted a tract that had belonged to the Mission Concepcion. Here he built his adobe house across one of the Mission's old irrigation ditches. In 1863, his daughter Vincenta married Ernest Edwards and was given the house and surrounding acreage. Vincenta Edwards and her daughter, Ernestine Edmunds, were known in San Antonio as exceptional educators. In 1961, Ernestine Edmunds bequeathed the house and adjacent mill to the San Antonio Conservation Society.

The single-story Yturri-Edmunds house is a fine example of adobe construction and shows a number of features common to Anglo-Territorial homes built during the period of the mid-19th century: a front facade veranda with square-shaped supports and balustrade, the six-over-six paned windows with shutters, and the double set of paneled doors. Oddly, the house has an extended hipped roof instead of the far more common flat roof. One room in the house has been restored to look like a school room in honor of Ernestine's career in education. The majority of the furnishings on display belonged to the family.

Additional Information

The Yturri-Edmunds Historic Site also contains the Postert House (1855), a block-and-stone rubble one room house which was moved here to save it from demolition, and the Oge Carriage House (1881) which originally stood in San Antonio's Historic King William District. The old stone mill on the property has been restored to working order, and is used by the Society for special occasions.

Ezekiel Cullen House

205 South Congress Street
San Augustine, TX 75972
(409) 275-5061

Contact: Ezekiel Cullen Chapter-Daughters of the Republic of Texas

Open: Thurs.-Sun. 1–4 p.m.; other times by appointment

Admission: $2.00 per person; special rates for school groups

Activities: Guided tours, annual April House Tour

Suggested Time to View House: 1 hour

Description of Grounds: Located on a half city block with large yard

Best Season to View House: Spring

Number of Yearly Visitors: 300

Year House Built: 1839

Style of Architecture: Greek Revival

Number of Rooms: 7

On-Site Parking: Yes **Wheelchair Access:** No

Description of House

The use of the Texas "Lone" Star motif in the center of the molding over the entry and also on the downspouts at either end of the porch suggests that this lovely Greek Revival-style home was built for a Texas patriot, and that the house has a history coincident with that of the State of Texas itself. The suggestion bears truth: the house was built for Ezekiel W. Cullen, a lawyer who fought at Bexar for independence from Mexico and later served the young Republic of Texas in a number of capacities—as Representative from San Augustine to the Third Congress, as First District judge, and as an Associate Justice of the Republic of Texas' Supreme Court. After Texas gained statehood, Cullen practiced law until President Taylor pressed him into national service as purser of the U.S. Navy. He returned to Texas in 1871 and died in Dallas some time later. After the Civil War, ownership of the house that Cullen built fell to the Elisha Roberts family, then, in 1900, to Mr. and Mrs. Saunders, who added a music room. In 1952, Mrs. Lillie Cranz Cullen bought the house as a birthday gift for her husband, Hugh Roy Cullen, grandson of Ezekiel W. Cullen. They commissioned Raiford Stripling, the noted San Augustine-born architect, to restore the house; when it was complete, they presented it to the Daughters of the Republic of Texas.

The Ezekiel Cullen House was built in 1839 by master builder Augustus Phelps. The mixture of elements which makes the Greek Revival such a graceful and harmonious style can be clearly seen here. Details include the porch gable with Doric columns, the wonderful window surrounds, and the fan-shaped windows at either end of the ballroom. All of the furnishings in the house reflect the initial years of the Cullen occupancy.

Notable Collections on Exhibit

One room of the house is filled with paintings by Seymour Thomas, a well-known portraitist who was born in San Augustine.

Additional Information

The Ezekiel Cullen House is listed on the National Register of Historic Places. It also serves as headquarters for the Medallion Homes and Historical Places annual tour. Other houses on this tour include: the 1890 Greek Revival-style Gatling House and the 1830 "Chinaberry Grove," a rustic log cabin.

Charles L. McGehee, Jr., Cabin

**Camino Real and
Old San Antonio Road
San Marcos, TX 78666
(512) 392-9997**

Contact: Heritage Association of San
Marcos, Inc.

Open: By appointment only with
authorized docent

Admission: Free

Activities: Guided tours

Suggested Time to View House: 45 minutes

Description of Grounds: 1000 acre ranch
located on old crossroads between
Camino Real and the town of Martindale

Best Season to View House: Spring-fall

Number of Yearly Visitors: 50

Year House Built: c.1850

Number of Rooms: 4

Style of Architecture: National, log cabin

On-Site Parking: Yes **Wheelchair Access:** Yes

Description of House

This modest log cabin was the first home of the wealthy San Marcos landowner, Charles L. McGehee. He built it for his bride, who was born in nearby Martindale, on land granted to his father by the Spanish Colonial Government. This land ran for four leagues along the San Marcos River and constituted an area which would be the last designated as a town under Spanish rule. In 1869, court papers identified this crossing of the San Marcos as the McGehee Crossing.

The Charles L. McGehee Cabin has been fully restored to its original appearance on its original site. It has four rooms, a shingled roof which extends over the full-width front porch, chimneys located at both end gables, and a glazed door with segmented sidelights. The cabin was built using the board-and-batten technique. It is furnished to represent an affluent home of the 1870s.

Charles S. Cock Museum

400 East Hopkins Street, P.O. Box 1806
San Marcos, TX 78666
(512) 392-9997

Contact: Heritage Association of San Marcos, Inc.

Open: Open every Fri. 11 a.m.–1 p.m.; open other times by appointment; closed months of August and December

Admission: Free

Activities: Guided tour, "Cottage Kitchen" luncheons, annual Tour of Distinction

Suggested Time to View House: 45 minutes

Description of Grounds: Small yard with shrubs and trees on the San Marcos River Walk

Best Season to View House: Spring-early summer

Number of Yearly Visitors: 3,000

Year House Built: 1867

Number of Rooms: 4

Style of Architecture: Rural Greek Revival

On-Site Parking: Yes **Wheelchair Access:** Yes

Description of House

Charles S. Cock and his wife came to Texas from Mississippi in 1851 at the urging of General Edward Burleson who, with Dr. Eli Meriman and William Lindsey, had laid out the town of San Marcos and settled there. When the Cocks got to San Marcos, they joined the Methodist Church, bought some land in Caldwell County near Maxwell, and started growing cotton with slave labor. Over the next two decades, despite the intervening Civil War, the family grew in prosperity and Charles became an influential member of the community. In 1877, he was elected the second mayor of San Marcos. Charles Cock died in 1897 and his wife moved out of the house to live with her daughter nine years later. This simple one-story interpretation of the Greek Revival style was built just after the Civil War out of limestone, pine, cedar, and elm. Though it has only two main rooms, one notices some charming details: the segmented transom and sidelights at the front door, the end gable chimneys, the six-over-six fenestration, and the full-facade and partial-width entry porch. The porch extensions appear to be a later addition; even the stone foundation differs from that of the main structure. The furnishings are primarily handmade Texas "primitive" pieces.

Additional Information

The Charles Cock Museum is listed on the National Register of Historic Places. The annual Tour of Distinction, organized by the San Marcos Heritage Association, is held in the first weekend of May and includes many houses and other historic buildings not open to the public otherwise. One especially noteworthy stop on the tour is the 1909 John A. Montgomery House.

Sebastopol House

704 Zorn Street
Seguin, TX 78155
(512) 379-4833

Contact: Texas Parks and Wildlife
Department-Sebastopol Historical Park
Open: Drop-in, Fri.-Sun. 9 a.m.–4 p.m.;
group tours available by reservation
Wed.-Sun. 9 a.m.–4 p.m.
Admission: Adults $2.00; students $1.00;
group rates available
Activities: Guided tours, special
seasonal events

Suggested Time to View House: 45 minutes
Description of Grounds: 2 acre manicured
lawn
Best Season to View House: Spring and fall
Number of Yearly Visitors: 4,500
Year House Built: Between 1854 and 1856
Style of Architecture: Greek Revival
Number of Rooms: 12
On-Site Parking: Yes **Wheelchair Access:** Yes

Description of House

The Sebastopol House is named for the famous Crimean War battle which
took place in 1854, the same year that construction began here. It was built by
Colonel Joshua Young for his wife, but she died shortly before its completion
and its first occupants were Colonel Young's widowed sister and her eight
children. They lived here for almost twenty years, at which time she sold the
property to Joseph Zorn, Jr., a local merchant who had married Nettie Watkins
three years earlier. Over the next forty years, Zorn served as alderman and
postmaster of Sequin, mayor for twenty years (1890-1910), and president of the
public school system. He died in 1923 and his wife fourteen years later; their
youngest son, Calvert, lived here until 1952.

Sebastopol is an unusual and significant residence, primarily because it is
built of "limecrete," an early form of concrete formed into load-bearing walls.
This particular use of concrete was patented by Dr. John E. Park, who'd come
to Sequin from Georgia in the late 1840s. Much of this original building material
remains in the house today; thus, Sebastopol is one of the best surviving
examples of early concrete construction in the whole of the Southwest. The
house boasts 4,200 square feet of living space on two levels shaped in a "T."
The floors are made of pine, the window and door frames of walnut. The floor
plan features a parlor, two bedrooms, and an office upstairs and the public
rooms downstairs. Exterior features include a flat roof line with a decorative
frieze and pilasters, nine-over-nine windows, a segmented transom and side-

lights at the main door, and a full-width, full-height wrap-around porch with squared supports and a simple railing. The interpretation is primarily architectural and not indicative of the various families' lives who occupied the house.

Notable Collections on Exhibit

Individual pieces of furniture are significant by virtue of their provenance or ownership—many belonged to the Zorns or LeGettes—and include a tall case clock possibly made by Ephraim Downs c.1818, two balloon-back chairs in the Rococo style, a mantel clock made by E. Ingraham of Bristol, Connecticut, and a pair of cane chairs which once belonged to John Ireland, a Sequin native who served as Governor of Texas from 1883 to 1887.

Additional Information

The Sebastopol House is listed on the National Register of Historic Places.

Miers Home Museum

Northeast Oak Street
Sonora, TX 76950
(915) 387-5144

Contact: Sutton County Historical Society
Open: Open by appointment
Admission: Donation accepted
Activities: Self-guided walking tour of the
town of Sonora
Suggested Time to View House: 45 minutes
Description of Grounds: Located on
Courthouse Square among other historic
buildings and markers
Style of Architecture: National,
board-and-batten
Best Season to View House: Spring and fall
Number of Yearly Visitors: 450
Number of Rooms: 3

Year House Built: 1889
On-Site Parking: Yes **Wheelchair Access:** No

Description of House

The history of Sonora and all of Sutton County is really the story of
man's dependence on water; in fact, the town came into being after the water
well was drilled in the late 1880s. Unfortunately, too often the story of water
is one of conflict. The builder of this house, Isaac Miers, was shot in a dispute
over the precious resource in 1891. It is recorded that the murder took place
on the courthouse steps, and that Isaac managed to stagger back to his home
before dying shortly thereafter. Prior to moving into the house, he and his
wife had lived in a tent in a sheep camp.

The Miers Home was one of the first to be built after the well was drilled;
the single wall, board-and-batten construction method that is used here is
often seen in the region's pioneer structures. Originally, the house consisted
of two floors with two rooms downstairs and a sleeping loft above. The
porches and parlor are later additions. It has been fully restored to its
appearance in the 1890s.

Notable Collections on Exhibit

The Miers Museum is a repository of Sutton County memorabilia.

Additional Information

The Sonora Walking Tour includes a number of historical sites well
worth visiting, among them the marker where the well was dug, the
Masonic Lodge, the Sutton County Courthouse, and the site of the shooting
of Will Carver, the infamous member of the Hole-in-the-Wall Gang.

J. D. Berry Cottage

525 Washington Street
Stephenville, TX 76401
(817) 965-5313

Contact: Stephenville Historical House Museum

Open: Fri.-Sun. 2–5 p.m.;
open anytime by request

Admission: Free

Activities: Guided tours, special group tours by reservation

Suggested Time to View House: 30–60 minutes

Facilities on Premises: Erath County history archives

Description of Grounds: 5½ acre area with eleven restored historic houses and buildings including the 1899 Church and Schoolhouse, the J. D. Berry Cottage and the John Tarleton Ranch House

Number of Yearly Visitors: 2,500

Best Season to View House: Early spring and fall

Number of Rooms: 6

Year House Built: 1869

Style of Architecture: Gothic Revival-style stone cottage

On-Site Parking: Yes **Wheelchair Access:** No

Description of House

Colonel and Mrs. J. D. Berry spent the early days of their marriage on the Mississippi; after the Civil War, however, they moved to Waco, Texas, where the Colonel started a mercantile business. After inheriting some money from relatives in Germany, they moved to Stephenville. At the time, the area around the settlement was still largely the province of Native Americans and the Berrys played a significant role in spearheading the development of the region—the Colonel was a land speculator, an insurance man, and a politician.

The cottage that the Berrys built here in 1869 is a center gable stone structure in the Gothic Revival style. The gables feature vergeboards designed in the style of a Mississippi showboat. Other exterior features include two end-gable chimneys, an entry porch with a second-story balcony, irregularly shaped quoins, and a Dutch "hex" symbol on the vents under the eaves. The walls are a very sturdy 18 inches thick over which plaster has been laid and painted a soft blue with dark trim. The "long room" which connects the kitchen to the rest of the house was added a year after the original construction was complete. The house is mainly furnished with turn-of-the-century pieces, most of which have been donated to the museum.

Notable Collections on Exhibit

There are two wall hangings done by Stephenville's first artist, a doll collection, some interesting children's furniture, a still life c.1900, and a print of General Lee and the Confederate high command.

Additional Information

The J. D. Berry Cottage is listed on the National Register of Historic Places.

Atkins House

416 North Jackson Street
Sulphur Springs, TX 75482
(903) 885-2387

Contact: Hopkins County Historical
Society-Heritage Park and Museum
Open: Wed.-Sun. 1–4 p.m.; closed
Thanksgiving and Christmas Day
through New Year's Day
Admission: Adults $2.00; seniors and
children $1.00
Activities: Guided tours by appointment,
special seasonal events including the
annual May Folk Festival, Civil War
Days, and "Christmas in the Park"
Suggested Time to View House: 30 minutes
Best Season to View House: Spring and fall
Year House Built: 1870s
Number of Rooms: 6

Description of Grounds: 11 acre Heritage
Park includes the Atkins House, a working
blacksmith shop, a smoke house, the 1870
Country Store and the Fishscale House
Facilities on Premises: Museum gift shop
Number of Yearly Visitors: 1,200
Style of Architecture: National, brick
On-Site Parking: Yes **Wheelchair Access:** No

Description of House

The story of the Atkins House—sometimes called the "Star House"—is the story of the Irish immigrant Sarah Hamilton and her two husbands. The first was James Crouch who is presumed to have died in the Civil War. Before he left Bright Star in 1861, he had given his wife power of attorney to transact business in his behalf. Sarah took this opportunity to become a successful businessperson in her own right; she owned a hotel on Main Street and the first coffee shop in Bright Star, appropriately called "Aunt Sarah's Shop." In 1873, she married Joseph Atkins, an Englishman who had a cobbler's shop and saddlery in town. Though the couple remained childless, they cared for and brought up many of the area's needy children. They willed their house to a nephew, Robert Sickles, who moved in with his family in 1900. The family took care of Uncle Joseph and Aunt Sarah until their deaths in 1906 and 1907, respectively. It is recorded that Sarah was buried in shoes that her husband had made for her. The house was moved from Bright Star to the Hopkins County Historical Society's Heritage Park in Sulphur Springs where it has been meticulously reassembled and restored.

Though the original structure had hand-pressed double brick walls, when the house was moved it was discovered that most of the bricks had deteriorated so badly that they needed to be replaced. Thus, the Society was granted permission by the Texas Historical Commission to rebuild the structure with single brick walls. The center of the house was a large hexagonal master bedroom with eight openings and a fireplace. The rest of the house branched out off four sides of this room. It was this unusual shape which gave the house its nickname, "Star House." When the cook's room was later added it broke up the star pattern.

Of the furnishings, only the dining room table and chairs, and a rocking chair, belonged to Sarah Atkins; the rest have all been donated to the museum.

Draughton-Moore,
The Ace of Clubs House

420 Pine Street, P.O. Box 2343
Texarkana, TX 75504
(903) 793-4831

Contact: Texarkana Museums System
Open: Nov.-March, Wed.-Fri. 10 a.m.–4 p.m.,
  Sat. 1–4 p.m.; Apr.-Oct., Wed.-Fri.
  10 a.m.–4 p.m., Sat. and Sun. 1–4 p.m.;
  closed national holidays
Admission: Adults $5.00; seniors $4.50;
  children and students with ID $2.50;
  mini-tour rate $3.50
Activities: Guided tours, 18 minute
  introductory video, workshops on period
  related activities and Victorian Tea Parties
Facilities on Premises: Gift shop

Suggested Time to View House:
  75–90 minutes
Description of Grounds: Large grounds
  with carriage house
Best Season to View House: Spring and
  summer
Number of Yearly Visitors: 3,000
Year House Built: 1885, remodeled c.1920s
Style of Architecture: Eclectic Italianate
  with Moorish-Spanish Revival elements
Number of Rooms: 12
On-Site Parking: Yes **Wheelchair Access:** Yes

Description of House

James Harris Draughton, a native Tennessean who'd come to Texarkana and found his success as a lumber man and dry goods merchant, is said to have enjoyed poker. It is further alleged that he once won an inordinately large pot with the winning card being the Ace of Clubs. So, when he built this wonderfully idiosyncratic (and expensive) Italianate-style home in 1885, folks understood perfectly when he called it the "Ace of Clubs House." Some ten years later, the house was purchased by a local attorney, Henry Moore, whose family occupied it for the next ninety-one years.

There are many splendid Italianate houses among America's historic homes but it is safe to say that none is built quite like this one. First, it is shaped like a playing card, Draughton's famous Ace of Clubs. This gives it twenty-two sides arranged on three floors with each floor consisting of three octagonal rooms and a long rectangular room joined to a large central octagon which houses the central stairway. Second, the house is surrounded by a dry moat which, responding to the opening and closing of the windows in the cupola atop the house, acted as a kind of air conditioner. The triple thick brick walls have been stuccoed and scored to resemble brownstone and the house features three entrances. The interiors reflect the different periods seen in each of the rooms as they were modernized. The ceilings, floors, walls, and trim were all restored using appropriate colors and materials.

Most of the furnishings are original; those that are not have been collected or come from the museum's private collection.

Notable Collections on Exhibit

Among the more notable items on display are: an Adam Mantel, an exquisite Directoire Mirror, an 1898 Steinway & Sons grand piano, and an incredible collection of over 500 pairs of size 4½B ladies shoes! The shoes were, for the most part, purchased by Olivia Smith Moore from Neiman-Marcus in Dallas. Some of them are displayed in Miss Olivia's fabulous Art Deco Bathroom and Dressing Room, along with other of her personal items.

Additional Information

The Draughton-Moore "Ace of Clubs" House is listed on the National Register of Historic Places.

Bonner-Whitaker-McClendon House

806 West Houston
Tyler, TX 75702
(903) 592-3533

Contact: Society for the Restoration and Historic Preservation of the Bonner-Whitaker-McClendon House

Open: Sat. 10 a.m.–5 p.m., Sun. 1–5 p.m.; closed during the holidays

Admission: $3.00 donation requested

Activities: Guided tours, Victorian Teas, Victorian Christmas Celebration

Suggested Time to View House: 30 minutes

Facilities on Premises: Souvenirs available

Description of Grounds: 2 acre grounds designed to replicate the Victorian period of the late 1800s

Style of Architecture: Victorian Queen Anne-Eastlake, bracketed

Best Season to View House: Early spring

Number of Yearly Visitors: 5,000

Year House Built: 1878

Number of Rooms: 10

On-Site Parking: Yes **Wheelchair Access:** No

Description of House

The Bonner-Whitaker-McClendon House stands on land originally acquired by Texas State Supreme Court Justice M. H. Bonner from the estate of his former law partner, Governor James Pickney Henderson. Bonner's daughter, Matilda, and her husband, Harrison Moores Whitaker, another lawyer whose partner was Governor R. B. Hubbard, purchased two acres of this land and built their Victorian dream house here in 1878. Whitaker and Hubbard convinced the St. Louis Railroad to service East Texas, thus keeping their region out of Jay Gould's clutches. The railroad contract was signed in the parlor of this house. Because of Whitaker's prominence in the area, the house became an important stop-over for visiting dignitaries and the center of Tyler social life. After Matilda's early death, Whitaker sold the house to her sister Annie and Annie's husband, S. S. McClendon. The youngest of that couple's nine children is Sarah McClendon, the noted Washington, D. C., news correspondent.

This superb two-story Victorian is framed with thirty-foot studs, thus allowing for fourteen-foot ceilings throughout. The exterior features exquisite detailing on the gables and lintels, a second floor recessed porch, and an elaborate shutter system. It is painted in yellow, red, and brown in accordance with its original appearance. Inside, the house features several innovations for its day: indoor plumbing, dual lighting fixtures which took either gas or electricity, and broad archways between rooms. When the house was restored, four decorators collaborated to bring the interior back to its full Victorian glory, from the reproduction wallpapers to the pink "ribbon" stenciling on the bedroom ceiling. Most of the furnishings are original to the house and have been donated by the McClendon family. Among the more interesting pieces is a Victorian parlor set purchased in New York by Mattie Whitaker and a rare walnut Box Piano.

Notable Collections on Exhibit

Many of the items on display are of museum quality, especially the beautiful wedding gown which was worn by Mrs. McClendon on her wedding day and has been restored with the assistance of the Smithsonian Institute.

Additional Information

The Bonner-Whitaker-McClendon House is listed on the National Register of Historic Places. It opened as the Designer Showcase for Historic Tyler's Heritage Tour in 1988.

John Nance Garner House– Ettie R. Garner Building

333 North Park Street
Uvalde, TX 78801
(512) 278-5018

Contact: Garner Memorial Museum

Open: Mon.-Sat. 9 a.m.–Noon, 1–5 p.m.; closed Thanksgiving, Christmas Eve and Day, New Year's Day

Admission: Adults $1.00; children (6-18) $.50; children (under 6) and public school groups free; adult group tours $20.00 flat rate

Activities: Guided tours for pre-scheduled groups

Suggested Time to View House: 1 hour

Facilities on Premises: Museum

Best Season to View House: Spring and fall

Description of Grounds: Small landscaped yard

Number of Yearly Visitors: 5,000

Number of Rooms: 10

Style of Architecture: Eclectic Southwestern Craftsman

Year House Built: 1920, remodeled 1952

On-Site Parking: Yes **Wheelchair Access:** No

Description of House

The John Nance Garner House is an extensively remodeled home which now serves as a museum relating the life and career of John Nance Garner. Garner, who was born in Blossom, Texas, on November 22, 1868, moved to Uvalde at the age of twenty-two. Here he practiced law and was part owner of the *Uvalde Leader*, the local newspaper. Later he became County Judge and was elected to the United States House of Representatives in 1903, during Theodore Roosevelt's Presidency. In the House, Garner won a reputation as a tough-but-fair negotiator who followed the courage of his convictions into some pretty good legislative battles. He was elected Democratic minority leader in the Seventy-first Congress and Speaker of the House at the next session. At the Democratic National Convention in 1932, Garner, who held some nominating votes, released them to Franklin D. Roosevelt and was himself nominated for the office of Vice-President. He served in that position with distinction during the first two of Roosevelt's four terms. John Nance Garner died in Uvalde in 1967 at the age of ninety-eight.

Notable Collections on Exhibit

The collections on exhibit here—mainly photographs, political cartoons, and campaign memorabilia—all pertain to the career of John N. Garner.

Additional Information

The John Nance Garner-Ettie R. Garner Building is listed on the National Register of Historic Places.

McNamara House Museum

502 North Liberty Street
Victoria, TX 77901
(512) 575-8227

Contact: Victoria Regional Museum
Association

Open: Thurs. and Fri. Noon–5 p.m., Sat.and
Sun. 1–5 p.m.; closed New Year's Day,
Easter, Fourth of July, Thanksgiving, and
Christmas

Admission: Free

Activities: Guided tours, fifth grade
educational programs, seasonal
programs

Suggested Time to View House: 30 minutes

Facilities on Premises: Carriage house
educational center

Description of Grounds: Restored 19th
century-style landscaped yard with
surrounding sidewalk

Best Season to View House: Spring

Year House Built: 1876

Number of Rooms: 8

Number of Yearly Visitors: 5,000

Style of Architecture: Late Gothic Revival

On-Site Parking: No **Wheelchair Access:** Yes

Description of House

The McNamara House is a good representation of the style and aspirations of a middle class family of coastal South Texas in the latter part of the
19th century. It was built in 1876 for William J. McNamara, an Irish immigrant and former resident of Port Lavaca, who dealt in hides, wool, and
cotton. Judging from the house, and its original furnishings, his business
was successful. He and his wife, Mary Ann Buckley McNamara, had four
daughters. One of them, Mary Ellen, married T. M. O'Connor; the house
remained in that branch of the family for over eighty years.

The McNamara house is a vernacular interpretation of the late Gothic
Revival; both the body of the house, and a separate rear wing, feature the
wide verandas, overhanging roofs, raised open foundation, and large windows found in many Southern coastal homes. However, here one also sees
some Victorian ornamentation, like the carved and hand-sawn porch post
brackets, the dormer fretwork, and the exterior color scheme showing
different natural hues. The house has been restored to the period of the late
19th century and the furnishings, original and collected, all date to that
period.

Notable Collections on Exhibit

The temporary gallery space in the house is given over to changing
exhibits which depict the social history of Victoria.

Additional Information

The McNamara House is listed on the National Register of Historic
Places.

Earle-Harrison House and Gardens

1901 North Fifth Street
Waco, TX 76708
(817) 753-2032

Contact: G. H. Pape Foundation
Open: Year-round, daily
Admission: Adults $2.00; children $1.00
Activities: Guided tours, Brazos River
Festival, "Christmas on the Brazos"
Suggested Time to View House: 1 hour
Description of Grounds: Two city blocks of
gardens with live oaks, pond and
fountain, and brick walks
Best Season to View House: Spring and
summer
Style of Architecture: Greek Revival,
peristyle
Number of Yearly Visitors: 2,500
Number of Rooms: 12

Year House Built: 1858
On-Site Parking: Yes **Wheelchair Access:** Yes

Description of House

The Earle-Harrison House stands on little over an acre of what once was the original eleven league land grant. It was built in 1858 by Dr. Baylis Wood Earle, a local cotton planter, and his wife, Eliza Ann Harrison Earle. Dr. Wood died shortly after the house was completed. In 1872, it was purchased by General Thomas Harrison, Eliza's brother. General Harrison was both a plantation owner and a lawyer who lived here until his death in 1891.

Some consider the Earle-Harrison House the best example of a Greek Revival, peristyle antebellum house still standing in Texas. Most impressive are the nine great cypress columns fashioned from timber that was hauled to Waco from East Texas. The house is thought to be built by a shipwright owing to the fact that the timbers are fitted rather than nailed. Materials used include: cypress, brick fired on the plantation, wide heart-of-pine for the floors, and locally-cut post oak. The bricks were probably made by Dr. Earle's slaves. Ceilings are an incredible sixteen feet tall downstairs and fourteen feet upstairs. The off-center front door and the position of the dining room fireplace suggest that the white Doric columns on either side of the house may only represent half of a planned peristyle that was never completed. The furnishings are all authentic to the antebellum period of Dr. Earle's residency.

Notable Collections on Exhibit

There are two items of note: the Governor Pat M. Neff Collection of early pioneer kitchen utensils, pottery, furniture, and glassware; and a large painting by Adolph Bougiseau (1825-1905).

Earle-Napier-Kinnard House

814 South Fourth Street
Waco, TX 76706
(817) 753-5166

Contact: Historic Waco Foundation

Open: Sat. and Sun. 2–5 p.m.; closed New Year's Day, Easter, Fourth of July, Thanksgiving, Christmas, month of December

Admission: Adults $2.00; seniors $1.50; children $1.00; additional $1.00 charge for each house

Activities: Guided tours, special seasonal events including Christmas on the Brazos and Brazos River Festival

Suggested Time to View House: 1 hour

Number of Yearly Visitors: 3,650

Best Season to View House: Spring and summer

Facilities on Premises: Gift shop located at Hoffman House-Historic Waco Foundation offices

Description of Grounds: Yard with "memory" and herb gardens surrounded by white picket fence

Year House Built: Started 1858, completed 1868

Style of Architecture: Greek Revival

Number of Rooms: 15

On-Site Parking: Yes **Wheelchair Access:** Yes

Description of House

Construction of this fine Greek Revival-style mansion was begun in 1858 by John Baylis Earle, a native Mississippian who came to Waco in 1855, married Emma Cynthia Nelson, and established the first cotton mill in Texas. There he produced cloth for Confederate uniforms. In 1869, John Smith Napier, an Alabama planter, bought the house and completed the second story. His daughter, Sarah, and her husband, the Reverend David Cannon Kinnard, began living here in 1880, followed by their daughter Ogilvie, who lived here until her death in 1957.

The house is built of native rose-colored brick and features a partial-width, two-story entry porch with a balcony supported by white fluted columns. Both the upper gallery and front porch show highly ornamented balustrades and the two doors are framed by a narrow band of ventilation windows—the main entry also features a segmented transom above the door. The front and side windows are flanked by black "plantation" shutters. Original elements inside include hardwood floors covered by antique Oriental carpets, fruit-motif wallpaper in the dining room, and antique gold walls. Upstairs in the rear gallery is a tine-footed bathtub heated by gas jets.

The house contains many furnishings which belonged to the Kinnards, including some fine Eastlake and Renaissance Revival-style furniture; in the parlor, there is a rosewood pianoforte manufactured by John Talman and Sons of Philadelphia.

Notable Collections on Exhibit
In addition to the original furnishings on display, the Earle-Napier-Kinnard Museum also features an extensive collection of dolls donated by house committee members.

Additional Information
The Earle-Napier-Kinnard House is listed on the National Register of Historic Places.

Fort House Museum

503 South Fourth Street
Waco, TX 76706
(817) 753-5166

Contact: Historic Waco Foundation

Open: Sat. and Sun. 2–5 p.m.; closed New Year's Day, Easter, Fourth of July, Thanksgiving, Christmas, month of December

Admission: Adults $2.00; seniors $1.50; children $1.00; additional $1.00 charge for each house

Activities: Guided tours, special seasonal events including Christmas on the Brazos and Brazos River Festival

Suggested Time to View House: 45 minutes

Facilities on Premises: Gift shop located at Hoffman House-Historic Waco Foundation offices

Description of Grounds: Small yard with original myrtle tree plantings and herb garden surrounded with wrought iron fence

Best Season to View House: Spring and summer

Number of Yearly Visitors: 3,500

Year House Built: 1868

Style of Architecture: Greek Revival

Number of Rooms: 15

On-Site Parking: Yes **Wheelchair Access:** Yes

Description of House

By the middle of the 19th century, much of the farm land of the South was exhausted, forcing a migration west in search of suitable fresh soil. The fertile hill country of central Texas attracted a great many of these southern farmers—five hundred of them were brought here by William Aldridge Fort and his partner W. W. Downs alone. Fort, who had come here from Alabama in 1854 and found the land good, moved into town when the area got settled, became president of the local bank, and took a prominent position in Waco society. He built this house for his family in 1868.

The exterior of this two-story pink brick structure features a full-height entry porch with an elliptical window in the pediment supported by fluted Ionic columns, a full-width porch and gallery in the rear, and black shutters. Inside, the original hardwood floors are covered in blue and red-toned Oriental rugs, the plastered walls are painted a putty color, and the window treatments feature swags and valances of burgundy velvet over Nottingham lace panels. Underneath the central stairway is an unusual closet. The house is furnished with Empire and middle Victorian-style pieces; there is also a rare locally-made tester bed. The Fort House Museum is listed on the National Register of Historic Places.

Notable Collections on Exhibit

The Fort House Museum contains several items original to the Forts: family portraits, two gilt vases, and a gilt mantel mirror. The Museum also houses the Heritage Collection, Historic Waco Foundation's assortment of over 3,000 fashion and textile items from which two semi-annual exhibits are mounted.

John Wesley Mann House, East Terrace Museum

100 Mill Street
Waco, TX 76706
(817) 753-5166

Contact: Historic Waco Foundation

Open: Sat. and Sun. 2–5 p.m.; closed New Year's Day, Easter, Fourth of July, Thanksgiving, Christmas, month of December

Admission: Adults $2.00; seniors $1.50; children $1.00; additional $1.00 charge for each house

Activities: Guided tours, special seasonal events including Christmas on the Brazos and Brazos River Festival

Suggested Time to View House: 1 hour

Number of Yearly Visitors: 3,550

Facilities on Premises: Gift shop located at Hoffman House-Historic Waco Foundation offices

Description of Grounds: Yard with large shade trees, brick walks and gazebo surrounded by brick fence

Best Season to View House: Spring and summer

Year House Built: 1873, additions 1880 and 1884

Style of Architecture: Italianate Villa, towered

Number of Rooms: 23

On-Site Parking: Yes **Wheelchair Access:** Yes

Description of House

John Wesley Mann built this large and lovely Italianate villa on the Brazos River out of pink brick fired in his own kilns. It came to be called "East Terrace" because of the brick walls and walks which lead down to the east bank of the river from the house. For Mann, who had come to Waco from Tennessee in the 1850s and served in the Confederate Army during the Civil War, brick-making was only one of his occupations; he was also engaged in railroading, ice-making and refrigeration, and lumber milling. His bricks were used in the construction of the first suspension bridge across the Brazos. In 1868, he married a native of Poughkeepsie, New York, Miss Cemira Twaddle, whose ideas greatly influenced the design of the house.

The two-story Italianate-style house features arched windows, a full facade porch and gallery with white columns, a turned balustrade, also white, and especially elaborate ornamentation on the soffits and brackets. The center tower afforded Mann a view of his brick-making, millwork, and ice-making enterprises. The tower's mansard roof sits in contrast to the hipped roof which covers the rest of the house. Inside, original details include wood floors covered in antique Oriental rugs and interior shutters. The window treatments feature swags and valances in gold damask and red velvet; the plaster walls are painted a pale putty color. The Mann house had the first interior bathroom in Waco; the tub drained out onto the rear terrace.

The furnishings include relatively small Eastlake-style pieces and larger, heavier pieces from the late Victorian period. Among the few original pieces are Mrs. Mann's desk, a pier mirror, a plum velvet platform rocker, and two bamboo chairs with a matching dresser. The John Wesley Mann House is listed on the National Register of Historic Places.

McCulloch House Museum

407 Columbus Street
Waco, TX 76706
(817) 753-5166

Contact: Historic Waco Foundation

Open: Sat. -Sun. 2–5 p.m.; closed New Year's Day, Easter, Fourth of July, Thanksgiving, Christmas, month of December

Admission: Adults $2.00; seniors $1.50; children $1.00; additional $1.00 charge for each house

Activities: Guided tours, special seasonal events including Christmas on the Brazos and Brazos River Festival

Suggested Time to View House: 1 hour

Facilities on Premises: Gift shop located at Hoffman House-Historic Waco Foundation offices

Description of Grounds: Garden surrounded by white picket fence

Number of Yearly Visitors: 3,500

Best Season to View House: Spring and summer

Year House Built: Started 1866, completed 1872

Style of Architecture: Greek Revival

Number of Rooms: 19

On-Site Parking: Yes **Wheelchair Access:** Yes

Description of House

In 1866 the small dwelling which would become the east wing of a much larger house was built by Mr. and Mrs. Josiah H. Caldwell. Five years later, Champe Carter McCulloch, a native Missourian who settled in Waco after the Civil War, bought the property and built the present Greek Revival structure. McCulloch traveled regularly between Waco and New York as a representative of Sherman Brothers, local hardware merchants. In 1867, he married Emma Basset and the couple raised seven children in this house. McCulloch also served as Mayor of Waco from 1890 to 1900. Members of the family lived here for over a hundred years.

The McCulloch House is one of three exceptional Greek Revival-style homes in Waco (the other two—the Fort House and the Earle-Napier-Kinnard House—are featured separately in this guide); like its sister homes, it is a two-story structure built of pink brick featuring a full-height front porch. This porch, and the balcony above, is supported by four fluted cypress columns painted white. To balance the smaller, earlier east wing, the main entry is placed off center; the glazed door is surrounded by a full segmented transom light and capped by a simple, elegant entablature. Other elements include a wide white exterior cornice and elongated floor-to-ceiling windows. The one-story east wing still has its original 1866 hardwood floors.

Furnishings include Federal-style pieces in the parlor, an American Empire-style dining room set with Chippendale chairs, and a pianoforte made of rosewood with ivory inlay. The McCulloch House Museum is listed on the National Register of Historic Places.

Notable Collections on Exhibit

On display here is the Dresden china collection assembled by Hallie Maude Neff Wilcox, daughter of former Texas Governor Pat Neff.

Plantation House Museum

Highway 35 and FM 2852
P.O. Box 696
West Columbia, TX 77486
(409) 345-4656

Contact: Varner-Hogg Plantation State Historical Park

Open: Wed.-Sat. 9 a.m.–11:30 a.m. and 1 p.m.–4:30 p.m., Sun. 1–4 p.m.

Admission: Adults $3.00; children (6-12) $1.50

Activities: Guided tours of house, self-guided tours of grounds, Spring Heritage Days Celebration

Suggested Time to View House: 45 minutes

Facilities on Premises: Park headquarters with visitor center

Description of Grounds: Park setting with antique fruit tree and rose plantings

Best Season to View House: Spring and fall

Number of Yearly Visitors: 80,000

Year House Built: 1836, remodeled 1920

Style of Architecture: Greek Revival, remodeled in the Eclectic Colonial Revival style

Number of Rooms: 9

On-Site Parking: Yes **Wheelchair Access:** Yes

Description of House

The history of the Plantation House begins before the house was built. Martin Varner, one of Austin's "Old Three Hundred" and a veteran of the revolution, moved to the four thousand acre league grant on the Brazos River in 1824. Here he raised livestock and planted sugarcane. Ten years later, he sold his headright grant to Columbus Patton and moved to Wood County. The log cabin that Varner and his family lived in stood on the same site as the present plantation house. The Patton family were participants in the struggle for an independent Texas. Columbus's older brother was assigned to guard General Santa Anna after his defeat at San Jacinto. For a short period, the General was kept at the Patton Plantation. Columbus Patton was declared insane and died of a probable brain tumor in 1856. After his death, the once successful plantation fell into a decline hastened by bad weather and the Civil War. In 1901, it was purchased by former Texas Governor James S. Hogg, who was convinced that another Spindletop oil field lay beneath his property. By the time of his death in 1906, many wells had been drilled without a strike. Then, in 1920, the West Columbia field was brought in and the Hogg family became rich.

The original structure was a modified Greek Revival house built of brick made by plantation slaves. It had the typical symmetrical floor plan, full-columned porches, and separate kitchen which marked the style during that period. In the 1920s, the house underwent a transformation as the Hoggs invested some of their oil wealth in restoration and remodeling. It now has a six-columned portico instead of the rear galleries, stuccoed walls, and an enlarged kitchen with a covered walkway which connects it to the main house. The Hoggs also "turned" the house to face the West Columbia road instead of Varner Creek. The interior was restored to the period of the mid-19th century and Ima Hogg collected many pieces of that era, focusing on two styles: Empire and Rococo Revival.

Notable Collections on Exhibit

The Hoggs did a wonderful job in restoring the house to the period of the great Gulf coast plantations, c. 1830 to 1850. Various rooms are dedicated to Zachary Taylor, George Washington, Sam Houston, her father, and the Confederacy. Among the items on display are: a number of Currier & Ives prints, Civil War firearms, copies of Martin Varner's 1824 land grant and the 1834 deed transferring the plantation to Columbus Patton, a collection of Staffordshire china, a Dutch tall case grandfather clock c. 1740, and memorabilia from Hogg's tenure as Governor of Texas.

Additional Information

The Plantation House Museum is listed on the National Register of Historic Places.

Kell House Museum

900 Bluff Avenue
Wichita Falls, TX 76301
(817) 723-0623

Contact: Wichita County Heritage Society

Open: Tues.-Fri., Sun. 2–4 p.m.; closed
major holidays except Fourth of July

Admission: Adults $3.00;
children (under 12) $1.00

Activities: Docent guided tours, rotating
local history exhibits, Annual Luncheon
Lecture Series, Fourth of July Celebration

Suggested Time to View House:
45–60 minutes

Description of Grounds: Over 1 acre
manicured lawns with pecan-tree-lined
driveway and native wildflower gardens

Number of Yearly Visitors: 9,000

Facilities on Premises: Carriage house
gift shop

Year House Built: Between 1908 and 1909

Number of Rooms: 12

Best Season to View House: Spring and
summer

Style of Architecture: Eclectic Neoclassical

On-Site Parking: No **Wheelchair Access:** No

Description of House

Frank Kell was a founding father of Wichita Falls who, along with his brother-in-law, Joseph Kemp, owned, operated, or had investments in a number of successful businesses: the Wichita Mill and Elevator Company which was sold to General Mills at a handsome profit, various railroad companies, an operator of electric streetcars, newspapers, and the local utility company. He was also involved in the Lake Wichita irrigation project and served as Director of the Federal Reserve Board from 1914 to 1927. When Frank Kell died in 1941, he was President or Chairman of six major companies. He and his wife, Lula Kemp Kell, built this house in 1909 and raised seven children here. Members of the Kell family lived here until 1980, when the property was sold to the Wichita County Heritage Society.

This three-story Neoclassical structure was designed by local architectural firm of Jones & Orlopp and stands as one of the few remaining buildings from the early years in Wichita Falls. It features a veneer of red brick over a wood frame, cypress porch columns, limestone window heads and sills, wide bracketed eaves, and a full-width porch echoed by two smaller circular side porches. The interior is interpreted to the late Victorian period of dark colors, heavy fabrics, marble fireplaces and stenciled plaster walls. Native red oak and gum is used extensively in the paneling and trim. All of the furnishings are original to the house and include some antiques which were purchased in New Orleans during the 'Twenties and 'Thirties.

Additional Information

The Kell House Museum is listed on the National Register of Historic Places.

Utah

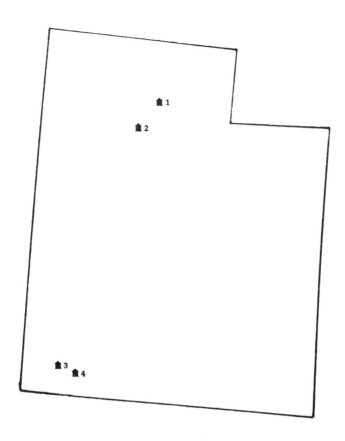

1. Ogden
Miles Goodyear Cabin and Pioneer Museum

2. Salt Lake City
Alfred McCune Home
Beehive House
Deuel Log Cabin
Historic Kearns Mansion, Utah Governor's Residence
James Glendinning Home
Wheeler Farm House

3. Santa Clara
Jacob Hamblin Historical Site

4. St. George
Brigham Young Winter Home

Miles Goodyear Cabin and Pioneer Museum

2148 Grant Avenue
Ogden, UT 84409
(801) 393-4460

Contact: Weber County Daughters of Utah Pioneers
Open: Mid May–mid Sept., Mon.-Sat. 10 a.m.–5 p.m.; closed major holidays
Admission: Free
Activities: Guided tours of house and museum
Suggested Time to View House: 1 hour
Facilities on Premises: Small gift shop

Description of Grounds: Located on the Temple Square
Style of Architecture: National-Folk, log cabin
Best Season to View House: Summer
Year House Built: c. 1845
Number of Rooms: 1
On-Site Parking: Yes **Wheelchair Access:** No

Description of House

This log cabin is the first permanent home built in Utah by a white man. Miles Goodyear (1817-1849), trapper, Indian trader, and mountain man, lived the hard life that his early death attests to. The young Miles was an orphan bound out to a Connecticut farmer who completed his bondage in 1834 and headed West. In Kansas he joined a group of missionaries and trappers—led by the redoubtable Thomas "Broken Hand" Fitzpatrick—who were going to the Oregon Territory. In Idaho, Goodyear quit the party and lived by trapping and trading in that region for the next three years, stopping at Fort Hall for supplies every so often. In 1840, he married the daughter of Ute chieftain Pe-Teet-Neet and they had two children over the next two years. In 1845, Goodyear decided to settle on the banks of the Weber River in the area of the Great Salt Lake and built this cabin of cottonwood logs there. Two years later, on his way home from trapping on the Yellowstone River and trading skins with John Frémont in California, he decided to name his settlement Fort Buenaventura since it now lay at the main crossroads of the Idaho-California Trail.

In that same year, however, Brigham Young ordered that a new settlement be platted at the juncture of the Weber and Ogden Rivers. After inspecting Fort Buenaventura, Young decided that it would not do to have a "gentile" living amongst the believers. So, in 1848, Captain James Brown of the Mormon Battalion bought Miles Goodyear out of his property for the huge sum of $1,950; Miles held on to some skins and the tools of his trade: traps and horses. He died of exposure and exhaustion a year later while driving a herd of horses from Missouri to California. Fort Buenaventura came to be called Brownsville and then, finally, Ogden. The Goodyear Cabin was moved to its present site in 1928.

Of the all the period items on display, only two are original to the cabin: a drop leaf table and a small set of shelves. The rest have been donated by descendants of Utah pioneers.

Notable Collections on Exhibit

The Daughters of Utah Pioneers Museum contains period rooms filled with artifacts from those early Utah settlements. Among the more interesting items are: a lounge handmade of native pine c.1868, a doll carriage, a copper tea set, and a harp which belonged to the French royal family and came to Utah in 1875. One can also view a superb collection of vintage photographs of pioneer families.

Alfred McCune Home

200 North Main Street
Salt Lake City, UT 84103
(801) 533-0858

Contact: Utah Heritage Foundation
Open: Reception center, Mon.-Thurs.
10 a.m.–Noon by appointment
Admission: $1.00 per person
Activities: Guided tours
Suggested Time to View House: 45 minutes
Description of Grounds: Urban setting,
house situated on grassy knoll

Best Season to View House: Spring and
summer
Number of Yearly Visitors: 1,200
Year House Built: 1901
Style of Architecture: Eclectic Period
Revival, Tudor with East Asian influences
Number of Rooms: 22
On-Site Parking: No **Wheelchair Access:** Yes

Description of House

This imposing twenty-two-room mansion was built by Alfred C. Mc-
Cune who had made his fortune building railroads, starting with the Utah
Southern Railroad, and went on to become one of the largest contractors in
the western United States. McCune, who was born in Calcutta, India, and
emigrated with his family to settle on a farm in Nephi, Utah, started his
career in railroad building at the age of twenty-one. His vast wealth can be
measured by the company he kept—his partners in a Peruvian mining
enterprise consisted of J. P. Morgan, William Hearst, and F. Vanderbilt.

In the late 1890s, McCune dispatched the architect S. C. Dallas on a
two-year mission to study various building styles and construction techniques throughout Europe and the United States. The result was this eclectic
design, whereupon Gothic and East Asian elements have been grafted onto
an essentially Tudor-style house. The result works, owing partly to the
materials employed—roof tiles from Holland, mahogany from San Domingo,
English oak, rare white mahogany harvested in South America—and partly
to the sensitivity with which the architect blended his details. The interiors
are opulent; here one can see walls hung with moiré silks, brocades, hand-
embroidered wool tapestry, and exotic leathers.

Additional Information

When visiting Salt Lake City's Marmalade District, one should stop at
the Thomas Quayle Home at 355 Quince Street. This superb example of the
Carpenter's Gothic style was built in 1884 by English immigrants who came
to America to follow the westward migration of the Mormon Church.
Originally built at the Grower's Market, the house was moved to its present
location by the Utah Heritage Foundation, where it now serves as that
organization's headquarters. The Alfred McCune house is listed on the
National Register of Historic Places.

Beehive House

Contact: Church of Jesus Christ of
  Latter-day Saints

Open: Mon.-Fri. 9:30 a.m.–4:30 p.m., Sun.
  10 a.m.–1 p.m.; closed Thanksgiving,
  Christmas, New Year's; all other holidays
  close at 1:00 p.m.

Admission: Free

Activities: Guided tours

Suggested Time to View House: 30 minutes

Facilities on Premises: Card shop

Description of Grounds: 1850s period
  English garden with period plantings and
  flowers. Portion of original cobblestone
  wall located on one side.

Best Season to View House: Spring-fall

Number of Yearly Visitors: 150,000

Year House Built: Between 1853 and 1855,
  remodeled 1888

Style of Architecture: Greek Revival

Number of Rooms: 27

On-Site Parking: No **Wheelchair Access:** Yes

Description of House

Built in 1854 by Brigham Young as his official residence, the Beehive House is Utah's most significant historic home; it is now a museum run by the Church of Jesus Christ of Latter-day Saints to honor its second president. Young followed Joseph Smith across nearly half the country in search of an end to the persecution of their church; when Smith was killed in 1846 in Illinois, Young led his followers west and they finally settled here, on the narrow plain between the Great Salt Lake and the towering Wasatch Mountains. Their ingenuity and hard work made the desert bloom and the settlement took on the aspect of the Promised Land, presided over by Brigham Young. In addition to serving as President of the Mormon Church until his death in 1877, Young also held the office of Utah's first territorial Governor, in the years 1850 to 1858. After Young, this house was occupied by two subsequent presidents of the church, Lorenzo Snow and Joseph F. Smith. From 1918 to 1961, when it became a museum, the Beehive House served as a working girls' dormitory.

The two-story adobe home, which was designed by Truman O. Angell, gets its name from the beehive-shaped cupola mounted atop the widow's walk. The restored exterior walls have been stuccoed and painted the original straw-color yellow; a two-story gallery, railed above and open below, flanks the main house. Inside, the house features wide-plank flooring, painted rooms, hand-grained woodwork, hand marbling, and, in the 1888 addition, period reproduction wallpaper. Many of the furnishings are in the Renaissance Revival style; the rest are relatively simple pine pieces characteristic of the early Mormon settlements. Young, who himself was a carpenter, built a rocking chair on display here and many of the other pieces belonged to him.

Notable Collections on Exhibit

In addition to the many significant personal items of Brigham Young's on display, one should also take note of the Deseret Alphabet books, hair wreath pictures, images of Joseph Smith, original monogrammed china, picture albums, school books, and the many important pieces of early Utah pine furniture.

Additional Information

At 63 East South Temple Street is the Lion House, a communal residence built by Young for his wife and children in 1856 which now serves as a reception center for the Brigham Young complex. This multi-gabled English Gothic Revival-style home features a number of fascinating details, including the eponymous lion which sits over the first-floor portico. Both the Beehive House and the Lion House are listed on the National Register of Historic Places.

Deuel Log Cabin

45 North West Temple Street
Salt Lake City, UT 84150
(801) 240-3310

Contact: Church of Jesus Christ of
Latter-day Saints

Open: Mon.-Fri. 9 a.m.–9 p.m., Sat. and
Sun. 10 a.m.–7 p.m.; closed New Year's
Day, Easter, Thanksgiving, Christmas

Admission: Free

Activities: Guided tours with costumed
interpreters

Suggested Time to View House: 15 minutes

Facilities on Premises: Gift shop located in
adjacent Museum of Church History
and Art

Description of Grounds: Sited on plaza
between two modern buildings with
native trees. Yard contains c.1840s
period vegetable and flower gardens.

Best Season to View House: Spring and
summer

Number of Yearly Visitors: 200,000

Year House Built: 1847

Number of Rooms: 1

Style of Architecture: Folk, log cabin
On-Site Parking: No **Wheelchair Access:** Yes

Description of House

This rough log cabin is one of only two remaining from the original 1847 settlement at the northern extension of the pioneer fort in Salt Lake Valley. It was first occupied by Osmyn and Mary Deuel, and Osmyn's brother, Amos, all native New Yorkers who followed the Mormon Church from Ohio to Illinois to Utah. Osmyn was a successful blacksmith, farmer, and land speculator. When the Deuels left this house after only six months, it became an armory. It was later acquired by Latter Day Saint apostle Albert Carrington. Carrington was Captain Howard Stansbury's assistant when the U. S. Army Corps of Engineers conducted their famous survey of Great Salt Lake in 1849-1850. The cabin was acquired by the Deseret Museum and kept on display at Temple Square from 1919 to 1976. It was then put into storage until 1984, when it was restored on its present site.

The fifteen-by-twenty-foot Deuel Log Cabin was built using the single-pen design out of locally-cut Douglas fir and lodgepole pine. The logs are squared and the ends are dovetailed where they come together at the corners. The cabin has a chimney fashioned out of adobe brick and a low, gabled sod roof. There is one door and an adjacent window in the front and one window in the rear. The period furnishings reflect the lives of the Deuels; these include a cast-iron stove, chests, trunks, table, chairs, bedsteads, and kitchen utensils.

Historic Kearns Mansion, Utah Governor's Residence

603 East South Temple
Salt Lake City, UT 84010
(801) 538-1005

Contact: State of Utah Governor's Mansion
Open: June-Nov., Tues. 1–4 p.m.; first week of December, Mon.-Sat. 1–5 p.m.
Admission: Donations welcome
Activities: Docent guided tours
Suggested Time to View House: 50 minutes
Style of Architecture: Eclectic Renaissance Revival in the French Chateau manner

Description of Grounds: Situated along Salt Lake City's famous South Temple Street known as "Millionaires' Mile" with informal gardens and carriage house
Best Season to View House: Summer
Year House Built: 1902
Number of Rooms: 24, 8 open to the public
On-Site Parking: No **Wheelchair Access:** Yes

Description of House

In 1879, at the age of seventeen, Thomas Kearns, who'd been born in Canada and raised in Nebraska, set out West to make his fortune. Two years later he wound up in Park City, Utah, where David Keith gave him a job in the mines. Keith would become a lifelong friend and business partner. In 1889, the two formed a partnership with John Judge, Albion Emery, and Windsor Rice to mine the Mayflower property in Park City; three weeks later they were rich. The vein they'd discovered propelled Kearns into public life—in the next few years, he served as city councilman, delegate to the Utah Constitutional Convention, and United States Senator. In 1901, the same year he went to Washington as senator, he also married John Judge's young niece, Jennie. They moved into this mansion the following year and almost immediately hosted President Theodore Roosevelt here. Kearns died in 1918 but Jennie lived here until 1937 when the house was deeded to Utah to serve as the Governor's Residence.

This elaborate three-story mansion was designed in the style of a French Renaissance chateau by Salt Lake City architect Carl M. Newhausen and is built of limestone quarried in central Utah's Manti Canyon. The symmetrical facade features two turreted towers with candle-snuffer roofs flanking an impressive entry showing garlands in the tracery. Other exterior details to look for include: the triple arch over the second-story balcony, the paired Corinthian columns under the first floor canopy, and the varied window treatments which include a unique pair of oval portholes on either side of the balcony. Inside, the opulence is almost unimaginable. Much of the woodwork is hand-carved by European artisans in a mixture of local and exotic woods. The twenty-four rooms include an all-marble kitchen, a bowling alley, a ballroom, a billiards room and separate vaults for jewelry, silver, and wine. Copies of famous artwork adorn many of the interior surfaces and the 18th century French furnishings are all authentic and original. Note the bronze figures on the newel posts; sculpted by Auguste Moreau, they were bought by the Senator at the Paris Exposition of 1900.

Notable Collections on Exhibit

Many of the furnishings and art objects on display are of museum quality.

Additional Information

Historic Kearns Mansion is listed on the National Register of Historic Places.

James Glendinning Home

617 East South Temple Street
Salt Lake City, UT 84102
(801) 533-5895

Contact: State of Utah and Utah Arts
Council

Open: Mon.-Fri. 8 a.m.–5 p.m.; closed all
weekends and major holidays

Admission: Free

Activities: Guided tours on request

Suggested Time to View House: 15 minutes

Facilities on Premises: Art gallery
specializing in regional art from the state
collection

Description of Grounds: Small front yard
with flower garden

Best Season to View House: Spring-fall

Style of Architecture: "Picturesque" Gothic
Revival with characteristics of the
Italianate style

Number of Yearly Visitors: 700

Number of Rooms: 10

Year House Built: 1883

On-Site Parking: Yes **Wheelchair Access:** No

Description of House

Robert James Glendinning was born in Scotland in 1844, emigrated with his family to New York City, received his education there, and, in 1866, began working his way across the United States. After stopping in Leavenworth, Kansas, he drove a mule team to Virginia City, Montana, then moved to Salmon, Idaho, the following year. In 1882, he moved to Salt Lake City and became a partner in a hardware company. Here Glendinning made his mark, first as founder of the Chamber of Commerce, then as Salt Lake City's tenth mayor, a position he held from 1894 to 1898, the period that Utah gained statehood. In 1901, he moved again, this time to Spokane, Washington, and sold his house to Henry Newell, president of King Hardware and Stove Company. The house was privately owned until 1975, when the state purchased the property; the Utah Arts Council took it over three years later.

This cottage was designed by John Burton in the "Picturesque" style made popular by the work of Andrew Jackson Downing. The various roof lines, over the main part of the house, the bay, and the porch, at one time featured wrought iron cresting which has since been removed; the roof itself is steeply pitched and has an open pediment. Other exterior details include: tap-style quoins and six-over-six windows capped by eyebrow-style hoods. This latter element is typical of the Italianate style. Inside, the flooring and most of the original moldings have been restored; the banister and parquet floor in the entry hall appear exactly as they did in the late 19th century. The interior is done in a color scheme of olive green and light brown walls with white ceilings and white trim.

Notable Collections on Exhibit

Currently the house serves as a multi-use building which includes an art gallery.

Wheeler Farm House

6351 South Ninth East Street
Salt Lake City, UT 84121
(801) 264-2241

Contact: Wheeler Historic Farm

Open: Year-round, daily

Admission: Adults $1.00; seniors and children (3-11) $.50

Activities: Guided tours, farm related skill demonstrations, special seasonal programs and events

Suggested Time to View House: 45-60 minutes

Facilities on Premises: Gift shop

Description of Grounds: 20 acre farm complex with field and wooded areas bordered by the Cottonwood Creek

Best Season to View House: Spring and summer

Style of Architecture: Victorian Queen Anne, masonry

Number of Yearly Visitors: 200,000

Number of Rooms: 10

Year House Built: 1898

On-Site Parking: Yes **Wheelchair Access:** Yes

Description of House

Utah natives Henry J. Wheeler and his wife, Sariah Hankinson Pixton Wheeler, built their house in 1898, only two years after the territory had become the forty-fifth state. Prosperous and well-established in the Salt Lake City community, the Wheelers and their six children operated a family dairy farm named "Rosebud" in addition to their commercial ice business. So affluent were the couple that Sariah could afford to travel extensively in Europe while her husband built a summer house on their property. The Wheelers were one of the first families in town to own the newfangled invention of their day, a motor car.

Small for a family of two adults and six children, the asymmetrical, two-story brick house contains only ten rooms. It features many of the typical elements of a late Victorian structure: a cross-gabled hipped roof, front and side entry porches detailed with turned balustrades and column porch supports, decorative trusses, and a squared two-story tower. It also contains an unusual design twist: in the attic, Wheeler installed a reservoir which provided the house with running water. The Wheeler Historic Farm is listed on the National Register of Historic Places.

Notable Collections on Exhibit

Up to now, the Wheeler Farm House has not been decorated with as much Victorian "clutter" as might be desired. Instead, it has been interpreted with only a few pieces of "Victoriana" and some furniture common to the period. Oil paintings executed by local artists adorn the walls and a Staffordshire figurine collection purchased by Sariah Wheeler in England is prominently displayed.

Jacob Hamblin
Historical Site

4 miles west of St. George
Santa Clara, UT 84770
(801) 673-5181

Contact: Church of Jesus Christ of
Latter-day Saints

Open: Daily including holidays
9 a.m.–7 p.m.

Admission: Free

Activities: Guided tours

Suggested Time to View House: 35 minutes

Description of Grounds: Large well-kept
lawns with seasonal flowers and cactus
plants

Best Season to View House: Year round

Number of Yearly Visitors: 40,000

Year House Built: Between 1862 and 1863

Number of Rooms: 7

Style of Architecture: National, stone

On-Site Parking: Yes **Wheelchair Access:** Yes

Description of House

At the age of twenty-two Jacob Hamblin converted to Mormonism and joined Brigham Young's pioneers as they came west in 1847. Hamblin, a rugged frontiersman, devoted father, and explorer, made a name for himself as a missionary for his church to the local Native American tribes. His fame spread when he negotiated the Treaty of Fort Defiance, New Mexico, in 1870; because he was able to effect a peace with the tribes who had learned to trust him, he would forever thereafter be remembered as the "great Indian peacemaker." Hamblin and his family lived in this house for seven years, until they moved to Kanab, Utah, and then even further afield as he followed his missionary work. He died in 1886 in New Mexico.

The pioneer home that Jacob Hamblin occupied was built by Mormon craftsmen out of Ponderosa pine and locally-cut stone. The two-story structure features side gables and roof lines which extend out over the second floor balcony in front and the lean-to kitchen in back. The floor plan consists of two bedrooms with fireplaces, a kitchen and eating room, a storage room, and a passageway downstairs; and a large public room upstairs which was typically used for church meetings and school classes. The rough, unfinished interior is interpreted to the period of Hamblin's residency.

Notable Collections on Exhibit

In addition to the homely items on display, one may view Jacob Hamblin's original saddle, and a classic weaving loom and spinning wheel.

Additional Information

The Jacob Hamblin Home is listed on the National Register of Historic Places.

Brigham Young Winter Home

**89 West 100 North Street
St. George, UT 84770
(801) 673-5181**

Contact: Church of Jesus Christ of
Latter-day Saints
Open: Memorial Day-Labor Day, daily
8:30 a.m.–8 p.m.; Labor Day-Memorial
Day, daily 9 a.m.–7 p.m.
Admission: Free
Activities: Guided tours
Suggested Time to View House: 45 minutes
Description of Grounds: White picket
fenced yard with old growth shade trees
and seasonal flowers
Best Season to View House: Year round
Number of Yearly Visitors: 70,000
Year House Built: c.1868, addition 1870
Number of Rooms: 9

Style of Architecture: Late Greek Revival
On-Site Parking: Yes **Wheelchair Access:** Yes

Description of House

Brigham Young, second President and Prophet of the Church of Jesus
Christ of Latter-day Saints, led his people to Utah in 1847 and founded a
commonwealth in the Great Salt Valley. While in Salt Lake City, he lived in
the Beehive House which is also listed and described in this guide. To escape
the occasionally brutal winters encountered there, he built this house in the
extreme southwest corner of Utah where conditions were far milder.

Young was a carpenter, glazier, and painter, and he designed this two-
story house in the Greek Revival style himself. A full-width porch featuring
fret-cut style supports and spindle-like balustrades runs along the front of
the main section and wing. The nine-over-six windows have simple, flat
lintels, the open eaves are heavily bracketed, and the glazed doors have a
segmented transom. The interior is plain—no wallpaper—and has been
painted to match the original colors as closely as possible; the wooden
fireplaces have been painted and scrolled to look like marble. A detail of note
is the way the pine throughout has been quilled to resemble hardwood. This
was done under Young's direct supervision.

The furnishings in the Brigham Young Winter Home are a mixture of
Victorian and early pioneer styles. Pieces include a clipper desk, a four-
poster bed and a sleigh-style bed, a Wheeler-Wilson sewing machine c.1860,
a Chickering grand piano, a cast iron stove, and a Victorian-style dresser
with carved acorn embellishments. This fully restored house is one of the
more important historical sites of the Mormon Church. The Brigham Young
Winter Home is listed on the National Register of Historic Places.

Notable Collections on Exhibit

When visiting the Brigham Young Winter Home, look for the china set
decorated with a gold band marked with the initial "Y."

Washington

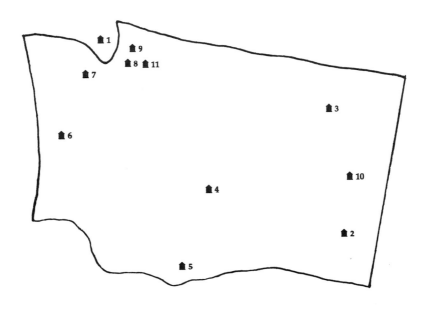

1. **Anderson Island**
Johnson Farm House

2. **Colfax**
Perkins House and Perkins Cabin

3. **Colville**
Keller House, "Lockwood"

4. **Ellensburg**
Olmstead Place

5. **Goldendale**
"Maryhill"

6. **Hoquiam**
Hoquiam's Castle

7. **Olympia**
Bigelow House

8. **Puyallup**
Ezra Meeker Mansion

9. **Snohomish**
Blackman House Museum

10. **Spokane**
Campbell House
Glover Mansion

11. **Sumner**
Sumner Ryan House Museum

Johnson Farm House

9306 Otso Point Road
Anderson Island, WA 98303
(206) 884-2135

Contact: Anderson Island Historical Society

Open: Memorial Day weekend-Labor Day weekend, Sat. and Sun. Noon–4 p.m.

Admission: Donation $1.00

Activities: Seasonal events such as the July Salmon Bake and the October Apple Squeeze

Suggested Time to View House: 30 minutes

Description of Grounds: 6 acres of gardens and several outbuildings

Best Season to View House: Summer

Number of Yearly Visitors: 1,000

Year House Built: 1912

Style of Architecture: Saltbox-style farmhouse

Number of Rooms: 6

On-Site Parking: Yes **Wheelchair Access:** No

Description of House

The Johnson family built this two-story, frame saltbox-style farmhouse in 1912 when there were but a few settlers on Anderson Island in Puget Sound. John Oscar Johnson and his wife, Alma Marie—both from Scandinavia—had homesteaded in the area as early as 1896. The couple and their four children lived in this simple house which was heated only by two wooden stoves, one in the kitchen and one in the front room. Three of the children remained in the house after their parents' deaths in 1924. The sons carried on the family dairy and egg business well into the 1970s and, since the business was lucrative, the sons expanded the farmstead to fourteen outbuildings on more than six acres.

The Johnson Farm House is furnished with many items familiar to a rural farmstead of the era including several antique quilts and toys, an old organ, and hand-made braided rugs. The barn and many of the outbuildings contain farm tools and implements used by the Johnsons in their daily work.

Additional Information

In order to reach the Johnson Farm House from the mainland, one has to catch the ferry from Steilacom. Please call for the current ferry schedule and fee information at (206) 581-6290.

Perkins House and Perkins Cabin

North 623 Perkins Street, P.O. Box 76
Colfax, WA 99111
(509) 397-2555

Contact: Whitman County Historical Society
Open: June-Aug., Thur. and Sun. 1–5 p.m.; other times by appointment
Admission: Free, donations appreciated
Activities: Guided tours by appointment, annual Ice Cream Social
Suggested Time to View House: 1 hour
Best Season to View House: Spring-fall

Facilities on Premises: Books and other items for sale
Number of Yearly Visitors: 1,100
Year House Built: c.1886
Style of Architecture: Modified Victorian Queen Anne
Number of Rooms: 10
On-Site Parking: Yes **Wheelchair Access:** No

Description of House

The "Father of Colfax," James Perkins, arrived in the territory of Washington when he came with his family from Illinois in 1861. They began their journey to the great Pacific Northwest in 1852, traveling by ox-driven wagons, stopping first in Oregon's Willamette Valley before settling in the Walla Walla area. Impatient with farm life, young James ventured out on his own and built a sawmill on the Palouse River in 1871. The operation was a success and began attracting other businesses to the area. In only two short years, the small settlement rapidly became a township and was named after Schuyler Colfax, Vice President of the United States under Ulysses S. Grant.

It was an era of "firsts." Not only did Perkins establish the first business in the town, but he also built the first house—the Perkins cabin—and was the first man to marry in Colfax. In 1873, Perkins and Miss Sarah Jane (Jennie) Ewart celebrated their nuptials and soon the small cabin had to be remodeled to accommodate their growing family; all four of the Perkins children were born in this "first" house. After enjoying success in real estate and banking, primarily as agent for the railroads, Perkins eventually became the mayor of his town and a prominent player in local Republican politics.

By 1884, it was time to build a new house; the Victorian-style Perkins House, modeled after house plans found in a pattern book popular at the time, was finished by 1886 and rapidly became the center of social and business affairs in Colfax. The Perkins House is an excellent example of period building methods and fashionable decoration; employing the "balloon" method of construction, it features twelve-and-a-half-foot ceilings, elaborate hand-carved window surrounds, exterior balconies on all sides of the upper story, a glazed front entry, and tongue-and-groove floor boards painted to resemble wood. The Perkins House is listed on the National Register of Historic Places.

Notable Collections on Exhibit

Though the beautiful marble fireplace and the family crystal chandeliers may catch the visitor's eye, it is the restored original wallpapers and period reproductions which are truly noteworthy. The local historical society carefully reproduced such wallpaper patterns as "Villa Montezuma" and the Arts and Crafts motif, "Honeysuckle," in various areas. If one looks closely at the cutaway section of the hallway, remnants of the original wallpaper will be seen.

Keller House, "Lockwood"

700 North Wynne Street
Colville, WA 99114
(509) 684-5968

Contact: Stevens County Historical Society, Inc.

Open: May 1-Sept. 30, daily 11 a.m.–4 p.m.

Admission: Free, donations accepted

Activities: Guided tours, Candlelight Tour on the first weekend of each month

Suggested Time to View House: 30–45 minutes

Facilities on Premises: Gift shop and bookstore

Best Season to View House: Spring-fall

Description of Grounds: 7½ acres with gardens, carriage house and various resettled historic buildings such as a schoolhouse building and trapper cabins

Number of Yearly Visitors: 3,000

Style of Architecture: Craftsman, "classic box" bungaloid style

Year House Built: 1910, rebuilt 1911

Number of Rooms: 8

On-Site Parking: Yes **Wheelchair Access:** No

Description of House

"Lockwood" was the name given to this house by J. H. "Harry" Young, a businessman of great determination; in the twenty-nine years that he lived in Colville, Young was able to influence the development of various local industries: real estate and land management, silver mining, newspaper publishing, banking, and insurance. Young married the cultured and educated daughter of a wealthy Spokane family, Anna Helberg. It was her mother's maiden name, Lockwood, which provided the inspiration for his naming their home. In a sad twist of irony, the house also bears the name of Keller, Anna's second husband, and not Young, who died in 1914, despite the fact that it was he who built it!

Rebuilt after a disastrous fire in 1911, the new "Lockwood" exemplified the Craftsman style. Beautiful bay windows with original beveled glass, gabled dormers, and exposed rafters with extended ends are only a few of this style's particular felicities. In addition, the interior woodwork was redone in red oak, quarter-grained and impeccably matched, wood beams were added to several rooms, and the oak flooring was sanded and waxed smooth in order to conform to the Craftsman ideal. The built-in bookcases and other remaining built-in pieces were produced in the style of Gustav Stickley; the wallcoverings of the dining room were executed in gilt paint over embossed paper and then stenciled in an Art Nouveau-style design. Perhaps the most interesting feature of this home can be found in the living room: placed on either side of the fireplace are two beveled and leaded windows which exhibit the "Josephine Knot" pattern; these are original to the 1910 house.

Notable Collections on Exhibit

Besides the wonderful built-ins, the Keller House features an original chandelier and several patterned shades made in the workshops of Louis Comfort Tiffany, and a piano and matching stool marked "Decker & Son-1856."

Additional Information

The Keller House is listed on the National Register of Historic Places.

Olmstead Place

Route 5, P.O. Box 2580
Ellensburg, WA 98926
(509) 925-1943

Contact: Washington State Parks
Open: Memorial Day-Labor Day, Sat. and
Sun. Noon–4 p.m.; other times by
appointment
Admission: Free
Activities: Guided tours
Suggested Time to View House: 30 minutes
Description of Grounds: 217 acre
homestead with outbuildings
Best Season to View House: Summer
Number of Yearly Visitors: 30,000-40,000
Year House Built: Cabin-1875, Smith
Residence-1908
Number of Rooms: Cabin-4, Smith
Residence-10
On-Site Parking: Yes **Wheelchair Access:** No

Style of Architecture: Log cabin, late Folk
Victorian farmhouse

Description of House

The Olmsteads were one of the fortunate families who traveled west, not by foot or ox-driven wagon, but by train, from Illinois to the Pacific coast. Once the family arrived in the new territory in 1875, they rode by horse to the Kittitas Valley; here they established their farmstead where Cooke Creek flows into the Yakima River. It was here the Olmstead family started cattle herding, then switched to a dairy and hay operation which remained in their possession for three generations.

On this several-hundred-acre homestead—now a state park—the original Olmstead cabin and farmhouse remain much the way these structures stood close to a century ago. Although the log cabin provided simple accommodations for the Omsteads as they started a new life in the Northwest wilderness, it does display both practical and curiously elaborate construction techniques. It was built with a complex dovetail joint system, chinked with newspaper stuffings, and with a stone and stick-style chimney. By 1908, when the farm operations had generated cash savings, the Olmsteads built a fancier two-story farmhouse detailed with Queen Anne-style trim and brackets typical of this rural folk version. The site of the Olmstead Place is listed on the National Register of Historic Places.

Notable Collections on Exhibit

Reminders of the early days of the Olmstead family can be seen in the many original furnishings and farm implements on display in the cabin and farmhouse, as well as in several of the outbuildings scattered over the property. Assortments of vintage clothing, simple and durable farm furniture, kitchen utensils and an authentic butter churn, and antique dolls provide a glimpse of pioneer life in the closing years of the last century.

"Maryhill"

35 Maryhill Museum Drive
Goldendale, WA 98620
(509) 773-3733

Contact: Maryhill Museum of Art
Open: March 15-Nov. 15, daily 9 a.m.–5 p.m.
Admission: Adults $4.00; seniors $3.50; children (6-16) $1.50
Activities: Guided museum tours, special programs
Suggested Time to View House: 1–2 hours
Facilities on Premises: Museum store and cafe
Best Season to View House: Early spring-fall

Description of Grounds: Large, expansive grounds with garden and picnic area are just a part of the original 7,000 acres
Number of Yearly Visitors: 80,000
Year House Built: Started 1914, completed 1917
Style of Architecture: Eclectic Renaissance Revival, Beaux Arts
Number of Rooms: 20+
On-Site Parking: Yes **Wheelchair Access:** Yes

Description of House

Many of the historic homes of the Pacific Northwest share similar stories, but the story of "Maryhill," a mansion designed by Washington, D.C., architects Hornblower and Marshall, is somewhat different. It is the story of four friends—Sam Hill, Loie Fuller, Queen Marie of Roumania, and Alma Spreckel—who, at different times in their lives, focused their creative energies and monies into the building of this magnificent house and art museum. Sam Hill (1857-1931), a businessman, diplomat, and son of Quaker parents, purchased 7,000 acres on the bank of the Columbia River in 1907 with dreams of establishing an agricultural religious community here. When his "utopia" did not materialize, he abandoned the mansion as a private residence and was persuaded by Loie Fuller to convert it into an art museum. Loie Fuller (1862-1928) was an avant-garde dancer at the Folies Bergére of Paris personally acquainted with many of the French painters and sculptors whose works formed the basis of the would-be museum's collection. Queen Marie of Roumania (1875-1938), granddaughter of Queen Victoria and Tsar Alexander II, and Red Cross humanitarian, provided the dedication in gratitude for Sam Hill's role in aiding the Roumanian people during World War I. And, finally, Alma Spreckels (1882-1968), the San Francisco heiress and founder of the Palace of the Legion of Honor, became the museum's principal benefactor and donated many additional pieces from her personal collection. It was under her sustained guidance that the fully realized museum called "Maryhill" opened to the public in 1940.

Notable Collections on Exhibit

The permanent collection includes bronzes and watercolors by the French artist Auguste Rodin, as well as Native American carvings, baskets, beadwork, and other artifacts. The Queen Marie Gallery includes pieces from Queen Marie's personal inventory: antique furniture, exquisite jewelry and vintage clothing. The gown that she wore to the coronation of Nicholas II is on display. The collection of rare 19th-century Russian icons was a gift from the Queen. Several schools of Dutch, British, and American painting are also represented.

Additional Information

"Stonehenge," a replica of the famous arrangement of megaliths in southern England, was built by Sam Hill as a tribute to the men of Klickitat County who lost their lives during the First World War. The monument is located at the original townsite, three miles east of the museum off Highway 15. "Maryhill" is listed on the National Register of Historic Places.

Hoquiam's Castle

515 Chenault Avenue
Hoquiam, WA 98550
(206) 533-2005

Contact: Hoquiam's Castle
Open: Summer, daily 10 a.m.–5 p.m.;
   winter-spring, Sat. and Sun.
   11 a.m.–5 p.m.; closed month of
   December
Admission: Adults $4.00; children
   (under 16) $1.00
Activities: Guided tours
Suggested Time to View House: 35 minutes
Facilities on Premises: Gift shop
Description of Grounds: Sited on hill with
   view of Grays Harbor
Best Season to View House: Summer
Number of Yearly Visitors: 17,000
Year House Built: 1897
Style of Architecture: Victorian
   Queen Anne
Number of Rooms: 15 open to the public
On-Site Parking: Yes
Wheelchair Access: No

Description of House

Robert Lytle and his brother Joseph owned and operated the first electric sawmill on the West Coast and made a fortune in the lumber industry which they helped establish. Lytle and his wife, Ida, built this impressive house in the rowdy port and milltown of Hoquiam on Grays Harbor off the Pacific Ocean in 1897. Lytle gave the house and all its furnishings to his niece, Theodosia Bale Pugsley, as a wedding present and she lived here until her death in 1956. At that time, it went on sale for $14,000 but wasn't purchased until 1960. The house was acquired by the Robert and Beryl Anne Watson in 1968 and they restored it and opened it for public tours in 1969. In 1992, attorney Jim Spencer bought the house and continues to keep it open.

Hoquiam's Castle is a large three-story structure built in a winning combination of the Queen Anne and Shingle styles on a rusticated stone foundation; prominent elements include a hipped roof with cross gables, a three-story tower extension with the uppermost story partially open and its turret supported by Classical-style columns and metal railing, and a smaller, cantilevered tower which cuts through the front roof line. This wonderfully balanced facade also features Shingle-style fenestration in varying iterations—same-sized sashes holding many panes above and single panes below, stained glass insets, beveled insets, and ribbon effects—a balcony, and Romanesque-style arched stone porch supports. The entire exterior is covered in bands of textured shingles.

The interior floor plan consists of an entry hall, main parlor, music room, and formal dining room on the ground floor; the family bedrooms on the second floor; and a 1,200 square foot ballroom and turn-of-the-century saloon on the third floor. The saloon features a curved-back bar shipped from New Orleans. Only three pieces are original to the house—the light fixture over the roulette table, the library in the ballroom, and the trunk in the maid's room—but the Watsons collected many authentic furnishings, including a Tiffany stained glass window, which give the interior its c.1900 appearance. The electric wiring, indoor plumbing, and central heating were all features originally installed by Robert Lytle.

Notable Collections on Exhibit

Among the items on display, of special note are the six hundred piece cut-crystal chandelier, the Lytle family photographs, and a collection of vintage clothing which includes a beaver skin top hat.

Additional Information

Hoquiam's Castle is listed on the National Register of Historic Places.

Bigelow House

918 Glass Avenue
Olympia, WA 98506
(206) 357-6198

Contact: Bigelow House Preservation
 Committee
Open: Anytime by appointment
Admission: Donations welcome
Activities: Guided tours
Suggested Time to View House: 1 hour
Facilities on Premises: Small music
 research library
Best Season to View House: Year round

Description of Grounds: 1 acre with
 woodshed and fruit trees not far
 from Budd Inlet
Number of Yearly Visitors: 900
Year House Built: 1854
Style of Architecture: Rural Gothic
 Revival-Carpenter style
Number of Rooms: 14
On-Site Parking: Yes **Wheelchair Access:** Yes

Description of House

One of the oldest frame houses in the State of Washington, the Gothic Revival-style Bigelow House still remains in the safekeeping of the descendants of Daniel Richardson Bigelow and his wife, Ann Elizabeth White. The story of their lives as early territorial pioneers is told in the many papers, books, and artifacts on hand at this charming home. It is a story of a young New York-born and Harvard-educated lawyer who settled in the Puget Sound area around 1851 and eventually became a powerful advocate for a separate Washington Territory, and for equal rights and women's suffrage. Ann Elizabeth White, who at the age of fourteen endured the road west with her family over the Oregon Trail, was one of the first teachers in the territory. Consequently, Daniel and Ann Bigelow and their family of eight children were host to many notable citizens such as George Bush, an early black pioneer, and Susan B. Anthony, the famous suffragist. The Bigelow House was also the site of the surrender of the great Snoqualmie chief, Patkanim, during the Indian Uprising of 1855 and 1856.

The Bigelow House is a two-story clapboard structure with many embellishments in the Carpenter style. This detailing can be seen in the center gable, scroll-design vergeboards without crossbracing, lancet-shaped doors, open-design porch supports, and spindle-like balustrades. In addition to the ground floor full-width porch, there is also a small secondary porch located to the right of the main entry, on one of the wing extensions. All of the furnishings are original to the Bigelow family and their descendants including an early rocker c. 1820 and four leather strip seat chairs c. 1853.

Notable Collections on Exhibit

In addition to the many historic documents, the Bigelow House is filled with more than twenty-eight zithers, four small organs, and several "primitive" scenic oil paintings.

Additional Information

The Bigelow House is listed on the National Register of Historic Places and is the center of the Historic Bigelow Neighborhood which comprises several restored historic houses built by the Bigelow and White families. Among them are the 1893 Pioneer-style Bigelow-Bailey House and the 1891 Queen Anne-style Byrd House.

Ezra Meeker Mansion

312 Spring Street
Puyallup, WA 98371
(206) 848-1770

Contact: Ezra Meeker Historical Society
Open: Mid Mar.-mid Dec., Wed.-Sun.
1–4 p.m.; closed Easter, Thanksgiving
Admission: Adults $2.00; seniors and
students $1.50; children (5-12) $1.00
Activities: Guided tours
Suggested Time to View House: 45 minutes
Facilities on Premises: Gift shop
Description of Grounds: 1½ acre with
various ornamental trees and rose
gardens
Best Season to View House: Spring and
summer
Number of Yearly Visitors: 11,000
Number of Rooms: 17

Year House Built: Started 1887,
completed 1890
Style of Architecture: Late Italianate, frame
On-Site Parking: No **Wheelchair Access:** No

Description of House

Ezra Meeker was born in Ohio in 1830 and married Eliza Sumner in his twenty-first year; a year later, in 1852, the couple and their young son Marion joined the waves of pioneers traveling west on the Oregon Trail. They finally settled in the Puyallup Valley in 1861 where Meeker—like many of his fellow farmers—began to plant hops. Soon he was the center of an annual $20 million hops industry and became known as the "Hop King of the World." Soon after completing this house in 1890, the ensuing decade's bank panics and crop failures substantially reduced Meeker's fortune and he turned his attention elsewhere, primarily to the preservation of the Oregon Trail. His efforts in this regard ended in success when President Hoover declared the Trail a National Historic Highway in 1931. Meeker is said to be the only man who traveled his beloved Oregon Trail by all four common modes of transportation: ox-drawn wagon, automobile, railroad, and airplane.

The two-story house is a fine late example of the Italianate-style villa, with its porch entry, side bay extension, hipped roof and widow's walk highlighted with wrought iron cresting, elaborately ornamented bracketed cornices and eaves, and bracketed windows in varied configurations. The porte cochere on the side is a later addition. Inside, there is a full basement and attic, several original stained glass windows, finely-crafted woodwork executed in numerous native woods, and six coal-burning fireplaces. The hand-carved fireplace mantels were manufactured "back East" and shipped by boat to Oregon via Cape Horn. Only some of the furnishings on display belonged to the Meekers; the rest are collected period pieces, mostly in the Victorian style. The Ezra Meeker Mansion is listed on the National Register of Historic Places.

Notable Collections on Exhibit

Among the items on display is a collection of vintage clothing, quilts, and Meeker family memorabilia.

Blackman House Museum

118 Avenue B
Snohomish, WA 98290
(206) 568-5235

Contact: Snohomish Historical Society

Open: June–Sept., daily Noon–4 p.m.;
March-May and Oct.-Dec., Wed.-Sun.
Noon–4 p.m.

Admission: Adults $1.00; seniors, children
and students $.50

Activities: Guided tours for groups

Suggested Time to View House:
30–60 minutes

Description of Grounds: Typical small
town lawn and perennial garden

Best Season to View House: Spring-early
summer

Style of Architecture: Victorian Queen
Anne-style cottage

Number of Yearly Visitors: 3,000

Number of Rooms: 9

Year House Built: 1878

On-Site Parking: Yes **Wheelchair Access:** No

Description of House

Hyrcanus Blackman, a successful local merchant and first mayor of Snohomish, a town not far from the Puget Sound, built this charming Queen Anne-style cottage in 1878. Blackman was one of three brothers who made the long journey west from the state of Maine. All of the brothers became involved in the lumber mill industry, specializing in the manufacture of house shingles. The Blackman House was inherited by Eunice Blackman, the only surviving child of Hyrcanus and his wife. A son had died in his early twenties. Eunice and her husband, Dr. Ford, lived here for many years.

The Snohomish Historical Society purchased the house in 1969; the Society has restored the Blackman House with its original woodwork and some original wallpaper still intact. The restoration has striven for authenticity, leaving much of the exterior and interior of the house unaltered. One of the more idiosyncratic features of the house can be seen in the various shingle textures found on the steep, cross-gabled roof, the multi-pane bay windows, and the small front entry porch. No doubt these shingles are representative of the type produced at the Blackman mill. The public is invited to walk through this little gem at their leisure and view the Victorian-style furnishings and personal items of Hyrcanus Blackman and his family displayed as if the occupants had just stepped away.

Campbell House

Contact: Eastern Washington State
Historical Society

Open: Tues., Thurs.-Sat. 10 a.m.–5 p.m.,
Wed. 10 a.m.–9 p.m., Sun. 1–5 p.m.

Admission: Adults $2.00; seniors and
students (6-16) $1.00; immediate family
$5.00; Wed. free

Activities: Guided tours, occasional
interpretive events including "living
history" demonstrations

Suggested Time to View House:
30–60 minutes

Facilities on Premises: Museum shop

Description of Grounds: Museum complex
and yard landscaped with various shrubs
and trees

Style of Architecture: Eclectic Period
Revival, Tudor

Best Season to View House: Year round

Number of Yearly Visitors: 40,000 - 50,000

Year House Built: 1898

Number of Rooms: 29

On-Site Parking: Yes **Wheelchair Access:** Yes

Description of House

Ohio natives Amasa Campbell and his wife, Grace Fox Campbell, commissioned Spokane architect Kirtland K. Cutter to design this twenty-nine room Tudor-style mansion in 1889. Amasa Campbell was a successful mine owner and operator who had made his fortune in the Coeur d'Alene mining district of northern Idaho; he could easily afford to hire this well-known designer of many local well-appointed mansions. Among Cutter's commissions was the Glover Mansion, which is also listed in this guide.

Under the direction of the Eastern Washington State Historical Society, the Campbell House and grounds are undergoing extensive restoration. This restoration is based upon careful readings of the original Kirtland architectural drawings and the 1898 decorator's plans, researching countless photographs of the original finished structure, and studying correspondence and records. Once completed, not only will additional rooms be open, but visitors will see a more personalized interpretation of a gracious turn-of-the-century home furnished with original family portraits and watercolors, decorative features such as authentic wall and floor coverings and window treatments, and Victorian-style furniture and accessories. "Modern" conveniences such as the telephone and call systems, the dumbwaiter, and the "cool room" will be restored to full operating condition.

Additional Information

Adjacent to the Campbell House is the Cheney Cowles Museum, also managed by the Historical Society. It provides research library and archive facilities and features rotating exhibits illustrating the history and culture of eastern Washington and the Inland Northwest. The Campbell House is listed on the National Register of Historic Places.

Glover Mansion

West 321 Eighth Street
Spokane, WA 99204
(509) 459-0000

Contact: Glover Mansion
Open: Mon.-Fri. 10 a.m.–5 p.m.
Admission: Free
Activities: Guided tours
Suggested Time to View House: 1 hour
Facilities on Premises: Restaurant
Description of Grounds: 1 acre
  landscaped grounds
Style of Architecture: Eclectic Period
  Revival, Tudor half-timbered
Best Season to View House: Year round
Number of Yearly Visitors: 1,000
Number of Rooms: 22

Year House Built: 1889
On-Site Parking: Yes **Wheelchair Access:** Yes

Description of House

When James Glover, known as the "Father of Spokane," hired the young architect Kirtland K. Cutter in 1888 to design his new home, Glover was taking a tremendous chance. The inexperienced architect was the nephew of a local banker and the Glover Mansion was his first commission. But Glover was hardly a stranger to risk; as a pioneer merchant and real estate developer, he owned Spokane's first general store, opened and became president of the First National Bank, and was elected second mayor of the city. But in the years following the Panic of 1895 Glover lost everything, including the mansion. From 1898 until 1929, ownership of the Glover Mansion lay in the hands of various Spokane businessmen. In 1929, it was purchased by the Spokane Unitarian Church, which owned it until 1992 when it was acquired by its present owners.

Originally sited on seven acres, the Glover Mansion is a beautiful example of the half-timbered Tudor style. It is evident that Cutter was anxious to demonstrate his skill as an up-and-coming architect. His extensive application of such exterior architectural devices as multiple overhanging gables, heavy-arched recessed entries, shed dormers, second story sleeping balconies, and casement window treatments including the "porthole" shape, are indicative of talent as well as youthful exuberance. But it was in the design of the interior that he proved himself master of his craft. The dramatic hall extends two stories high and includes a mezzanine with balconies, Syrian-style carved archways, and wainscotting of golden oak. The open airways of the library and the dining room are embellished with highly decorative segmented transoms; the one in the library shows a hand-carved three-section with a floral and vine motif; in the dining room, a stained glass five-section with a floral design. The elaborate staircase has a ground floor alcove containing built-in furniture. A decorative curiosity of note is the marble fireplace in the main hall which is guarded by two carved lionheads on either side of the mantel. In order to bring the house back to its past grandeur, the present owners are undertaking a major restoration. The Glover Mansion is listed on the National Register of Historic Places.

Sumner Ryan House Museum

1228 Main Street, P.O. Box 517
Sumner, WA 98390
(206) 863-5567

Contact: Sumner Historical Society

Open: Apr.-Oct., Sat. and Sun. 1–4 p.m.;
open any time for special tours

Admission: Adults $1.00; seniors $.50;
children $.25; groups free, donation
appreciated

Activities: Guided tours

Suggested Time to View House: 45 minutes

Description of Grounds: Grounds kept in
perfect condition by the city

Style of Architecture: National frame
farmhouse, rural Classical Revival style

Best Season to View House: Spring

Number of Yearly Visitors: 1,000

Number of Rooms: 10

Year House Built: 1875; addition 1885
On-Site Parking: Yes **Wheelchair Access:** No

Description of House

The Sumner Ryan House Museum was built on the site where the town's first plat was made in 1883; it was also the home of Sumner's first mayor, George Ryan, and his wife, Lucy. The house is one of those all too infrequent examples of a home which has been lived in by only one family for over fifty years, remains unaltered for that entire period, and thus serves as a living museum of the period during which it was built and first occupied.

This frame farmhouse with some Classical Revival-style detailing was built of local cedar and contains exquisite hand-carved woodwork throughout the original section of the building. Architectural elements such as the staircase banisters, exterior transoms, and colored glass windows have survived the decades.

Notable Collections on Exhibit

Many visitors have praised the immense collection of archival-quality photographs depicting the city of Sumner in its early days, and local history books published prior to 1900. Also on exhibit is a model of a Sumner schoolhouse c.1891 built entirely to scale.

Additional Information

The Sumner Ryan House Museum is listed on the National Register of Historic Places.

Wyoming

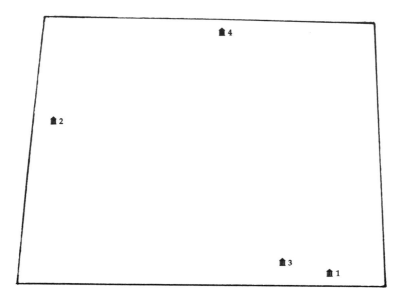

1. Cheyenne
Historic Governors' Mansion

2. Jackson
Miller House and Log Cabin

3. Laramie
Ivinson Mansion

4. Sheridan
"Trail End" State Historic Site

Historic Governors' Mansion

300 East Twenty-first Street
Cheyenne, WY 82002
(307) 777-7878

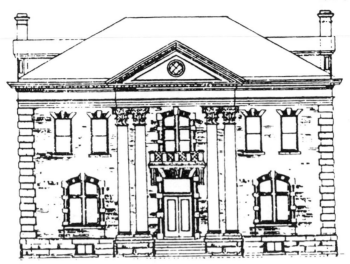

Contact: Wyoming State Museum, Division of Parks and Cultural Resources

Open: Year-round, Tues.-Sat. 9 a.m.–5 p.m.; closed Saturdays of three-day holiday weekends

Admission: Donations accepted

Activities: Self-guided tours, introductory video, Holiday Candlelight Tour

Suggested Time to View House: 30 minutes

Description of Grounds: City lot with blue spruce and juniper

Best Season to View House: Summer

Number of Yearly Visitors: 10,000

Year House Built: 1904, additions 1937 and 1959

Style of Architecture: Eclectic Colonial Revival in the Georgian manner

Number of Rooms: 18

On-Site Parking: Yes **Wheelchair Access:** Yes

Description of House

Scarcely had two decades passed before the wild cattle town of Cheyenne—founded in 1867 as a division point of the Union Pacific Railroad—had become the "civilized" capital of the new state of Wyoming. While the nearby outposts of Hecia and Sherman become "ghost towns," the more than one thousand residents of Cheyenne built gracious Queen Anne-style homes in neatly-ordered middle class neighborhoods. This civic pride became the driving force behind the erection of a governor's residence in 1904.

Designed by Charles Murdock and built at a cost of $33,253, this was the residence to which Governor Bryant B. Brooks brought his wife and five children in 1905. His family would be the first of many to live in the impressive two-and-one-half story-Georgian Revival-style mansion. The exterior features a full-height, pediment-topped portico supported by four Corinthian columns and defining limestone quoins. The interior reflects the tastes and the manners of Wyoming's various First Families; although several rooms have been added or remodeled over the years, some have been enhanced with period furnishings and artifacts reminiscent of the early days of statehood. The last room to be refurbished is the Governor's Den of Milward Simpson (1955-1959). Every item in this room speaks of Wyoming and its history, from the hand-made furniture designed and constructed by a Cody resident to the Wyoming Centennial Quilt on display. One of the more charming rooms is the Children's Bedroom which once belonged to the sisters Lena and Melissa Brooks. Located on the side of the house closest to the carriage house—home of the girls' pet pony—this room is furnished with Victorian Eastlake-style furniture and decorated with family photographs and a "calling card" or "memory quilt" listing the names of some eight hundred Cheyenne citizens.

Notable Collections on Exhibit

Furnishings include a mahogany library table and cane-topped table c.1905, and a round pedestal table made by a local rancher for the Wyoming exhibit at the 1904 St. Louis World's Fair. There is also a collection of photographs depicting the former Territorial and State Governors and First Families from the period 1905 to 1976.

Additional Information

Nellie Taylor Ross, the first woman governor of the United States, resided here, initially as First Lady, and then as Governor after winning a special election after her husband's death.

Miller House and Log Cabin

National Elk Refuge, P.O. Box C
Jackson, WY 83001
(307) 733-8084

Contact: U.S. Fish and Wildlife Service, National Elk Refuge

Open: Public access status under evaluation; restored house and grounds can be viewed from roadway

Admission: Park fee

Activities: Viewing only

Suggested Time to View House: 15 minutes

Description of Grounds: National Elk Refuge

Best Season to View House: Late Spring-early fall

Year House Built: 1898

Style of Architecture: Folk Victorian, log

Number of Rooms: 10

On-Site Parking: No **Wheelchair Access:** No

Description of House

Robert E. Miller, rancher and first supervisor of the Teton Forest Reserve, was a man of perseverance who, at the age of twenty-one, arrived in the fertile valley of the Grand Tetons from the small Wisconsin settlement of Argyle. Here he proceeded to homestead on eighty acres and some additional land purchased from the local outlaw, Teton Jackson. In 1885, Miller built a meager one-room log cabin—still intact—on this site. Later, in the early 1890s, he built a second house near Flat Creek; this one was a two-story folk-style structure, cross-gabled with two wings and matching porches. Although this house was also made of logs, Miller eventually replaced the animal bladder window "panes" with glass ones in order to provide a semblance of civilization for his wife. For many years, the Miller House was the center of social activity for the settlers of Jackson Hole, especially when Robert Miller assumed the position of supervisor in 1908 and the house served as both area post office and election center.

Though Robert E. Miller is long deceased, the survival of the Miller House and Log Cabin, one of the area's oldest houses and said to be "one of the most significant historic resources in Jackson Hole," is a very "live" issue among federal agencies and local historical societies. Over the years, funds have become available to stabilize the exterior in order to prevent deterioration but the interior so far has been only upgraded for "adaptive use." If the perseverance of its first occupant is emulated, then the Miller House and Log Cabin will once again be a center of local interest as an interpretative historical site illustrating the life and times of individuals like Robert E. Miller.

Additional Information

The Miller House and Log Cabin are listed on the National Register of Historic Places.

Ivinson Mansion

603 Ivinson Avenue
Laramie, WY 82070
(307) 742-7763

Contact: Laramie Plains Museum
Association, Inc.

Open: Summer, Mon.-Sat. 9 a.m.–7 p.m.,
Sun. 1–4 p.m.; winter, Mon.-Sat. 1–3 p.m.

Admission: Adults $4.00; seniors $3.00;
students $2.00; children under 6 free

Activities: Guided tours

Suggested Time to View House: 1 hour

Facilities on Premises: Community center

Description of Grounds: A full city block of
landscaped grounds with gardens a
carriage house and a log schoolhouse

Best Season to View House: Summer

Year House Built: 1892

Style of Architecture: Victorian Queen
Anne-Eastlake

Number of Rooms: 19

On-Site Parking: Yes **Wheelchair Access:** No

Description of House

It was in the "rough-and-tumble" frontier town of Laramie in the
territory of Wyoming that colonial-born and British-educated Edward Ivinson and his wife, Jane Wood Ivinson, decided to settle in 1870. Having
purchased some land from the Union Pacific Railroad, this apprentice from
Lord & Taylor in New York City applied his mercantile skills to the acquisition of ties and timbers for that same railroad. Soon Ivinson became involved in serious land management and banking; profits from his
investments would provide the couple with enough wealth to insure their
own high standard of living and improve the quality of life for all of
Laramie's citizens. He became treasurer of the University of Wyoming's first
Board of Trustees and senior warden of St. Matthew's Cathedral, while she
became the moving force behind the formation of the Episcopal Parish and
Laramie's first public school.

As prominent Laramie residents, Edward and Jane Ivinson called upon
the noted architect W.E. Ware of Salt Lake City to design and build their
home. The three-story, half-timbered mansion is a unique example of the
Queen Anne style, based on an asymmetrical floor plan with two full

three-story towers, one triangular and the other conical. The interior features doors and windows glazed with leaded glass, some fine examples of stained glass panes, original tile insets, and a marvelous "floating staircase."

Notable Collections on Exhibit

What remains of the Ivinson family furniture is a dining room set carved by inmates at the Wyoming territorial prison. A number of period rooms are filled with decorative art objects and household and ranch implements, ranging from a set of exquisitely hand-painted oyster plates made in Paris, to a butter bowl hand-hewn from an entire piece of wood log, to a unique horsehair quilt made by America's last train robber, Bill Carlisle, who did "time" in Laramie.

Additional Information

The historical significance of the Union Pacific Railroad and its role in the development of the Wyoming territory can be seen in the exhibits at the new Laramie Plains Railroad Museum located at First Street and Kearney. The Ivinson Mansion is listed on the National Register of Historic Places.

"Trail End" State Historic Site

400 Clarendon Avenue
Sheridan, WY 82801
(307) 674-4589

Contact: Wyoming State Parks and Historic Sites

Open: Apr.-mid Dec., daily 2–5 p.m.; June-Aug., daily 9 a.m.–6 p.m.

Admission: Free

Activities: Self-guided tour, guided tour by appointment, Holiday Open House

Suggested Time to View House: 1 hour

Facilities on Premises: Post cards for sale

Best Season to View House: Spring and summer

Description of Grounds: 3½ acre landscaped grounds in the "natural" style with over 200 trees, tennis courts and sunken rose garden

Number of Yearly Visitors: 12,500

Year House Built: Started 1908, completed 1913

Style of Architecture: Eclectic Colonial Revival in the Flemish manner with some Neoclassical styling

Number of Rooms: 33

On-Site Parking: Yes **Wheelchair Access:** Yes

Description of House

Between 1908 and 1913, John Benjamin Kendrick—soon to be Governor of Wyoming—built "Trail End," the Flemish-style mansion which stands in the shadow of the Bighorn Mountains outside the town of Sheridan. "Trail End" was an apt name for an estate owned by a man who had wandered long and far from his native roots in Texas. Orphaned early and restless in youth, Kendrick left the care of his relatives, became a cattle rover, and made his way to the territory of Wyoming. After several years of living the cowboy life, he married Eula Wulfjen and settled down on the OW Ranch. Later, the ranch would be renamed the Kendrick Cattle Company, by then an enterprise stretching over 200,000 acres.

The couple commissioned Montana architect Glenn Charles McAlister to design their new home but acted as their own general contractors. Construction of the three-story mansion took over five years, due to fluctuations in the cattle market which affected Kendrick's finances and "back East" union strife which slowed completion of the custom-made furniture and woodwork. Finally, in 1913 "Trail End" was completed and the result was a beautiful and unique architectural accomplishment. Based on a symmetrical plan, the dominant features of "Trail End" include a steep-pitched tiled roof, rusticated masonry, an elaborate front facade with curved limestone front-gabled parapets, and a main entry embellished with a Neoclassical-style portico. The exterior was built of materials gathered from several Midwest sites: brick and roofing tiles hand-made in Kansas and Missouri; limestone and granite quarried in Indiana and Montana. The Edwardian-style interior, designed by D. Everett Waid, was fitted with paneling, built-in cabinets, stairs, and ornamentation made mostly out of oak with piano-finish mahogany highlights. Hallways were papered in a brilliant oak leaf design, and ceilings were hand-painted in coordinating color schemes.

Notable Collections on Exhibit

Although the Kendricks lived in the house for only one year after its completion, they continued to use it as their summer place for years. After the death of her husband in 1933, Eula Kendrick lived at "Trail End" with her son and family until 1961. Because of this continuous one-family occupancy, much of the original custom-made furniture manufactured by Berkey & Gay of Grand Rapids, Michigan, remains in excellent condition.

Additional Information

In 1914, John Benjamin Kendrick was elected Governor of Wyoming, and resided for the next two years in the Governors' Mansion in Cheyenne. In 1916, Kendrick was elected to the United States Senate and from that time until 1933, he and his family lived in Washington, D.C.

Index

🏛 *Alaska*

🏛 *Arizona*

🏛 *California*

🏛 Colorado

🏛 Hawaii

🏛 Idaho

🏛 Montana

🏛 Nevada

🏛 New Mexico

🏛 Oregon

🏛 Utah

🏛 Washington

🏛 Wyoming

🏛 *Alaska*

	Photo or illustration courtesy of
House of Wickersham	Alaska Department of Natural Resources, Division of Parks and Outdoor Recreation
Independence Mine Manager's House	Alaska Department of Natural Resources, Division of Parks and Outdoor Recreation
Oscar Anderson House	Anchorage Historic Properties, Inc.
Rika's Roadhouse	Alaska Department of Natural Resources, Division of Parks and Outdoor Recreation

🏛 *Arizona*

Adobe Annex, Captain Jack Mellon House	Arizona Historical Society
Arizona Territorial Governor's Mansion	Sharlot Hall Museum and Historical Society
Bonelli House	Mohave Museum of History and Arts
Century House Museum and Gardens	Arizona Historical Society-Yuma
Hubbell Home	Hubbell Trading Post National Historic Site
Riordan Mansion	Riordan State Historic Park
Rosson House	Heritage Square Foundation, Inc.
Slaughter Ranch Museum	Johnson Historical Museum of the Southwest
Sosa-Carrillo-Fremont House	Arizona Historical Society

🏛 *California*

Alvarado Adobe	San Pablo Historical and Museum Society
Avila Adobe	El Pueblo de Los Angeles Historic Monument
Bidwell Mansion	Bidwell Mansion State Historic Park
Call-Booth House	Paso Robles Art Association
Camron-Stanford House	Camron-Stanford House Preservation Association
Casa de la Guerra	Santa Barbara Trust for Historic Preservation
La Casa Nueva	Workman and Temple Homestead Museum
Castro-Breen Adobe	San Juan Bautista State Historic Park
Cooper-Molera Adobe	Joshua Freiwald
Fenyes Mansion	Pasadena Historical Society
Fernald Mansion	Santa Barbara Historical Museums
Filoli	National Trust for Historic Preservation
Fischer-Hanlon House	Benicia State Park Interpretive Volunteers
Frank Lloyd Wright's Hollyhock House	City of Los Angeles Cultural Affairs Department
Gamble House	University of Southern California
General Phineas Banning Residence Museum	City of Los Angeles Department of Recreation and Parks, Friends of Banning Park
Governor's Mansion	Governor's Mansion State Historic Park
Hearst Castle	California Department of Parks and Recreation, Hearst San Simeon State Historical Monument
Held-Poage Memorial Home	Mendocino County Historical Society, Inc.
Hoffmann House	Escondido Historical Society
House of Happy Walls and Wolf House	California Park Service
Joel Clayton House	Clayton Historical Society
Kearney Mansion Museum	Fresno City and County Historical Society
Kimberly Crest House and Gardens	Kimberly-Shirk Association
Leland Stanford Mansion State Historic Park	California Department of Parks and Recreation
Luther Burbank Home and Gardens	Luther Burbank Home and Gardens Board

	Photo or illustration courtesy of
Lyford House	Richardson Bay Audobon Center
McConaghy House	Hayward Area Historical Society
Meux Home Museum	Meux Home Corporation
Muir House	National Park Service, John Muir National Historic Site
Octagon House	National Society of the Colonial Dames of America in California
Pardee Home Museum	Pardee Home Foundation
Rancho Los Alamitos Historical Ranch	Rancho Los Alamitos Foundation
Rancho Los Cerritos Historic Site	Rancho Los Cerritos Historic Site
Rotchev House and Kuskov House	Fort Ross State Historical Park
Sepulveda House	El Pueblo de Los Angeles Historic Monument
Scotty's Castle-Death Valley Ranch	National Park Service
Stow House and Sexton Museum	Goleta Valley Historical Society
Sun House	Grace Hudson Museum
Tao House	Eugene O'Neill National Historic Site
Tor House and Hawk Tower	Robinson Jeffers Tor House Foundation
Tournament House	Pasadena Tournament of Roses
Trussell-Winchester Adobe	Santa Barbara Historical Museums
William Heath Davis House and Park	Gaslamp Quarter Foundation
William S. Hart Museum	Los Angeles County Museum of Natural History
Winchester Mystery House	Winchester Mystery House Gardens and Historical Museum
Workman House	Workman and Temple Homestead Museum

🏛 Colorado

1870 Meeker Home	City of Greeley Museums
Avery House and Carriage House	Poudre Landmarks Foundation
Byers-Evans House	Colorado Historical Society
Cozens Ranch House Museum	Grand County Historical Association
Edinger-Shumate House	Frontier Historical Society and Museum
Grant-Humphreys Mansion	Colorado Historical Society
Harbeck-Bergheim House	Boulder Museum of History
H.A.W. Tabor House Museum	McVicar Family
Hiwan Homestead Museum	Jefferson County Open Space
McAllister House Museum	National Society of Colonial Dames in the State of Colorado
Miramount Castle Museum	Manitou Springs Historical Society
Molly Brown House Museum	Historic Denver, Inc.
Orchard House	Colorado Springs Park and Recreation Department, White House Ranch Historic Site
Staley House	Frisco Historical Society
Rosemount Victorian House Museum	Rosemount Victorian House Museum, Inc.
Wheeler-Stallard House Museum	Aspen Historical Society

🏛 Hawaii

Baldwin Home Museum	Lahaina Restoration Foundation
Chamberlain House	Mission Houses Museum
'Iolani Palace	Friends of 'Iolani Palace
Lyman Mission House	Lyman House Memorial Museum
Queen Emma Summer Palace	Daughters of Hawai'i

🏛 Idaho

Bishops' House	Friends of the Bishops' House, Inc.
McConnell Mansion	Latah County Historical Society
Standrod House	Pocatello Historic Preservation Commission

🏛 Montana

	Photo or illustration courtesy of
Charles M. Russell Residence	C.M. Russell Museum Complex, the Montana Federation of Garden Clubs
Daly Mansion	Daly Mansion Preservation Trust
Grant-Kohrs Ranch House	National Park Service, Grant-Kohrs Ranch National Historic Site
I.G. Baker House	River and Plains Society
Moss Mansion Museum	Billings Preservation Society
Original Governor's Mansion	Montana Historical Society
William Andrews Clark House	Copper King Mansion

🏛 Nevada

Beckley House	Clark County Southern Nevada Museum and the Junior League of Las Vegas
Giles-Barcus House	Clark County Southern Nevada Museum
Historic Bowers Mansion	Washoe County Parks and Recreation Department
House of the Silver Door Knobs	The Castle
MacKay Mansion	MacKay Mansion
Townsite House	Clark County Southern Nevada Museum

🏛 New Mexico

Dr. Woods' House	Lincoln County Historical Society and Lincoln County Heritage Trust
Ernest L. Blumenschein Home	Kit Carson Historic Museums
Las Golondrinas Placita House	El Rancho de las Golondrinas
La Hacienda de Don Antonio Severino Martinez	Kit Carson Historic Museums
J.P. White House	Historical Center for Southeast New Mexico
Kit Carson Home	Kit Carson Historic Museums

🏛 Oregon

Brunk House	Polk County Historical Society
Burrows House Museum	Lincoln County Historical Society
Captain George Flavel House Museum	Clatsop County Historical Society
Historic Barlow House	Historic Barlow House
Historic Bush House	Salem Art Association
Historic Hughes House	Friends of Cape Blanco State Park
Hoover-Minthorn House	State of Oregon, National Society of Colonial Dames in America
McLoughlin House Museum	McLoughlin Memorial Association
Mission Mill Village	Mission Mill Village Association
Moyer House	Linn County Historical Museum
Pittock Mansion	City of Portland Bureau of Parks and Pittock Mansion Society
Schminck Memorial Museum	Oregon State Society of Daughters of the American Revolution
William L. Holmes House	Rose Farm Museum

🏛 Texas

1839 Samuel May Williams Home	Galveston Historical Foundation
1859 Ashton Villa	Galveston Historical Foundation
Alley Log Cabin	Magnolia Homes Tour, Inc.
Atkins House	Hopkins County Historical Society–Heritage Park and Museum
Beard House	Beard House

Bonner-Whitaker-McClendon House	Society for the Restoration and Historic Preservation of the Bonner-Whitaker-McClendon House
Captain Charles Schreiner Mansion	Hill Country Preservation Society, Inc.
Carl Baetge House	New Braunfels Conservation Society
Carrington-Covert House	Texas Historical Commission
Charles L. McGehee, Jr., Cabin	Heritage Association of San Marcos, Inc.
Charles S. Cock Museum	Heritage Association of San Marcos, Inc.
DeGolyer House	Dallas Arboretum
Dilue Rose Harris House Museum	Magnolia Homes Tour, Inc.
Downes-Aldrich House	Historical and Cultural Activities Center of Houston County, Texas, Inc.
Draughton-Moore, The Ace of Clubs House	Texarkana Museums System
Earle-Harrison House and Gardens	G. H. Pape Foundation
Earle-Napier-Kinnard Museum	Historic Waco Foundation
E. B. Black House	Deaf Smith County Historical Museum
Eddleman-McFarland House	Historic Fort Worth, Inc.
Eisenhower Birthplace State Historical Place	Texas Parks and Wildlife Department
Ezekiel Cullen House	Ezekiel Cullen Chapter-Daughters of the Republic of Texas
Farrell-Wilson Farmstead	Heritage Farmstead Association
Fort House Museum	Historic Waco Foundation
Fulton Mansion, "Oakhurst"	Fulton Mansion State Historical Park
Galvan House of Heritage Park	City of Corpus Christi Parks and Recreation Department
George House at Old City Park	Dallas County Heritage Society, Inc.
Historic Freeman Plantation	Historic Freeman Plantation
"House of the Seasons"	House of the Seasons
Howard-Dickinson House	Rusk County Heritage Association
J.D. Berry Cottage	Stephenville Historical House Museum
John Jay French House Museum	Beaumont Heritage Society
John Nance Garner House-Ettie R. Garner Bldg.	Garner Memorial Museum
John Wesley Mann House	Historic Waco Foundation
Jose Antonio Navarro House	José Antonio Navarro State Historical Park
Kammlah House at the Pioneer Memorial Museum Complex	Gillespie County Historical Society, Inc.
Keith-Traylor House, "Lura"	Magnolia Homes Tour, Inc.
Kell House Museum	Wichita County Heritage Society
Kellum-Noble House	Harris County Heritage Society
Kreische Homestead and Brewery	Monument Hill and Kreische Brewery State Historical Park
Ledbetter Picket House	Albany Chamber of Commerce
Lewis-Wagner Farmstead and House	University of Texas at Austin-Winedale Historical Center
Lon C. Hill Home	Rio Grande Valley Museum
Lyndon B. Johnson Birthplace	National Park Service and the Lyndon B. Johnson National Historical Park
Lyndon B. Johnson Boyhood Home	Lyndon B. Johnson National Historical Park
Magoffin Home State Historic Site	Texas Parks and Wildlife Department
McCulloch House Museum	Historic Waco Foundation
McFaddin-Ward House	McFaddin-Ward House, Inc.
McGregor-Grimm House	University of Texas at Austin-Winedale Historical Center
McNamara House Museum	Victoria Regional Museum Association
Miers Home Museum	Sutton County Historical Society

Moody Mansion	Moody Mansion and Museum
Neill-Cochran House	National Society of Colonial Dames of America
Nichols-Rice-Cherry House	Harris County Heritage Society
O. Henry House	City of Austin Parks and Recreation Department and O. Henry Museum
Old Place	Harris County Heritage Society
Pillot House	Harris County Heritage Society
Plantation House Museum	Varner-Hogg Plantation State Historical Park
Sam Rayburn House	Texas Historical Commission
Senftenberg-Brandon House Museum	Magnolia Homes Tour, Inc.
Sidbury House	Junior League of Corpus Christi
Sam Bell Maxey House State Historical Park	Texas Parks and Wildlife Department
San Felipe Cottage	Harris County Heritage Society
Sebastopol House	Texas Parks and Wildlife Department
Spanish Governor's Palace	City of San Antonio Department of Parks and Recreation
Staiti House	Harris County Heritage Society
Starr Family State Historical Park	Texas Parks and Wildlife Department
Sterne-Hoya House	Sterne-Hoya House Library and Museum
Steves Homestead	San Antonio Conservation Society
Stinson Home	Governor Hogg Shrine State Historical Park
White-Pool House	Ector County Historical Commission
Woodland Home and the Steamboat House	Sam Houston Memorial Museum
Yturri-Edmunds Historic Site	San Antonio Conservation Society

🏛 Utah

Alfred McCune Home	Utah Heritage Foundation
Beehive House	Church of Jesus Christ of Latter-day Saints
Brigham Young Winter Home	Church of Jesus Christ of Latter-day Saints
Deuel Log Cabin	Church of Jesus Christ of Latter-day Saints
Historic Kearns Mansion	State of Utah Governor's Mansion
Jacob Hamblin Historical Site	Church of Jesus Christ of Latter-day Saints
James Glendinning Home	State of Utah and Utah Arts Council
Wheeler Farm House	Wheeler Historic Farm

🏛 Washington

Blackman House Museum	Snohomish Historical Society
Campbell House	Eastern Washington State Historical Society
Ezra Meeker Mansion	Ezra Meeker Historical Society
Glover Mansion	Glover Mansion
Hoquiam's Castle	Hoquiam's Castle
Johnson Farm House	Anderson Island Historical Society
Keller House, "Lockwood"	Stevens County Historical Society, Inc.
"Maryhill"	Maryhill Museum of Art
Olmstead Place	Washington State Parks
Sumner Ryan House Museum	Sumner Historical Society

🏛 Wyoming

Historic Governors' Mansion	Wyoming State Museum, Division of Parks and Cultural Resources
Ivinson Mansion	Laramie Plains Museum Association, Inc.
"Trail End" State Historic Site	Wyoming State Parks and Historic Sites